Elizabeth,

I hope you

enjoy adi

1570 Here page.

Jac 10 0620

FEMALE ENTREPRENEURS

The comparative numbers between male- and female-led start-ups are stark. Ninety-one per cent of venture capital money continues to fund businesses founded solely by men, with only one per cent of venture capital money invested in businesses founded solely by women. Yet being a female entrepreneur is not the preserve of Wonder Woman. It's for every woman who wants to make it happen.

Female Entrepreneurs: The Secrets of Their Success encourages every woman who has dreamt of being an entrepreneur but hasn't yet taken the leap to take the first steps towards realising her dreams – as well as encouraging every woman who has not yet thought about running her own business to consider it. Additionally, it encourages governments and the corporate world to recognise and embrace the huge value that female entrepreneurs bring to society and the economy.

John Smythe and Ruth Saunders reveal the secrets of the success of fifty-two female entrepreneurs. They outline wisdom and insights to inspire budding entrepreneurs to take the leap and offer practical advice on what to think about when setting your business up for success as well as when considering whether to scale. They also provide top tips on how to play to women's inherent strengths and avoid the weaknesses women face – as well as how to stay sane and enjoy the journey. This practical, unique guide provides the encouragement, support and motivation any aspiring female entrepreneur could need to make those first steps towards the realisation of their ambitions.

John Smythe and Ruth Saunders are both entrepreneurs themselves and regularly advise start-ups on how to launch and scale up for growth.

JOHN SMYTHE spent his early career in corporate and government relations and then set up a pioneering leader and employee engagement consultancy, SmytheDorwardLambert. He has three books to his credit: *The Velvet Revolution at Work*, *The CEO: The Chief Engagement Officer* and *Corporate Reputation: Managing the New Strategic Asset*.

RUTH SAUNDERS uses her thirty years of experience as a strategy consultant at McKinsey & Co, marketer at P&G, advertising planner at Saatchi & Saatchi and market researcher at Mars Inc. to help clients develop, to get board buy-in and to implement innovative marketing strategies that deliver tangible business growth. She is author of *Marketing in the Boardroom* and is a trainer, speaker and coach.

"This book is a MUST HAVE for any budding entrepreneurs – male or female. It's an essential 'how to' guide, offering insights and endless pearls of wisdom that give you the courage to jump in and go for it. If only it had been available when I started my business…" – *Gemma Greaves*, Founder, Cabal and Chief Executive, The Marketing Society

"There's never been a better time for women to start their own business. Whether you simply want to work for yourself or you're driven to build the next big thing in tech, you'll find inspiration in these stories." – *Sarah Turner*, Co-founder & CEO, Angel Academe

"Packed with great case studies and examples, this book highlights the key pathways – and obstacles – to success for female entrepreneurs and helps you to navigate them." – *Ann Francke*, Chief Executive, Chartered Management Institute

"As an entrepreneur, I know how hard it can be to start from nothing – especially if you've had a significant corporate role beforehand. Be prepared to ask for lots of help and keep asking – you'll be amazed how prepared people are to help. Take your input from a wide range of sources – this book is a good place to start with lots of sage advice. And don't believe in luck – success comes when opportunity meets experience!" – *Steven Mendel*, Founder, Bought By Many

"One of the recurring themes in this book is just how much better women are at communicating with their teams – engaging with them in an authentic and empathetic approach that really can't be faked. Good communication does not guarantee success, but there is not one example here that mimics the command and control ethic of many male entrepreneurs we have too long revered." – *Marc Wright*, Founder, simplycommunicate

"Why do so many women thrive after they've left corporate life and reinvented themselves as successful entrepreneurs? What is the corporate world getting so wrong that such a significant talent base prefers to work and achieve elsewhere? Read on! Rich with insights and detailed real-life advice from interviews with 52 successful women entrepreneurs, Smythe and Saunders – no mean entrepreneurs themselves – have produced a highly readable and very timely examination of what it means to set up and run your own successful business, and what that means for women entrepreneurs specifically. "Yes, she can" – and they are. If only all that entrepreneurial spirit, courage and creativity could find a home in most organisations too." – *Richard Goff*, Chair, www.peopledirector.org

FEMALE ENTREPRENEURS

THE SECRETS OF THEIR SUCCESS

John Smythe and Ruth Saunders

Routledge
Taylor & Francis Group

LONDON AND NEW YORK

First published 2020
by Routledge
2 Park Square, Milton Park, Abingdon, Oxon OX14 4RN

and by Routledge
52 Vanderbilt Avenue, New York, NY 10017

Routledge is an imprint of the Taylor & Francis Group, an informa business

British Library Cataloguing-in-Publication Data
A catalogue record for this book is available from the British Library

Library of Congress Cataloging-in-Publication Data
Names: Smythe, John, 1951- author. | Saunders, Ruth (Marketing
    consultant), author.
Title: Female entrepreneurs : the secrets of their success / John Smythe
    and Ruth Saunders.
Description: Abingdon, Oxon ; New York, NY : Routledge, 2020. |
    Includes index.
Identifiers: LCCN 2019053693 (print) | LCCN 2019053694 (ebook) |
    ISBN 9781138337824 (hardback) | ISBN 9780429442131 (ebook)
Subjects: LCSH: Businesswomen—Great Britain—Case studies. |
    Entrepreneurship—Great Britain—Case studies. | Women-owned
    business enterprises—Great Britain—Case studies. | Success in
    business—Great Britain—Case studies.
Classification: LCC HD6054.4.G7 .S69 2020 (print) | LCC HD6054.4.G7
    (ebook) | DDC 658.4/21082—dc23
LC record available at https://lccn.loc.gov/2019053693
LC ebook record available at https://lccn.loc.gov/2019053694

ISBN: 978-1-138-33782-4 (hbk)
ISBN: 978-0-429-44213-1 (ebk)

Typeset in Minion Pro
by Swales & Willis, Exeter, Devon, UK

Printed and bound by CPI Group (UK) Ltd, Croydon, CR0 4YY

CONTENTS

ABOUT THE AUTHORS

John Smythe and **Ruth Saunders** are both entrepreneurs themselves and regularly advise start-ups on how to launch and scale up for growth.

John Smythe has advised public and private sector clients on the engagement of leaders and employees in developing and executing strategy, change and transformation globally, at one time leading up to 130 consultants and psychologists in London and Boston, U.S.A., under the brand name SmytheDorwardLambert. Previously John worked in corporate communication positions within U.S. corporations and is the author of three previous books: *The Velvet Revolution at Work, The CEO: The Chief Engagement Officer* and *Corporate Reputation: Managing the New Strategic Asset.*

Ruth Saunders uses her thirty years of experience as a strategy consultant at McKinsey & Co, marketer at P&G, advertising planner at Saatchi & Saatchi and market researcher at Mars Inc. to help clients develop, to get board buy-in and to implement innovative marketing strategies that deliver tangible business growth. She has worked with a range of corporate companies and start-ups across a wide variety of sectors, helping them to build a strong platform for growth. She is author of her first book *Marketing in the Boardroom: Winning the Hearts and Minds of the Board* (2017) and is also a trainer, speaker and coach.

PROLOGUE

The idea for this book emerged in Autumn 2017. On a bright spring morning John Smythe, for no reason he can recall, idly jotted down the names of all the female entrepreneurs he knew personally to some degree. To his surprise the list comprised twenty-six names. He could barely list ten male counterparts.

He was probably subconsciously prompted by the increasing press interest in female entrepreneurs. Women like Justine Roberts, founder of Mumsnet, who had addressed one of John's Groucho Club breakfasts. Hers was a story of relentless determination and zeal. It took them eight years to turn a profit. That's courage.

On a whim, he invited the twenty-six to supper at London's Groucho Club in October 2017. They came, they dined and had a jolly evening. There was no agenda aside from curiosity and hospitality.

However, towards the end of the evening, one guest suggested that there must be a book to be written about female entrepreneurs, by way of encouragement to others. A call to Jonathan Norman at Gower, John's publisher of two previous works, followed shortly after and, soon enough, agreement was reached with Taylor & Francis, which had acquired Gower/Ashgate. Jonathan took the opportunity to switch careers and Amy Laurens became the publisher. In the course of events, John approached his long-time friend Ruth Saunders to ask if she would consider being co-writer. She readily agreed. Both John and Ruth had (separately) been published by Gower/Ashgate.

As the months went by, the cause of women in business was being reported on more frequently in the press. First on the under-representation of women on executive boards and then, as writing commenced, also on the under-representation of women in the entrepreneurial world.

The objective of the book is to encourage women who have never even considered becoming an entrepreneur, as well as women who have considered it but feel constrained by extrinsic and intrinsic barriers, to do so. Additionally, we want to encourage the corporate world, particularly investors, to recognise and embrace the huge value that female entrepreneurs bring to our society and economy.

For us, entrepreneurship means any enterprise, commercial or social or both, of any size. Attention tends to focus on the big names because they make for a great story. But they all started as unknowns.

We've focussed on the experiences of female entrepreneurs rather than entrepreneurship in general as it seems to us that the world of work has been significantly shaped by men for men. The press has reported on the differences that men and women face when raising capital. Investors are still mainly male and discrimination by male investors towards women is real. Just 1% of VC capital goes to businesses founded by all-female teams, 9% to businesses with at least one female founder and 91% to businesses founded by all-male teams.[1]

Happily, with the rise in the number of successful female entrepreneurs, there are more female as well as male investors investing in female entrepreneurs. Why wouldn't they as female start-ups are often more profitable? We hope this increase continues. But there is still a long way to go. We expand on the statistics in Chapter 1 but the overall message is that a vast source of potential lies largely untapped in the U.K., with women in the U.S. twice as likely to be active in a new entrepreneurial venture.[2]

In their previous books, John and Ruth wrote as subject experts. Ruth on marketing at boardroom level and John on employee communication, engaging employees in developing business strategy and organisational change and corporate reputation. Neither are subject experts on this topic, although Ruth is obviously more so than John.

So, mostly what you read here is the opinion and experience of the fifty-two female entrepreneurs we interviewed. We started with the original twenty-six and many of them kindly recommended other female entrepreneurs for us to talk with. We've peppered each chapter with quotes and vignettes from our interviewees. Whilst not all interviewees are quoted, all are acknowledged and each has a mini bio. The last chapter, Chapter 12, is the only one where John and Ruth reflect on what they heard. Thanks and appreciation to them all. It's typical that busy entrepreneurs found the time to be interviewed and tell us their stories.

We met female entrepreneurs who started their businesses both before the age of ten and into their sixties. Some were showing signs of entrepreneurship as children, others had conventional careers and started late. Others solved a personal challenge such as postnatal depression and realised that there must be a vast market of others who could benefit from their discovery. We counted six major catalysts that led these fifty-two women to 'have a go', which are expanded on in Chapter 2.

We interviewed women from all social backgrounds, including some with first-, second- and third-generation refugee backgrounds.

We also included women at all stages of their entrepreneurial journey, with some just starting their first business, some in the thick of growing their business, some who had been running established businesses for some years, some who have successfully sold out and some who are serial entrepreneurs who can't help throwing themselves back into the ring again. Indeed a section on 'knowing when to stop' is the shortest in the book!

Having undertaken the fifty-two interviews, our view is that anyone of any age can make it as an entrepreneur if they have enough self-belief and determination. These qualities seem to rank above having a great idea, as great ideas may occur in a flash but they are just as likely to emerge over time and testing with friends and advisors. Entrepreneurship is open to all.

Separately John and Ruth analysed the interviews to identify the common themes, which were then used to fashion the chapter structure of the book:

Chapter 1 – Why this book?
Chapter 2 – Getting started
Chapter 3 – Discovering and honing your business idea
Chapter 4 – Building the confidence to take the first steps
Chapter 5 – Surrounding yourself with the right people
Chapter 6 – Scaling up a business to be successful
Chapter 7 – Failure comes with the territory
Chapter 8 – Embracing the natural advantages that women have
Chapter 9 – Overcoming the natural challenges that women face
Chapter 10 – Making work work around life: the personal agenda
Chapter 11 – Making work work for women: the female agenda
Chapter 12 – Yes, she can: authors' reflections

We haven't tried to demarcate the differences between male and female entrepreneurs aside from offering some thoughts provided to us by interviewees. For sure, many of the interviewees' experiences and insights will be as relevant to men as women.

John's contribution to the book is dedicated to his mother Eileen and father Frank, and Ruth's to her parents Sydney and Rachel. We also dedicate the book to all fifty-two female entrepreneurs who generously and candidly told us their stories 'warts and all'.

One further aside. Robert Caro is writing the definitive biography of Lyndon Bird Johnson in five Pulitzer-winning instalments. The last of this monumental endeavour is yet to be published. In between volumes he wrote a short work on the art of writing biography called *Working*, a highly readable tract. In it he mentions the significance of describing the locations of his subject in some detail to enable readers to time travel to them and become immersed in the story. The significance of place.

Prompted by this revelation of the significance of place we thought we would note that many of our fifty-two interviews took place in London's

Groucho Club which, for those unfamiliar, is set in the heart of London's creative (and party) heartland, Soho. There's no sign outside and no indication externally of what lies within.

Inside are young and charming staff, a brasserie, a quieter restaurant, two bars, an outside deck, masses of contemporary art (many by members) and legions of members drawn from the creative industries, notably music, theatre, cinema, TV, advertising, design and the like. There are plenty of nooks, crannies and snugs including one with a log fire to hunker down in front of and interview people. There are quaint signs in the restrooms reminding people that the taking of illegal substances will result in permanent expulsion!

There are two Groucho clubs at the same location. The first is a relatively quiet and calm place where business gets done until around 5 p.m. when the other Groucho Club takes over. From calm and quiet, it almost instantly becomes a noisy inferno of garrulous gossip and, in the older sense, gaiety. All interviews were conducted before this transition. Though admittedly some strayed into it!

Step inside the Club with us.

NOTES

1   *The Alison Rose Review of Female Entrepreneurship*, 2019.
2   Harding, R., *State of Women's Enterprise in the UK*, www.prowess.org.uk/facts.

CHAPTER ONE
Why this book?

As mentioned in the prologue, our purpose in writing this book is to inspire wannabe entrepreneurs of all ages and life stages to take the entrepreneurial leap. Particularly women but also men – both those who have never given a thought to being an entrepreneur and those that have but have been held back by real or imagined barriers.

It's not a 'paint by numbers' how-to handbook. There is no model path. But, as you will see, there are plenty of commonalities shared by successful female entrepreneurs. As Stephanie Wray, founder of Cresswell Associates, put it: 'We are all making it up as we go'. We are sure that the disclosures, stories, successes, missteps and frustrations shared by our fifty-two female entrepreneurs will inspire others to have a go. Early on, we learnt that very few new enterprises are instant hits. Mostly it's a labour of love and commitment over time when few are rooting for you except yourself and close family and advisors.

In Chapter One we cover:

1. *Setting the scene.*
2. *The state of female entrepreneurship today.*
3. *What do the research and data tell us?*
4. *What does global best practice tell us?*
5. *What is the solution?*
6. *How this book came about – introducing Eileen and Sydney and Rachel.*

SETTING THE SCENE

Before we look at how well female entrepreneurs are doing today, let's look briefly at the meaning of entrepreneurship (and social entrepreneurship) and other variants of it, such as intrapreneurship, self-employment and interim executive work.

ENTREPRENEUR

According to etymologist David Lerner the term entrepreneur is loaned from French. The French word *entreprendre* means 'to undertake' with *entre* deriving from Latin and meaning 'between'. It's also close to a Sanskrit word meaning 'self motivation'. Apt!

Entrepreneurs are defined as 'people who set up and run their own business (or businesses) taking on financial risks in the hope of profit'. They work with and between others. They are a go-between, a collaborator, a connector, a builder of ideas, dreams and, occasionally, of bubbles.

Research by Score's 'The State of Women Entrepreneurs' helpfully groups entrepreneurs into six categories:

- **Potential entrepreneurs**: those who see opportunities in their environments and have the desire and capabilities to start businesses.
- **Intentional entrepreneurs**: those who intend to start a business in the next three years.
- **Nascent entrepreneurs**: those who have taken steps to start a new business but have not yet paid salaries or wages for more than three months.
- **New entrepreneurs**: those who are running new businesses that have been in operation for between three months and forty-two months.
- **Established business owners**: those who are running a mature business, in operation for more than forty-two months.
- **Discontinued entrepreneurs**: those who, for whatever reason, have exited from running their own business.[1]

INTRAPRENEUR

Being an entrepreneur is a different but related state to being an intrapreneur. An intrapreneur is employed by an organisation and is given space to act like an entrepreneur, perhaps to develop ideas for new products and services and new approaches for their organisations.

The organisation takes all of the risk and losses, as well as, in most cases, the financial gain. Intrapreneurs benefit from the experience, which may encourage them to become an entrepreneur themselves in the future with their new-found knowledge and confidence.

Many entrepreneurs begin this way, believing that there is much to be learnt from established organisations that have been founded by an entrepreneur. Many household names started as 'acorns', such as Mars, Bechtel, Rowntree, Amazon, Facebook, Aldi, Dassault, JCB, Porsche, VW and many more.

SELF-EMPLOYED OR FREELANCER

Being self-employed or a freelancer is also a popular choice – with self-employed people needing to accept risk in a similar way to entrepreneurs, as well as to find a gap in a market that they can make a living from. Many, if not most, are content with their self-employed status and remain as a single-person entity, in contrast to entrepreneurs who work with and through others.

Like entrepreneurs, the self-employed are often willing to take more risk in the hope of creating more reward. However, none of our interviewees said they were setting up their own business just for the financial reward. As you will see in Chapter Two, there are many catalysts, triggers and life events that lead people to become entrepreneurs.

Self-employment may develop into entrepreneurship when an idea takes off and the individual decides to ride its coat tails.

INTERIM EXECUTIVE

Of increasing popularity is the interim executive role lasting weeks, months and sometimes longer. It's popular with people who have worked in the corporate world as they can take a fleeting look at what it's like to be self-employed. Some choose to do this role long-term to give them flexibility. Others choose it because they enjoy the variety, the often higher reward and some contractual security.

IN SUMMARY

The significance of these categories is to encourage people to reflect on which type of work will play to their strengths, ambition, constraints and needs.

For example, one of our interviewees built a successful artisan business employing no others. She then hatched a plan to grow and developed a business plan to realise this aspiration. But when thinking through the plan, she realised that growth would mean her having to step into managerial shoes away from her loved artisanship. Spelling out the plan gave her valuable insight on what this would mean for her day to day and it wasn't attractive.

Wannabe entrepreneurs should spell out their aspirations before setting up their business – to help them see beyond the gleaming spires of their dreams down into the day-to-day detail on where they will be spending most of their time.

One final thought is the rise of the independent associate (essentially a self-employed freelancer). Many of the interviewees didn't employ people but instead used associates who valued their independence. The associate path limits the ever-increasing risks and burdens of employing people and provides flexibility for everyone. For example, one of our entrepreneurs, Melanie Chevalier, uses over 2,000 associates around the world, all choreographed from London.

THE STATE OF FEMALE ENTREPRENEURSHIP TODAY

So now we have defined who female entrepreneurs are, let's look at some of the recent research and data on female entrepreneurialism.

To put the research into context it's worth referring to a recently published book by Caroline Criado Perez: *Invisible Women: Exposing Data Bias in a World Designed for Men*. Caroline opens the book with: 'Seeing men as the human default is fundamental to the structure of human society. It's an old habit and it runs deep'.

The work covers many examples of how the world is biased against women. For example, at a more trivial level:

- Conference organisers providing microphones with the assumption that the user will be wearing a suit jacket and trousers.
- Female employees shivering in offices set to a male temperature norm.

- Women struggling to reach a top shelf set at a male height norm.
- Children's TV being dominated by male characters – with only 13% of children's non-human TV characters being female, rising to only 32% of children's human TV characters.
- Gender-neutral terms really meaning male, e.g., in Wikipedia, the 'England national football team' page talks about the men's national football team, whilst the women's page is called the 'England women's national football team'.

And at a more life-threatening level:

- Car driver seats with safety measures that don't account for the average female torso.
- Clinical trials lacking gender disaggregation, leading to
  - dangerous assumptions about dosages which can cause harm and, in some cases, fatality;
  - female heart attacks going undiagnosed because the symptoms are deemed 'atypical'.
- Town planners prioritising snow clearance on roads (which men are more likely to use) over pavements (which women are more likely to use), resulting in the majority of cold-weather injuries being experienced by women who have fallen on icy or snowy surfaces.
- U.S. universities giving parents an extra year to earn tenancies – with the number of women attaining tenancy in their first job declining by 22% as women spent the year being mothers whilst men used it to do more research.

Caroline's argument, supported by scores of examples, is that policy influencing the workplace and life in general is designed, largely unconsciously, by men for men. She explains that the men (and it nearly always is men) who create this gender bias 'didn't deliberately set out to exclude women. They just didn't think about them. They didn't think to consider if women's needs might be different'.

She argues that this gender bias is only going to get worse, as the advent of big data is fast accelerating the problem with algorithms designed with a male bias. Google's speech recognition is 70% more likely to recognise male than female speech.

This gender bias is very prevalent in the entrepreneurial world. You only have to look at the levels of investment by venture capitalists to see the problem. Just 1% of VC capital goes to businesses founded by all-female teams, and 9% to businesses with at least one female founder. In contrast, 91% of VC capital goes to businesses with all male founders.[2]

Based on Caroline Criado Perez's premise, it's not surprising to learn that only 13% of senior people on U.K. investment teams are woman and almost half (48%) of investment teams have no women at all. So, investment decisions are being made (in Caroline's words) 'largely unconsciously by men for men'.[3]

Women end up having to 'lean in' to this male world of work or 'lean out' and leave. And that's what's happening to the detriment of employers. Many of our interviewees left the corporate world to become entrepreneurs in part because of the male gender bias they experienced every day at work. Be it the impossibility of having a fulfilling career *and* being at home most days for their children. Or the difficulty of conforming to the male stereotypes expected in the workplace. Or the lack of desire to break through the still very existent 'white male glass ceiling'. For many of them, becoming their own boss and creating the cultural values and day-to-day flexibility to which they aspired was the only viable solution – resulting in the corporate world losing out on vital female talent.

The rules of the corporate world continue to be primarily defined by white males for white males. It's improving but if employers want to retain their top talent then much more needs to be done to create workplaces where people of all genders, ethnicities and classes can thrive and succeed.

WHAT DO THE RESEARCH AND DATA TELL US?

THE POSITIVE SIDE

On the positive side, female entrepreneurship is growing, both overall and at a faster rate than male entrepreneurship. The number of new businesses set up by female entrepreneurs is large and growing, creating a valuable asset for global and U.K. economies:

- Between 2016 and 2017, 163 million women worldwide started businesses, with 111 million women currently operating established businesses.[4]
- In 2015, 126,000 businesses were created by women in the U.K. – twice the level of 2006 (58,000) – resulting in 77,000 new jobs and an estimated £3.5 billion contribution to the U.K. economy.[5]
- Between 2009 and 2012, the proportion of women starting a business nearly doubled from 3.7% to 7.1% of the U.K.'s female working population.[6]
- Globally, between 2014 and 2016, women's intention to start a business increased by 16%.[7]

Female entrepreneurship is growing at a faster rate than male entrepreneurship:

- Historically, women accounted for just over 25% of the self-employed, but since 2008, 58% of the newly self-employed have been female, rising to 70% in 2014.[8]
- Between 2015 and 2016, the proportion of women involved in owning or running a business less than 3.5 years old grew by 10% and the proportion owning established businesses grew by 8%. This resulted in the gender gap ratio of women to men participating in entrepreneurship decreasing by 5%.[9]

Female entrepreneurs favour the more caring professions:

- Over half of female entrepreneurs in innovation-driven economies are in the government, health, education and social services fields, with women 2.25 times more likely than men to start businesses in these sectors.[10]

Women who take the leap are much more likely than men to cite 'family reasons' and 'necessity' as the key reasons to become self-employed:

- One fifth of women chose to work as self-employed to help combine 'family commitments' and 'wanting to work at home' with employment in a flexible manner. Conversely, men were almost twice as likely than women to say that a key reason why they became self-employed was to 'make more money'.[11]
- At every level of entrepreneurship, women are at least 20% more likely than men to cite 'necessity' rather than 'opportunity' as their motivation.[12]

Studies suggest that businesses run by women deliver a higher Return on Investment (ROI):

- In the U.S., First Round Capital's review of their own holdings found that female-run businesses deliver a 63% better ROI than male-run ones.[13]
- A Barclays Bank report states: 'When they do secure investment, women's businesses show returns of 20% more revenue with 50% less money invested'.[14]
- An RBS report states: 'When firm characteristics (size, sector, age, funding) are controlled for, women-owned firms outperform those by their male counterparts'.[15]
- Chief Executive of the Small Business Service in the U.S., Martin Wyn Griffith, said that: 'A pound invested in developing women owned enterprise provides a greater return on investment than a pound invested in developing male owned enterprise'.[16]

THE NEGATIVE SIDE

However, on the negative side, U.K. female entrepreneurship is still struggling to match the level of its male counterparts, with women at almost every stage less likely to become entrepreneurs. The overall number of female entrepreneurs is still a long way behind the number of male entrepreneurs:

- In 2017, women in the U.K. made up only one third of all entrepreneurs and less than 20% of leaders of small to medium-sized enterprises (SMEs).[17]
- In 2016, women led 20% of SMEs with employees and 22% of SMEs without employees.[18]
- An RBS study shows that almost 1.5 million women in the U.K. are self-employed, with women accounting for just 17% of business owners.[19]

Women in the U.K. are less likely than their male counterparts to start their own business:

- In 2016, the proportion of women involved in the owning or running of any business that is less than 3.5 years old was half the level of men (6% versus 12%).[20]

Women in the U.K. are less interested than their male counterparts in starting their own business:

- In 2017, only 9% of U.K. women were interested in starting an enterprise, compared with 14% of men. This compares with 20% of women in Canada, 15% in the U.S. and 13% in Australia.[21]
- Even in early years, school-age boys are 50% more likely to be interested in starting their own business than girls.[22]

Female founders are less likely to scale up their business than their male counterparts:

- Female-led businesses are only 44% of the size of male-led businesses, with an average Gross Value Added (GVA) of £56K per year versus £126K for male ones.[23]
- Female-led businesses also tend to be smaller with 19% of them employing five people or more compared with 27% of businesses owned by men.[24]
- Once established, 29% of male entrepreneurs will eventually achieve £1–50 million turnover, compared with only 13% of women. This is despite the fact that women are as successful as men in sustaining a business once established, with 73% of entrepreneurs of both sexes running businesses older than 3.5 years.[25]

Women are trailing their male counterparts in the more successful sectors:

- Female-owned enterprises represent less than 25% of business in the U.K.'s five most productive sectors, i.e., those that generate an average output of £50+ per hour, such as financial services, IT and manufacturing. In contrast, women are more likely to start a business in lower productivity sectors such as education (2.5 times more likely than men) and service (2.1 times more likely than men).[26]
- Women still remain less prominent in information and technology, with fewer than 2% of women starting businesses in this sector – almost four times less than the percentage of men.[27]
- Across the science, engineering and technology sectors, there are ten times as many male-owned than female-owned businesses.[28]
- Sadly, female-owned businesses win less than 5% of corporate and public sector contracts.[29]

U.K. FEMALE ENTREPRENEURSHIP ALSO LAGS BEHIND LEVELS ACHIEVED IN OTHER COUNTRIES

The U.K. lags behind other countries in the world, with U.K. women being more hesitant than their global female counterparts to set up their own business:

- Only 6% of U.K. women run their own businesses, compared with 15% of women in Canada, almost 11% of women in the U.S. and over 9% of women in Australia and the Netherlands.[30]
- The U.K.'s gender parity – the ratio of female entrepreneurs to male entrepreneurs – is only 0.46, i.e., for every ten male U.K. entrepreneurs, there are fewer than five female entrepreneurs. By comparison, gender parity in the Netherlands is almost 0.9, Spain sits above 0.8 and Australia, the U.S., Canada, Israel, Sweden and Greece have gender parity ratios of 0.6 or more.[31]
- Women in the U.S. are twice as likely to be active in a new entrepreneurial venture as women in the U.K. In contrast, men in the U.S. and U.K. are roughly at the same level.[32]

The failure of the U.K. to embrace female entrepreneurs is costing the U.K. economy:

- If women started businesses at the same rate as men, then the Minister for Women and Equality between 2003 and 2005, Jacqui Smith, suggested that the U.K. would have 150,000 more start-ups each year.[33]
- A NatWest report said that if the U.K. had emulated the level of female entrepreneurship in Canada in 2015, it would have provided the U.K. economy with an additional £1.35 billion boost.[34]
- RBS calculated that boosting female entrepreneurship could result in a boost of £60 billion to the U.K. economy.[35]
- Deloitte estimates that targeted help for female founders could provide a £100 billion boost to the economy over the next ten years.[36]

WHAT IS CAUSING FEMALE ENTREPRENEURSHIP TO LAG?

The primary reason for the lower levels of female entrepreneurship is the continued struggle that women have when seeking funding versus their male counterparts.

- Start-up funding is the number one barrier mentioned by women who aren't entrepreneurs – with almost twice as many women mentioning this as men (38% versus 21%). On average, women start businesses with 53% less capital than men, are less aware of funding options and are less likely to take on debt. Similarly, women are 81% less likely than men to feel that they can access the necessary start-up funds.[37]
- Consequently, female entrepreneurs are more likely than male entrepreneurs to:
  - self fund, with a NatWest study stating that 72% of female start-ups are funded by themselves or family with many loading themselves with very expensive credit debt at high interest rates;[38]
  - crowd fund, with women being 32% more successful than men.[39]

- In contrast, male entrepreneurs are more likely to raise venture capital money:
  - in the U.K., just 1% of start-up funding goes to businesses founded by an all-female team and a further 8% to businesses founded by at least one female. Consequently, male entrepreneurs are 86% more likely than female entrepreneurs to secure venture capital funding and 56% more likely to win the backing of an angel investor.[40]
- This will be in part due to the lack of senior females on U.K. investment teams:
  - only 13% of senior people on U.K. investment teams are women and almost half (48%) of investment teams have no women at all;[41]
  - a survey of U.S. investors found that they were twice as likely to believe that female-owned businesses perform below market-average than male ones (8% versus 4%);[42]
  - Nisha Dua, co-founder and partner of BBG Ventures which invests in female-led companies, says: 'Many people think there just aren't that many female founders. But the opposite is true. Most VCs just don't see those founders – women aren't in their network – or VCs don't understand their ideas'.[43]
- This will also be in part due to the lack of networking opportunities female entrepreneurs have:
  - women value access to networks more than men (31% versus 21%);[44]
  - yet only 36% of all-female founding teams are warmly introduced to VCs, versus 40% of teams with mixed gender and 42% of all-male teams;[45]
  - women are less likely than men to know other entrepreneurs (30% versus 38%) or to have access to sponsors, mentors or professional support networks, with 26% of women citing their lack of networks as a significant barrier.[46]
- This is hindering women's ability to succeed:
  - an RBS Group report says: 'Women start businesses under-capitalised. It's not just lower financial capitalisation, women also have lower levels of human (management training and experience) and

social (effective networks) capital. This under-capitalisation hinders women's prospects and also their ability to start a business'.[47]

- This is not just a U.K. issue. In the U.S.:
  - of the $58 billion that was invested by venture capitalists in 2016, only $1.5 billion reached female-led companies. So, while female-led businesses are increasingly being funded, access to capital for female entrepreneurs is far from reaching parity, in part due to women not being on the radars of VCs, nor being trained in how to raise capital;[48]
  - U.S. firms that receive VC funding tend to be founded and led by white and Asian men. Indeed, fewer than 5% of all VC-funded firms have women on their executive teams, and only 3% have a female CEO.[49]

A second barrier to women starting a business is 'family care', namely still being the primary carer for children and ageing parents:

- For female entrepreneurs with children, the number one reason for starting a business is to achieve a more flexible work–life balance.[50]
- However, the primary reason why women with children do not start a business is 'family care', with women twice as likely as men to cite this.[51]
- Additionally, rates of female entrepreneurialism fall sharply after the age of thirty-five, with no equivalent drops for men.[52]

A third barrier to budding female entrepreneurs is their perceived lack of confidence and fear of failure versus their male counterparts:

- Women are less likely to believe they possess the necessary entrepreneurial skills, such as financial management and market development, to be successful, with only 39% of women confident in their abilities versus 56% of men.[53]
- Women typically have higher risk-awareness than men, with women being 55% more likely than men to cite 'fear of failure' as a primary reason to not start a business.[54]

- An internal report at Hewlett-Packard revealed that women only apply for jobs if they think they meet 100% of the criteria listed. Men apply if they think they meet 60% of the requirements. As Sheryl Sandberg states: 'Women need to shift from thinking "I'm not ready to do that" to thinking "I want to do that – and I'll learn by doing it"'.[55]

WHAT DOES GLOBAL BEST PRACTICE TELL US?

The good news. Women are racing up the entrepreneurial league tables but have to fight hard for presence and funding. Happily, more and more women are creating successful businesses and, in turn, are investing in women.

Countries such as Canada, U.S. and the Netherlands have been leading the way in helping female entrepreneurs start up their own businesses through a series of coordinated and sustained policies and initiatives over the past ten years.

Canada's female versus male entrepreneurship ratio increased by circa 33% between 2006 and 2017, driven by a number of large-scale sustained initiatives including:

- The tracking and publishing of the allocation of funding by gender by the Official Development Assistance (ODA).
- Ernst and Young's 'Winning Women' programme supporting high-potential female entrepreneurs in rapidly scaling their companies through help in finding customers, suppliers and capital, as well as masterclasses on business strategy.
- The state-owned Business Development Bank of Canada's commitment to increasing lending to majority female-led businesses to $1.4 billion.
- The BDC Capital Women in Technology Venture Fund increasing its investment to $200 million.
- A parental leave policy and childcare programme being implemented in Quebec.

- The GoSponsorHer campaign challenging senior leaders to publicly sponsor a high potential woman in their network and to encourage others to do the same.
- Canada's innovative entrepreneurship portal, with centralised content, personalisation, ease of searching and direct application to funding.

Similarly, the U.S. has increased the number of female entrepreneurs by 20% and its female versus male entrepreneurship ratio by 6% since 2008, also through a number of large-scale initiatives including:

- The tracking and publishing of the level of female funding by HBR and other U.S. papers.
- The Women's Business Enterprise National Council's (WBENC) certification of any business that is at least 51% controlled by women who are U.S. citizens as female-owned. Once certified, these businesses are eligible for the £100m+ of investment capital provided by the Women-Owned Small Business (WOSB's) Federal Contracting Programme, as well as for the 5% of all federal contracts that are awarded by the Government to female-owned businesses.
- 110 Women Business Centres (WBCs) across the U.S. providing training, advice and mentoring to circa four million women at each stage of the entrepreneurial journey.
- BridgeCare Finance's loans to professional parents that help to reduce monthly childcare payments.
- SheEO's entrepreneur network where participants can spend fifteen seconds asking for help. Experienced volunteers then sign up to contribute support. The model has been rolled out in conferences and through digital platforms to great success.
- The Women in Science STEM Camp for Girls programme encouraging female high school students to study STEM subjects through hands-on experiments in engineering, chemistry, robotics and coding.

Additionally, the Netherlands has focussed on supporting all entrepreneurs, with female entrepreneurs benefitting the most. This has resulted in its female versus male entrepreneurship ratio increasing by circa 35% between 2008 and 2017, primarily driven by:

- Tax deductions for SMEs and start-ups.
- Centralised information for entrepreneurs that is easily accessible on the National Enterprise Agency website.
- Greater access to micro-financing and start-up capital, with four banks committing €30m.
- Entrepreneurship being embedded into the national qualifications framework and curricula, including interactive courses and Certificate Entrepreneurship.

Other countries have also implemented initiatives to help drive female entrepreneurship. For example:

- In Japan, the ~£1.1 trillion Government Pension Investment Fund allocates 10% of its passive domestic equity to ESG indices, including the MSCI Japan Empowering Women Index that tracks companies that encourage women to work.
- In Sweden, one of the country's four main state pension funds, AP2, has invested in gender equality social bonds issued by the World Bank.
- In Australia:
  - The Future Female Entrepreneurs initiative is a A$7.2 million programme that builds the digital literacy and business acumen of Australian girls and young women, particularly in rural and regional communities. Courses are delivered through a digital platform and in-person workshops.
  - The Australian business portal offers a comprehensive online 'Business Guide' that leads users through the steps of setting up a business.[56]

WHAT IS THE SOLUTION?

Given the U.K. statistics, there is increasing talk of the U.K. Government and financial institutions needing to follow the lead of these countries and do more to support women in making the entrepreneurial leap.

The Alison Rose Review of Female Entrepreneurship is one of the reports spearheading this change. In March 2019, the report made eight recommendations, leveraging best practice learnings from those countries leading the way.

Four of the recommendations aim to increase funding to female-run businesses. For example:

1. Promote greater transparency in U.K. funding allocation to ensure that female entrepreneurs get the funding they need.
2. Create investment vehicles that increase funding to women.
3. Encourage U.K.-based institutional and private investors to support and invest in female entrepreneurs.
4. Launch new banking products aimed at entrepreneurs with family care responsibilities.

The other four recommendations aim to increase mentoring and support to female entrepreneurs. For example:

5. Expand existing mentorship and networking opportunities for women.
6. Give entrepreneurial females greater access to entrepreneurial expertise.
7. Develop and expand entrepreneurship-related courses in schools and colleges.
8. Develop the U.K.'s first comprehensive digital information shop for entrepreneurs.[57]

Whilst there is a very long way to go before women are on an equal entrepreneurial footing to men, the following chapters contain many stories of females who have started and are successfully running their own businesses today that we hope will inspire others.

But before we go there, here are two very personal stories that inspired us to write this book.

THE STORY OF HOW THIS BOOK CAME ABOUT – INTRODUCING EILEEN AND SYDNEY AND RACHEL

Eileen (Morton) was John's mother. Events resulted in her becoming his single parent in the 1950s in post-WW2 Britain. John's father was known as 'Frankie' or 'Frank' (officially Francis Patrick). He was a pilot by profession.

Eileen and Frank left the Republic of Ireland like so many others in search of work – Ryanair wasn't even a glint in Michael O'Leary's eye back in the early 1950s. Frank found work with BEA (British European Airways), the forerunner of British Airways before it was merged with BOAC (British Overseas Airways Corporation), the global British state airline, as it was then before privatisation.

He also joined the Royal Air Force reserve. In the spring of 1953, John's mother saw an official-looking cyclist approaching their rented house. She froze as this was the norm for advising next of kin that their spouse had been killed on active service. Her fears were confirmed as the fateful telegram was given to her by the bearer of bad news.

John knows little of the circumstances except that his father was flying a single engine training aircraft (type unknown) which suffered engine failure. He was killed in the subsequent emergency landing, allegedly landing the wrong way in a ploughed field.

The RAF has steadfastly refused to provide details despite requests by John. A letter of sympathy from BEA dated 9 April 1953 confirmed it was an RAF accident.

That short telegram shattered three lives. Eileen's dream of leading the life of a reasonably comfortable pilot's wife came to an abrupt end. As did the income that went with it. Suddenly she was alone with a young child in a foreign country with very limited funds. Frank was buried in the family plot at the church at Kilmacanogue (pronounced Kilmacanock) at the foot of the pyramid-like Sugar Loaf mountain south of Dublin.

A story John's mother repeated as she became old and frail was that as Frank lay in his coffin a troop of IRA men galloped into the cemetery and replaced the Union Jack with the Irish Tricolour – almost certainly a myth as the family had nothing to do with the IRA as far as he knew.

John heard much about Frankie from Eileen and his Irish relatives and his father's siblings, especially John's aunt Philomena who was very close to Frankie.

There was no work to be had in Ireland so Eileen and child returned to England. Eileen's mother had worked in service in London and Eileen took positions as housekeeper and school matron across the south of England. It was no life for her but she succeeded in her purpose of keeping John out of the hands of the state. As for John, he knew no other life and was none the worse for it.

John has vivid memories of the homes he could be seen but not heard in. There were some ogres but many were kind. The most memorable person was the founder of fridge maker LEC, Charlie Purley. Rumour had it that he came by a blueprint and set the business up and owned a handsome property on the English South coast off the back of it. Rumour also had it that the windows of the house and the Bentley were bullet-proof! But John remembers him as being kind and inviting him on runs in the Bentley, which gave John a sense of 'if he can, I can'. There were to be twelve years in the North Sea oil industry where John sought strong father figures before striking out with his own start-up at age thirty-two.

It was only in recent years that John fully realised that Eileen was driven to that lonely life to protect him from the hands of the state. She was not a commercial entrepreneur but she had a mission which she succeeded with. She was a 'mumpreneur'. So John's contribution to this work is dedicated to her. Having interviewed fifty-two female entrepreneurs, he sees common attributes across that group that he realised years on that Eileen also demonstrated.

INTRODUCING SYDNEY AND RACHEL

Sydney and Rachel were Ruth's parents, both of whom were brought up on farms in Devon during the war.

Sydney was made to leave school when he was fifteen years old to work on a working class farm in the middle of Devon (in 'the back of beyond') with no running water or electricity. He hated it. So, when his father sadly died young, Sydney sold the farm and retrained as an accountant by getting a degree by post – something that was rare at that time, particularly for someone who had left school so young. Sydney spent his working years as an accountant – mostly freelancing with small businesses in Exeter.

Sydney was determined that his two daughters (Joy and Ruth) would have the education that he never had, to set them up for a solid foundation for life. So he encouraged them to study hard and go to university. Ruth fortuitously inherited her father's mathematical brain and so, after university, she went to London to do the type of consultancy work that her father would have loved to have done – which made him very proud. He felt that he had travelled half the distance from the 'back of beyond' to the city of Exeter and that Ruth had travelled the other half from Exeter to London.

Rachel studied needlework and cookery at school with the aim of being a farmer's wife. She married young at twenty years, as was expected of her, and sadly never became the farmer's wife she hoped to be.

It soon became clear that Rachel needed to support Sydney in generating cash flow. So she turned her hand to a number of things to make that happen – most notably growing and selling fruit and vegetables to the local market, taking in foreign exchange students and caring for elderly people – anything that could generate a little cash.

Rachel was determined that her two daughters (Joy and Ruth) would enjoy the freedom and choices that she felt she never had. So she encouraged them to be independent at a very young age. They walked a mile to school on their own from the age of six. They were sent to stay on one of the nearby family farms every summer from the age of seven. And they were encouraged to work for their pocket money, and learn how to budget it, from the age of twelve. Rachel's view was that you get out of life what you put into it and so it's important to take responsibility for yourself and what you do.

Sydney and Rachel forged their own path throughout their life together, rather than following the herd. So both daughters have never felt the need to follow the traditional path or fit into the rules created by society.

Looking back, Ruth can see just how limited Sydney and Rachel's choices were and how much greater freedom and independence she has had in life – much of which was created by them, for which she is very grateful. So Ruth's contribution to this book is dedicated in thanks to them.

WHO WE ARE AND WHO OUR INTERVIEWEES ARE

THE AUTHORS, JOHN AND RUTH, ARE BOTH ENTREPRENEURS

Ruth is the founder and leading partner of Galleon Blue, a consultancy that helps global companies develop, get senior level buy-in and implement innovative brand, marketing and customer-led strategies that drive tangible business growth. In 2017, she published her first book *Marketing in the Boardroom: Winning the Hearts and Minds of the Board.*

John built and sold SmytheDorwardLambert, a consultancy specialising in engaging employees in developing business strategy and organisational change. At its height, it employed 130 people in London and Boston. He went on to found Engage For Change with partner Jerome Reback and published *The CEO, The Chief Engagement Officer: Turning Hierarchy Upside Down to Drive Performance* (2007) and *The Velvet Revolution at Work: The Rise of Employee Engagement, The Fall of Command and Control* (2013).

THE FIFTY-TWO INTERVIEWEES WHO FEATURE IN THIS WORK ARE ALL ENTREPRENEURS WHO WE KNEW OR TO WHOM WE WERE KINDLY INTRODUCED

Some are successful serial entrepreneurs who have built and sold large companies, some are a few years into their journey of growing a sustainable and successful business and some are just starting out on their way.

Sarah Ali Choudhury	Easy Curry
Kate Andrews	Loco2
Alex Beer	Feed The Soul Vegan Café
Di Burton	Cicada Communications Limited
Aurée de Carbon	CARRHURE
Helen Caton	The Forton Group
Mélanie Chevalier	Creative Culture
Bridget Connell	Thinking Partnerships
Elizabeth Cowper	WoMo Network
Helen Dunne	Hardy Media
Liann Eden	Eden McCallum
Verity Drew Firth	Limes House Films
Tamara Gillan	Cherry London
Gemma Greaves	Cabal
Kate Grussing	Sapphire Partners
Rebekah Hall	Botanic Lab
Mursal Hedayat	Chatterbox
Emma Hill	Redefine Hair Salon
Julia Hobsbawm	Editorial Intelligence
Carolyn Hopkins	The Truckle Truck
Rowena Ironside	Women on Boards
Melina Jacovou	Propel London
Michaela Jedinak	Michaela Jedinak
Alice Johnsen	Alice Johnsen Life Coaching
Maria Kempinska	Jongleurs Comedy Club
Renou Kiefer	Rewrite the Narrative
Martha Lane Fox	Dot Everyone
Etty Laniado	Chef Laniado
Melanie Lawson	Bare Biology
Phoebe Lebrecht	Glass Digital Media
Vicki Willden-Lebrecht	Bright Agency
Sophie Le Ray	Naseba
Lindsay Levin	Leaders' Quest
Dena McCallum	Eden McCallum
Sandra Macleod	Echo Research

Maya Magal	Maya Magal Jewellery
Victoria Mellor	Melcrum Publishing
Lara Morgan	Pacific Direct; Scentered
Jane Mosley	Granny Olive's Kitchen
Fionnuala O'Conor	OpDem
Ellena Ophira	Weddingly
Claire Randall	Claire Randall Consulting
Sherry Roberts	The Longest Stay
Naomi Sautter	Naomi Sautter Weddings & Events
Hilary Scarlett	Scarlett & Grey
Gabriella Sugg	The Ella-Phant Kitchen
Sian Sutherland	Mama Mio
Sarah Turner	Angel Academe
Tash Walker	The Mix
Susie Watson	Susie Watson Designs
Sarah Wood	Unruly
Stephanie Wray	Cresswell Associates; RSK Biocensus

NOTES

1 www.score.org/blog/state-women-entrepreneurs.

2 *The Alison Rose Review of Female Entrepreneurship*, 2019.

3 *The Alison Rose Review of Female Entrepreneurship*, 2019, www.forbes.com/sites/davidprosser/2018/09/24/where-are-all-the-uks-female-entrepreneurs/#2df5dda05665.

4 *The Global Entrepreneurship Monitor (GEM) 2016–17 Women's Report*, www.gemconsortium.org/report/49860.

5 NatWest's *The Female Entrepreneur Economy* report, www.weconnecteurope.org/sites/default/files/documents/The_Female_Entrepreneur_Economy_NatWest_March_2017.pdf.

6 The NatWest study 2017 as above and www.independent.co.uk/Business/indyventure/uk-women-start-own-business-female-entrepreneur-number-proportion-drop-international-figures-a7603246.html.

7 www.score.org/blog/state-women-entrepreneurs.

8 Women's Budget Group, 2016, www.prowess.org.uk/facts and Labour Force Survey, ONS, 2015.

9 www.gemconsortium.org/report/49860.

10 Score's report on 'The State of Women Entrepreneurs', www.score.org/blog/state-women-entrepreneurs.

11 *ONS Regional Trends, Women in Business*, 2009,www.ons.gov.uk/employmentandlabourmarket/peopleinwork/employmentandemployeetypes.

12 www.prowess.org.uk/facts.

13 http://10years.firstround.com.

14 Untapped Unicorns, Female Founders Forum, Barclays, 2017.

15 *Women In Enterprise: A Different Perspective*, RBS Group, 2012.

16 Martin Wyn Griffith speaking at the National Dialogue for Entrepreneurship, Washington DC, March 2005, www.prowess.org.uk/facts.

17 *Forbes*, www.forbes.com/sites/davidprosser/2018/09/24/where-are-all-the-uks-female-entrepreneurs/#2df5dda05665.

18 *Women and the Economy*, March 2018, http://researchbriefings.files.parliament.uk/documents/SN06838/SN06838.pdf.

19 RBS Group: 'Women in Enterprise: A Different Perspective', www.prowess.org.uk/facts.

20 Global Entrepreneurship Monitoring Consortium, http://researchbriefings.files.parliament.uk/documents/SN06838/SN06838.pdf.

21 *The Alison Rose Review of Female Entrepreneurship*, 2019, citing Global Entrepreneurship Monitor, 'Global Entrepreneurship. Women's Entrepreneurship 2016/2017 Report', 2017.

22 'Enterprise Insight Impact Evaluation', 2009, https://www.prowess.org.uk/facts.

23 *The Alison Rose Review of Female Entrepreneurship*, 2019, citing The Federation of Small Businesses (FSB) 'Women in Enterprise: The Untapped Potential' (2016), Department of Business, Energy and Industrial Strategy (BEIS), Business Population Estimates for the UK and Regions 2018 (2018), YouGov 2017 Business Survey, RBS Analytics.

24 *The Alison Rose Review of Female Entrepreneurship*, 2019, citing Jonathan Dimson et al., *Productivity: The Route to Brexit Success*, report for McKinsey & Company, December 2016.

25 *The Alison Rose Review of Female Entrepreneurship*, 2019, citing The Federation of Small Businesses (FSB) 'Women in Enterprise: The Untapped Potential' (2016), Department of Business, Energy and Industrial Strategy (BEIS), Business Population Estimates for the UK and Regions 2018 (2018), YouGov 2017 Business Survey, RBS Analytics.

26 *The Alison Rose Review of Female Entrepreneurship*, 2019, citing *Labour Productivity, UK: April to June 2018*, UK Office for National Statistics (ONS), 20 February 2019.

27 www.score.org/blog/state-women-entrepreneurs.

28 *Labour Force Survey*, Q4 2006, ONS; www.prowess.org.uk/facts.

29 www.prowess.org.uk/facts.
30 *The Alison Rose Review of Female Entrepreneurship*, 2019, citing Global Entrepreneurship Monitor, *Global Report 2017/2018*, 2018.
31 *The Alison Rose Review of Female Entrepreneurship*, 2019, citing Global Entrepreneurship Monitor, *Global Report 2017/2018*, 2018.
32 Harding, R., 'State of Women's Enterprise in the UK'; www.prowess.org.uk/facts.
33 2nd Prowess conference, 2004; www.prowess.org.uk/facts.
34 www.weconnecteurope.org/sites/default/files/documents/The_Female_Entrepreneur_Economy_NatWest_March_2017.pdf.
35 www.theguardian.com/media-network/media-network-blog/2013/apr/10/female-business-owners-banks-help.
36 Eleanor Steafel, 'I was told I didn't look the part', *Telegraph*, 8 March 2018, www.telegraph.co.uk/women/business/told-didnt-look-part-funding-gap-preventing-millions-women.
37 *The Alison Rose Review of Female Entrepreneurship*, 2019, citing the UK VC & Female Founders report commissioned by Chancellor Philip Hammond in 2017 and released to the press in February 2019, www.british-business-bank.co.uk/ female-start-up-founders-missing-out-onbillions-in-funding).
38 www.telegraph.co.uk/women/business/two-thirds-british-female-business-owners-say-still-not-taken.
39 http://fortune.com/2017/07/20/women-better-men-crowdfunding-study.
40 *The Alison Rose Review of Female Entrepreneurship*, 2019; www.forbes.com/sites/davidprosser/2018/09/24/where-are-all-the-uks-female-entrepreneurs/#2df5dda05665.
41 *The Alison Rose Review of Female Entrepreneurship*, 2019.
42 *The Alison Rose Review of Female Entrepreneurship*, 2019.
43 www.entrepreneur.com/article/298142.
44 *The Alison Rose Review of Female Entrepreneurship*, 2019.
45 *The Alison Rose Review of Female Entrepreneurship*, 2019.
46 *The Alison Rose Review of Female Entrepreneurship*, 2019.
47 *Women in Enterprise: A Different Perspective*, RBS Group.
48 www.huffingtonpost.com/entry/women-entrepreneurs-are-driving-economic-growth_us_59f7c3dce4b04494283378f3?guccounter=1.
49 https://hbr.org/2017/09/the-comprehensive-case-for-investing-more-vc-money-in-women-led-startups.
50 *The Alison Rose Review of Female Entrepreneurship*, 2019.
51 *The Alison Rose Review of Female Entrepreneurship*, 2019.
52 *The Alison Rose Review of Female Entrepreneurship*, 2019.
53 *The Alison Rose Review of Female Entrepreneurship*, 2019.
54 *The Alison Rose Review of Female Entrepreneurship*, 2019.
55 Sheryl Sandberg, *Lean In: Women, Work, and the Will to Lead*.
56 *The Alison Rose Review of Female Entrepreneurship*, 2019; Global Entrepreneurship Monitor.
57 *The Alison Rose Review of Female Entrepreneurship*, 2019.

CHAPTER TWO
Getting started

First off, let's debunk the myth that entrepreneurship is the unique preserve of thrusting youth with a 21st-century proposition. Well, it can be that but, as we found from our interviews, the bug can strike at any age, triggered by a variety of self-determined catalysts or responses to circumstances – or a mixture of the two.

In Chapter Two, we review some of our interviewees' stories of how they started and from this deduce:

- *The six self-determined and circumstantial catalysts that caused our interviewees to take the entrepreneurial leap.*
- *When is the best age to start.*

THE CATALYSTS THAT ENCOURAGE WOMEN TO BECOME ENTREPRENEURS

In our interviews with fifty-two female entrepreneurs we found six underlying catalysts that encouraged them to take the leap. These were:

1. Building on childhood experiences.
2. Combining career with caring for a family.
3. Creating a better, more flexible and collaborative work environment.
4. Out of necessity to overcome difficulties.
5. Having a great idea.
6. Following a passion.

Many of our interviewees cited more than one of these catalysts in their stories. So, similarly, you may identify with one or more of them as you read this section.

CATALYST ONE – BUILDING ON CHILDHOOD EXPERIENCES

Entrepreneurial and (or) supportive family role models are widely reported as influential, with many of our interviewees citing them as a positive influence when choosing an entrepreneurial route. The distinction between entrepreneurial family role models and supportive role models is significant in that many of our interviewees had supportive family role models that were not entrepreneurial. So, whilst the combination of the two is powerful, it's not essential.

Tash Walker, Tamara Gillan, Mursal Hedayat, Lindsay Levin and Mélanie Chevalier are five examples of people who were stimulated by their childhoods to be entrepreneurial.

Tash Walker, founder of The Mix, had an entrepreneurial calling in childhood in part driven by her entrepreneurial mother:

> The idea of trying your hand at business was probably part and parcel of my childhood, whether it was buying and selling filing cabinets or making cakes, my mother tried it all to make a buck. They weren't necessarily always successful but I definitely thought that it was entirely plausible to have a go at running a business. I also always had the itch to work for myself someday. I'd seen my mother being in control, and liked the idea of me being in control.

Tash started her career in a small independent marketing agency. But it didn't take her long to realise that she didn't want to be part of the corporate world:

> I really liked the businesses I worked in. But if you've got that slight itch to want to be the one calling the shots and you can't see that path evidently in front of you in a male-dominated business, then it is probably inevitable that you will go off and do it yourself.

She identified a gap in the industry that none of the established players had seen and that the independent agency didn't want to go after. 'That was it really, that was the moment where I suddenly thought "OK, I could do something about that". So she took her chance and made the leap, resigning the next Wednesday and starting her own marketing agency, The Mix, three weeks later.

Tamara Gillan, founder of marketing agency Cherry London, credits her parents with having a big influence on her decision to be an entrepreneur. In her own words:

> My father had a really interesting background in that he comes from the East End where his father was a bare-knuckle fighter after the war. He went into the film industry in Soho early on as a lighting man making his own way in the world, and then he became a property developer. He married my mother who comes from a bright academic family from New Zealand and was over here travelling on what Kiwis call their 'overseas excursion'. Mum went to a school for gifted children, and became a journalist. And she married this self-made entrepreneur, not so much a wide boy but one who made his own way.

> I love that background because it gave me from my dad's side a belief that I would be an entrepreneur and take risks, and I would do it – along with the academic rigour and creative flair on my mother's side. So I think I have this lovely alchemy that set me up to do my own thing.

Tamara did a degree in New Zealand and then came to London to work in marketing. Yet she always knew she would be an entrepreneur.

> I always had a plan that when I turned thirty, after I'd worked in marketing agencies and as a client, I would start my first agency. And that's what I did. After working in London for some years, I started Cherry London and I just sort of threw myself in.

Mursal Hedayat, founder of Chatterbox, started her own business in response to the challenges that she saw her parents face as new migrants to the U.K. Mursal decided at the end of her university degree that she didn't want to be part of the corporate world.

> I'd been tracking my own success against society's metrics for so long, wanting to graduate at the top of the class with the best grades and go into a graduate programme that everyone thought was excellent. But it didn't work out that way. For the first time in my life, I failed at something. I hadn't graduated with a first, I hadn't secured that internship or postgraduate role at a top bank or whatever it was that I thought was the logical next step in my life.

At some level I wanted to be in one of those big businesses as that's what society deems as successful. But on another level I knew that I didn't want to be part of this quite corrupt 'sucking of value' but instead wanted to 'create value'. My failure sort of freed me from the corporate path and, looking back, it was so much of a blessing.

On completing university, Mursal decided to help refugees who faced similar challenges to her parents. And so she joined a year-long educational programme where she studied social innovation and entrepreneurship. When this finished, she started up her own social enterprise, the very aptly named 'Chatterbox', employing refugees as language tutors to help them rebuild their shattered lives in the U.K. She saw at first hand the challenges that her parents had had to face as new migrants to the U.K. – and so was in a great place to help new waves of refugees overcome similar challenges.

Lindsay Levin founded Leaders' Quest, a business which hones leaders' leadership skills. As she says herself, the roots of her business were embedded in her childhood. Lindsay recalls:

> My childhood is very relevant to what I do today. My dad was a car dealer and I worked in the business every school holiday. I worked a lot from a young age in very down-to-earth, gritty environments such as car repair shops and petrol stations. I was a petrol pump attendant in the days when you held the pump.

> I've always been hard-working and driven, but also really curious about people. So part of what I got in that childhood was a respect for all kinds of people. I learnt at a young age that everyone is connected, and that relationships and how you treat one another matter.

After Cambridge and a stint at strategy consultancy Bain, Lindsay joined the family's car dealership business and made CEO in her twenties. She recalls:

> I really threw myself into the business and ended up at a very young age with an unusual level of responsibility. I worked hard, made plenty of mistakes but learnt a lot. I rediscovered my childhood

experiences at work and realised I was entrepreneurial, full of ideas and interested in what makes people tick. I learnt how to help people be happy with their work and make a difference to customers.

At the time this was quite unusual in the car industry. We did a lot of pioneering things which got attention in the industry. Volkswagen even wrote a book about what we were doing called *Changing Gear* which was the story of our pioneering practices in our dealerships. And I became a speaker on leadership because of what we were doing in the business which at its heart was very simple – treat other people as you wish to be treated and try to inculcate that in the culture of your company.

Lindsay shows that it's possible to translate early experiences of a very gritty, male and conservative industry into a thought leader coaching business operating at the highest level.

But to reassure those who don't have entrepreneurs in the family, the absence of entrepreneurial parents or family members doesn't seem to be a barrier. As one of our interviewees said: 'What you haven't experienced you don't miss'. Our final example demonstrates this.

Mélanie Chevalier is a French woman living in London. She and colleagues have spent ten years building Creative Culture which helps multinationals to localise global marketing campaigns so that the language and tone align with the local host country's culture. Mélanie's childhood was spent with her family in many countries around the world. Mélanie had no entrepreneurial family role models. The influences on her were her supportive family and the experience of living her childhood on four continents and observing the cultural differences.

Mélanie says:

My childhood definitely determined what I'm doing today. I was raised overseas and spent the first ten years of my life on four different continents going from Taiwan to Brazil, Cameroon and then back to France. I then stayed in France for ten years before studying in Spain for a year and then moving to London where I've been for nearly fifteen years. The essence of what the business does is very much related to how I grew up and being surrounded by different countries, cultures and languages. I never really knew what I was going to end up doing but when I saw what transcreation was all about – helping adapt advertising, marketing and promotion across different countries – it immediately made sense to me. Yes, my childhood definitely helped determine that. Not so much the entrepreneur side of things because I don't have any entrepreneurs in my family, but it certainly defined the essence of Creative Culture.

CATALYST TWO – COMBINING CAREER WITH CARING FOR A FAMILY

This proved to be a much-cited catalyst, with many of our interviewees leaving the more male-dominated corporate world to care for young children or other family relatives. Starting a business gives the owner more flexibility to decide where and when they work and how to create the optimal work–life balance. For example, some women are in roles where they are forced to travel regularly, which can be impossible when children are very young. Some are expected to do a lot of out-of-hours hospitality or weekend conferences, which can make the work–family balance unacceptable. And some even reported veiled or overt male disapproval for sticking to their domestic timetable.

Many of our interviewees are managing this balance. We were staggered by some stories where women were managing a full-time day job, running their own business in their spare time and caring for a family, sometimes as a single mother. And others spoke of caring for family whilst building a global business but rarely missing iconic school-gate moments, birthdays and the like. Those that are already successful get (expensive) help – but of course this is mostly unaffordable in the early phases of a start-up.

Many had much advice to offer. The key to making it work, we were told, is to be able to multitask and manage time very effectively. Women seem wired to do that after centuries of coping and adapting. But as important is knowing the split you want between work and family and what resources you need to strike the balance.

Dena McCallum, Liann Eden, Melanie Lawson, Elizabeth Cowper, Claire Randall and Hilary Scarlett are all women who took the entrepreneurial plunge when faced with having children or other family members to care for. As you'll see, they were also driven by other catalysts such as having a great idea or following a passion – but having a child was often the trigger that made them take the entrepreneurial leap.

Liann Eden and Dena McCallum, the founders of Eden McCallum, were two women who took the entrepreneurial leap to keep doing the fulfilling work they loved as well as caring for their children. They met at Insead in 1991 and became good friends through their shared love of horse riding. After Insead, corporate life beckoned and Liann worked at Unilever and then McKinsey and Dena worked at McKinsey and then Condé Nast. They both ended up living in London and having children at a similar age. And both quickly realised that their senior-level corporate roles involved too much travel for them as new mums.

Dena was Director of Strategy at Condé Nast where she had to spend two weeks in six in Asia. And Liann was working at McKinsey where she was continuously travelling long-haul on projects. Both wanted to do rewarding work rather than play more supportive corporate roles, but in a way that gave them more control over their lives and put them in the driving seat when making decisions that affected their families. So they decided to leave the corporate world, with their respective corporations losing valuable female talent, and start their own business.

At Condé Nast, Dena had wanted to hire McKinsey-type support, but the budgets and team were too big. So why not set up a strategy house resourced with self-employed associates around the world that could deliver McKinsey-style work at a better price? Dena and Liann went through their rolodexes to find ex-McKinsey consultants they could use. There were many! The consultants too confirmed that they loved the consulting work but also wanted more control over decisions about their working hours and lives, and wanted to focus on delivering great projects rather than on firm admin and business development. They tested their business idea with clients – and the clients also liked the idea of retaining more control of the process whilst working with bespoke teams selected and supplied by Eden McCallum. And so Eden McCallum was born. Dena and Liann could lessen their travel and so be at home most nights and choose what to prioritise each day, including their children's school events. So this was a win–win. The consultants were happy, the clients were happy, the children were happy – and none more so than Dena and Liann. Of course, there were plenty of tough trade-offs, but they were in control.

Theirs is a story of starting a business after starting a family. It also illustrates the point that a business may have its genesis in the experience that you've gained when employed by others. It's a tale not so much of filling a gap, as recognising and acting on one that fits the way you and others around you want to work.

Melanie Lawson is the founder of Bare Biology – a premium Omega 3 fish oil supplement brand. Like Dena and Liann, Melanie started her business to have a more fulfilling life whilst also having the flexibility to care for her children. She says:

> I graduated in the mid nineties and got a job as an account executive in a sales promotion agency. I worked in that industry for ten years but I never really liked having a boss. After a few years the shine of being paid to go out drinking with clients wore off and I realised how dull it was. It felt pointless. I had no intention of being in that long-term or working my way up to the top. I knew pretty quickly that I wasn't very good at doing the 'political sucking up to the right people' thing and keeping my mouth shut when I had to.
>
> So my partner and I decided to have children. It was a nice way of getting out of doing that job! I was a full-time Mum for seven years but found that I needed something else in my life to give me a sense of purpose and achievement outside of just being a mother. I remember vividly sitting in a horrible playgroup with my toddler and my newborn, and saying to a friend 'I can't wait for this to be over, I'm going to start a business and want you to come and work for me, and then we'll have a bit of our old lives back'. And that's what I did.

In 2013, Melanie launched her premium Omega 3 supplement business, Bare Biology, as a way to combine fulfilling work with being a mother. We'll learn more about how she made this happen later on in this chapter. Melanie goes on to talk about how her entrepreneurial venture has made her much happier.

> I know that I am a better mother for having my own life and my own business. And I also know that my kids are really proud of me – especially my daughters as I'm showing them first-hand that women can do all the stuff that men do. But at the same time I make sure I am around for the important things. I always take them to school and when they get home there's a cooked dinner (cooked by me!) waiting for them. I never miss sports days – it's important to me to be there for them.

Elizabeth Cowper is the founder of WoMo and her story illustrates the enormous lengths women go to to take care of family and succeed in business. She says:

> I didn't naturally take to motherhood. I didn't find it easy and I didn't have this overwhelming maternal instinct. My mum had never been a stay-at-home mum. She's a radiographer, that's her career. But she helped a friend out with a smoked salmon business and helped another mate doing something else, and then she'd go back into radiography. She never worked full-time. But she never stopped, she always had stuff going on. So sixteen years ago, I was at home with my first baby thinking: 'What am I going to do now? I don't want to be a full-time mother'. Back then it was a bit of a taboo subject to say: 'I don't want to be a full-time mum'. Some people would say 'Go out and a get job' and others would say 'No, you need to be at home with your baby'.

> When my baby was five months old, I decided I was going back to work. I got a job working on the Change Team at Network Rail transferring in 15,000 people, which was a huge project and very demanding. The only way I could cope was by hiring a full-time nanny which cost me more than my salary. I was losing money every

month. My ex-husband wasn't hugely into the idea that I was going off to work every day, leaving our child and making no money. But I was really motivated even though everything I earned went to the nanny. I just thought I'm going to build a career and if I'm going to have a future I have to do this and suck it up.

I think it took just over a year before I made any money for me. By this point I was pregnant with my second one. When I was off on maternity leave, I got approached for a job at Fenn Wright Manson, the women's fashion brand, as their Head of HR. So I was going back to work with a second one at home, to another job. Then it started making sense because I was earning more money and paying for a nanny for two children. This got me thinking about how as a HR leader I could support other women who have had a baby going back into work.

Which was the genesis for Elizabeth's online support community (WoMo) for working mothers.

Elizabeth went on to be HR Director at other companies like LVMH and Planet Organic which inspired her further.

Planet Organic has a really good holistic approach – not just about eating organic food and living your life in a sustainable way, but also for its people. It has a much better approach to looking after people with long-term sickness or those who have a baby but want to work more flexibly.

This inspired Elizabeth to start WoMo, which, in her words:

Helps women through the process of finding out you're pregnant, going on maternity leave and coming back to work – including how you as an individual can manage it yourself, and how the company and HR leader can help that woman through the process in a really positive way that benefits the company and the employee.

Claire Randall (founder of Claire Randall Consulting) wanted to be a great mother as well as have a successful career. Her story illustrates the loss that corporates are suffering by sticking with their more male-oriented work cultures that make it difficult to balance both. She started out as a TV producer at Saatchi & Saatchi which she loved. But she recalls:

> As a TV producer in large corporates, you end up working long hours in often faraway places shooting ads. When I began thinking about starting a family, I realised it would be good to have something more flexible – where it's my time and I can choose how to manage it. Once I had my son I realised I could never go back into an agency because it wouldn't give me the flexibility I needed. It wasn't my plan to have my own business so early on. One of my biggest clients at this time asked me to work for them. They couldn't hire me as they didn't have the headcount plus there was no career path for me in TV production there. So I set up the company just to work for them, and I literally haven't stopped working since.

Claire Randall Consulting was born as an outsourced production consultancy for one large global advertiser. Interestingly, Claire's workforce is predominantly female:

> We employ mostly women, not as a policy, but because the women like the flexibility we offer. A lot of them are working four days a week instead of five. They can do the job from home if they need to and the hours are more manageable than those in production. I've only had four people leave in twenty-three years so we must be doing something right!

What a great testament for creating a flexible work culture.

One of our interviewees was forced to leave the corporate world to care for family members. Hilary Scarlett was a management consultant and director with the firm founded by John Smythe (SmytheDorwardLambert). But she had no choice but to leave her employment and work from home when her sister died leaving a daughter to be cared for and, subsequently, her partner was rendered into a coma as a result of a cycling accident. She started up Scarlett & Grey, a groundbreaking company that applies neuroscience to business, with the aim of enabling employees to perform at their best. Her new venture gave her the flexibilty to manage these responsibilities as well as make a good living and which has subsequently been built into a very successful business.

John says:

> Looking back, having listened to all of these tales, I'm not sure now that we did anything like enough for Hilary at the time. With a young team everyone's lives seemed effortless and I don't think we took in the gravity of what befell Hilary. She faced her situation with courage and calm.

As these stories ably demonstrate, entrepreneurship is proving a very successful way to combine a fulfilling career with being there for your family.

CATALYST THREE – CREATING A BETTER, MORE FLEXIBLE AND COLLABORATIVE WORK ENVIRONMENT

Many of our interviewees talked about their desire to leave the more male-dominated corporate world to create a more female-friendly working environment. As we saw in the last section, some did this out of necessity – driven by starting a family and needing to be at home more in the evenings or being able to work more flexible hours to be more available for their children. Others wanted to create a more female-friendly working environment with flexible hours, an absence of male banter (and worse) and greater collegiality than some more competitive male cultures. In more extreme cases, some left due to issues that they experienced in the workplace including bullying, deferred promotion and bias in remuneration.

A number of women talked about the male bias in the corporate world being a key reason why they decided to do their own thing, illustrating the huge talent loss that corporates are facing by not being more female-friendly. Four examples are Rebekah Hall, Tamara Gillan, Sandra Macleod and Mursal Hedayat.

Rebekah Hall, founder of Botanic Lab, talked about life in the corporate world.

> When I look back now there are a lot of things that weren't right about my corporate experience. One example is when I finally made the decision to leave the company I was in, and work for a client. It was bonus season where everyone gets rated on a scale of one to four. The top 1% of your peer group are ones and bonuses are stratified on that basis. My best friend, who is a guy, got a lower rating but a higher bonus than me. In the end, that's why I resigned. They didn't really know what to do with the tools because they could only allocate so much money and so many one ratings around. So they made the choice that the rating would be more important to me and the money more important to him. Now with the benefit of experience, I can see that that's not right. It's a blatant example of sex discrimination that would make people cringe now.

We will go on to learn more about how Rebekah built her business later in this chapter.

Similarly, Tamara Gillan, who we met previously, left the corporate world to start her own marketing agency, Cherry London, as she didn't want to have to waste her energies battling her way through the glass ceiling. She says:

> So one of the reasons I started my agency was the 'glass ceiling'. I was then in Orange and if you looked around, 65–70% of marketing were women, yet the leadership were men. I thought: 'There is an easier way to do this by my own rules rather than trying to break through that corporate environment'. And it's ironic because I think as a leader and a woman you've got so many more tools in your toolkit.

Sandra Macleod was given the impetus to start her own business, Echo Research, when she was ousted from a company when pregnant.

> I was about to go off and have my first child and I remember my boss saying to me: 'We have too many chief executives and you obviously won't want to carry on working'. So they gave me a handshake and

wished me good luck. I wanted to continue working so I asked if I could take a franchise I'd won (CARMA) with me, and my boss said: 'Well it's not going to come to anything, so yes you're welcome to it'. I said thank you and hugged him and left. So I took on the franchise as no one was interested in it, rebranded it to Echo Research, and grew it into an eight million dollar company.

Thinking about the conversation that kicked it all off, Sandra recalls: 'I look back on it and think: "Gosh, if I had that conversation now it would probably have been very different"'.

Internships may be the first taste young people have of working for others. Though the pay may be low or nothing, they provide an opportunity for young people to see what work is and what it is to work for others. For Mursal Hedayat (the founder of Chatterbox who featured earlier in this chapter) it helped her to see that working for a corporate organisation was definitely not for her. She says:

> At eighteen, I was making quite a significant amount of money for someone my age. Every summer and winter, I was invited back to a City of London financial firm as an intern. It struck me, at one point, that the longer I stayed the more they gave me real work. And I remember sitting in the back office and looking at the rows of people on either side of me and realising that some of the people were significantly older than me and were still doing the same job as me, years on. People in there were selling their youth and time for money, so that they could do what I was doing – buying stuff on Oxford Street that they didn't need. It was a personal light bulb moment that really put me off a corporate lifestyle and led me on the path of becoming my own boss. Lots of my university peers had been hoping for a well-paid corporate life. I'd seen the underside and realised that it was a terrible and unfullfiling compromise and wasn't for me. I learned that at age eighteen – and am grateful to that internship for showing me.

Other interviewees wanted to create a more female-friendly work environment that they and fellow women would prefer to work in. Melina

Jacovou and Vicki Willden-Lebrecht are two examples of people who left the corporate world to do this.

Melina Jacovou, founder of Propel, left a company due to a clash of values with a desire to build a company that treated people, particularly women, with respect. She recalls:

> I was a Board member in this business but over time realised that the founders didn't have the same values as me. We had very different beliefs about the way we should be, what we should do and the way we should treat people – not just our clients but also the people who worked within our organisation. There were a number of incidents where I didn't think that they were being authentic or treating people in the way they should be treated, especially women.
>
> For me, their beliefs and behaviours were unacceptable. I couldn't justify being part of that environment, so I left and started Propel. I literally went from riches to ruins. I was earning the most money I had ever had in my life, I had smart cars and had just bought a flat. And then I decided to set this up, and had no salary, no cars, and I nearly lost my flat.

Propel finds top talent for high growth technology companies. She continues:

> We emphasise culture a lot here. Our Head of People makes sure we take on the right type of people. We have a Propel Playbook which outlines how to treat clients and candidates, and ensures that our message remains current and consistent across the whole business. This in turn makes the company more scalable and increases employee retention. I love working with people who are excited about the future. But the key to me is really helping other people succeed, not just men but women as well. And really making the environment that I work in a diverse, inclusive one.

Similarly, Vicki Willden-Lebrecht started her own business, The Bright Agency, to escape a company with principles and values that she couldn't buy into. Vicky recalls:

I was pulled in and given a reprimand for spelling mistakes and I thought 'I'm in the wrong place'. I didn't feel comfortable that they were focussing on my weaknesses and not my strengths. And their approach to agenting was just different to mine. I wanted to help the artist more, I wanted them to be the best that they could be. I didn't feel listened to. The important realisation was that I couldn't work passionately for an organisation when I didn't agree with their values and principles. I felt restricted and it was impossible to stay. And, at twenty-three, I left and set up Bright.

Vicki is now the leader of one of the fastest-growing and most established children's literary and illustration agencies.

The combination of a great idea and creating a more agreeable work environment are attracting more women to go their own way to the detriment of corporates. What started as a trickle of female talent flowing out of corporates is fast accelerating into a torrent.

Some corporates respond by offering a few transactional benefits, thinking that will do the trick. They fail to recognise that the challenge lies deep in the cultural memory of their organisation, requiring root and branch change to attitudes, presumptions, equality, language, tone, behaviour, practices and, frankly, male entitlement. Many senior leaders, mostly males, lack insight on the issue and refuse to admit that their organisations must change if they want to remain attractive to half the working population. Our prediction is that change will come from the outside as the new workplace designed by women for women increasingly attracts the best talent across the genders. Cynics say this new workplace culture is soft on performance. To this we say: 'Nonsense – look at the research summaries in Chapter One where statistics show that female start-ups are outperforming male counterparts'.

It's significant that many of our cohort reported hiring other women, sometimes exclusively, because women understood the deal. They need to get the work done but choose, within reason, the how and when.

CATALYST FOUR – OUT OF NECESSITY TO OVERCOME DIFFICULTIES

We all face difficulties and challenges in life – as did many of our interviewees. For some of them, the key reason why they started a business was out of necessity – as a way to overcome difficulties. These included:

- Finding a way to succeed as a new U.K. migrant.
- Re-building their life after relationship difficulties, an illness or depression.
- Wanting to prove themselves after doing badly at school or wanting to please a critical parent.
- Needing to make money.

Etty Laniado and Sarah Ali Choudhury are two people who wanted to prove themselves after having their confidence knocked – with Etty also needing to earn money when migrating to the U.K.

Etty Laniado is Israeli and spent her childhood and much of her adult life in Israel bringing up two children. She then came to London to study professional cooking and went on to launch Chef Laniado, a high-end hospitality company. She tells her story.

> As we say in Hebrew: 'to progress you need to break with your past'. There came a point in my life where I had to make a break with everything. So, with my marriage broken, I decided to leave the country. I needed to prove to myself that I could do something on my own and be successful. And I needed to do something for myself. So I came here, went to culinary school for nine months and started my own business. So here I am, doing OK, actually a bit better than OK. So, yes, I'm a successful migrant. I'm Israeli, that's what we do!

Etty goes on to recall a childhood beset by dyslexia and trying to shine for her father.

> I have dyslexia which adversely affected my grades. I was growing up in a time when dyslexia wasn't recognised. If you were dyslexic you were considered stupid or slow or lazy. These were the words that I

heard, which damaged my self-confidence. Dyslexia can be worked on and it's something that I have worked on all of my life, especially when I was young. But at that age I didn't know that other people suffered from it and that I wasn't alone. It was tough to see the disappointment on my father's face when I got the reports at the end of every term.

She goes on to say:

My father was the figure I most wanted to impress, yet the person I felt I had disappointed most. But, on reflection, it's thanks to him that I'm where I am today. It galvanised me to get on and succeed in something he loved – food. I can thank him for that even if it was hard to bear at the time as I wanted so much to please him. I visited him in hospital when he was fading away from us. He opened his eyes and woke up for a moment. I told him that I had won a place on MasterChef and that my business was taking off. He smiled and I knew that he was proud of me. It was a memorable moment. I felt a surge of self-confidence and got some peace from closing the circle.

Sarah Ali Choudhury also set up her business to rebuild her confidence and self-respect, having been brought up in a culture where men are used to being the sole breadwinner. Sarah's Indian parents owned and ran the Taj Mahal Restaurant in Bridport in Dorset, a stone's throw from co-author John Smythe's cottage. Sarah went on to found Easy Curry, continuing the family tradition of professional hospitality. The inspiration came when she was in her late thirties, after having worked for years for others. Sarah's children announced that they preferred mum's cooking to eating out in Indian restaurants – and so a business idea was born.

Sarah found that working for herself built her confidence in all aspects of her life, which helped repair her relationship with her husband who had previously tended to take the upper hand. Sarah says:

My children kicked the idea off but it was an incident at their school that ignited the idea. One of the parents filmed me cooking my signature chicken curry and vlogged it and it went viral on Youtube. It made me think: 'What do I most wish I could do with my work life?'.

And I thought I'd like to become a vlogger about Indian cuisine to help others cook Indian food. It led to a monthly column in a local newspaper, *The Bournemouth Echo*, a widely read and well-regarded newspaper on Britain's (occasionally) sun-soaked south coast.

It also led me to cook for local homeless people on a large scale every month. And contrastingly it resulted in a contract to cook for the polo matches on Britain's version of the Hamptons, Sandbanks, home to the most expensive properties in the U.K. with celebrities including footballers vying for vast houses perched on tiny plots. More significantly, my business helped to save my marriage. My professional journey motivated me to take control over the rest of my life and take an equal place in my relationship with my husband. That's not an easy transition to make in a culture where the man is used to having the upper hand. But my husband reacted positively to my rising confidence and self-respect. So I can say to other women that running my own business has had a healing effect on my family life and my own sense of self, to everyone's benefit.

Sherry Roberts and Di Burton are two people who have overcome illnesses caused, at least in part, by life in the corporate world, to start and successfully build their own entrepreneurial businesses.

Sherry Roberts, founder of The Longest Stay, was forced to leave her corporate job due to illness that was in part prompted by working in an aggressive male environment. She had to find another way to make money. Sherry says:

> I was sent by an architectural hardware company to Pittsburgh to learn the business with a distributor of theirs. It was a very male-dominated environment with the behaviour of some colleagues making it uncomfortable. I went through a lot of bullying and inappropriate comments that were a form of sexual harassment. I dodged *Playboy* on every desk and constantly had comments made about my clothes. I was twenty-two years old and, due to the stress, I became gravely ill with a condition called Chronic Fatigue Syndrome, now referred to as ME.

I ended up suing the company and settling out of court. I was probably one of the youngest women in the United States to sue a company for sexual harassment in 1992. I was left with an illness that no one really understood. A doctor told me that I was lazy and making it up as I didn't want to go to work. I spent many months trying to figure out what I had.

Eventually a psychologist said I had CFS/ME and ADD, a learning disability. It explained why I'd struggled in school and university, why I get bored so easily, and why I find it difficult to concentrate. The doctor said that it's very debilitating and that I probably wouldn't work again in my life because she hadn't seen anyone really recover. After a while, I decided that I would go back to work. I had got to the stage that it didn't matter what state I was in. I picked up the phone, put my finger on a travel company in the *Yellow Pages* phone book and dialled the company. An hour later, I had a job in Alaska working for a cruise line – which worked out well as a transition to more demanding jobs as my health improved.

Sherry went on to graduate with an MBA at one of the top universities in the United States, Northwestern University, and then on to the top hotel school in Switzerland as an Entrepreneur in Residence. This enabled her to realise her ambition of running her own business in the hospitality sector, encouraged by her Italian husband, Giovanni. Her idea has turned into a great success. Sherry's company furnishes hotels and then enables people to buy what they see in their rooms online, resulting in the world's first shoppable hotels.

Di Burton, founder of Cicada Communications, also needed to find work after being signed off when suffering from suspected MS. She recalls:

I got my first job very quickly in a public relations company in Harrogate in 1985, because I had my PR diploma. I was generally very successful there. One of our clients was a major food supplier and they had found a coating for battered fish. I got them onto the then leading tech TV show *Tomorrow's World*, and my boss couldn't believe it. He spoke to a researcher and said 'How did she do it?'. And the researcher said that I never gave up, I just kept phoning.

Within that first year I got approached by another company to head up their PR division. So I moved to Leeds, and won a major energy client for them in the lead up to their privatisation – again a spectacular success. But, at the time, I was getting stress-related physical symptoms and they thought I had MS. So they wrote me off on sick leave. I got paid a huge salary for a year for doing nothing. I just went horse riding. But I then thought: 'Come on Di, this is no good'. So I set up on my own.

Di went on to found and build her own very successful communications and PR agency, Cicada Communications, specialising in B2B clients. She also set up a PR degree at Leeds Trinity, where she was made Consultant Fellow and Honorary Fellow, and gained a Master's Degree for the GCS network and the COI where she worked directly with Peter Mandelson and Alistair Campbell. Amazing stuff from a person signed off for a year with suspected MS.

Aurée de Carbon used the impetus of losing her jobs (not once but multiple times) to kick-start herself on her entrepreneurial journey. She recalls:

I started working in an international advertising and media firm in France and really enjoyed the marketing piece. But then the company was bought out and went bankrupt, everything collapsed. And after that I thought 'What am I going to do now?'. My father was an economist, working with the developing world. So I sent my application to BNP Paribas and I was lucky enough to be hired as a private advisor. I worked hard and really liked it. After two years, I left the bank to join HSBC. That was a disaster. I couldn't adjust myself to their products and the way they worked. So I worked for them for six months and then left. So again I asked myself: 'What am I going to do now?'. A guy in an executive search company approached me saying he would like to do something with me. He came to Paris with a manual, it was two hundred or so pages long. He said to read it over the weekend and if I wanted to join, then great. I read the manual over the weekend and I said to my husband: 'My god, this is the job of my life. This is my place'. So I said 'OK, I'll join'. I developed their business and became a partner. And then we had an argument and I had to leave. It was a bit of a shock because it was a family business and I really enjoyed working there. Being rejected and forced to resign after giving your heart and soul twelve hours a day for three years, including the weekend, was very hard.

I left and joined a competitor firm. Shortly after I joined, one of their associates left the company and so I was asked to buy shares. I said no, and they weren't happy. And so they discontinued our collaboration. It was a bit of a shock, a bit brutal. So, I left and again said: 'What am I going to do now? It's been twice that I've started to work with others and neither worked. So maybe it's time to start working for myself'.

So Aurée set up her own leading executive firm, CARRHURE, headquartered in Paris, which prides itself in helping not-for-profit organisations hire the best of the best.

Finally, Lara Morgan, founder originally of Pacific Direct and now well-being investor of Scentered, had to make enough money to survive when she started out. She recalls:

It was 1991, I was twenty-three years old, and I needed a job in the recession. Being an 'entrepreneur', especially as a woman, was unknown then. It was a dirty word in the U.K. – whereas in America it was exalted. I couldn't get a job so I started a little business with one objective – to make enough money to eat and pay the bills. There was no other plan because I never expected to run a business long-term. I simply needed a job to pay my hockey subs and other costs, and to live while my other half did his MBA at Cranfield.

It was a tough start for Lara but she went on to do great things. She built Pacific Direct, which manufactured and sold brand-licensed toiletries and amenities to the hotel industry and sold for a great deal of money. She then backed other start-ups including her own, 'Scentered', which we will learn more about later in this chapter.

Throughout our interviews we have been very impressed by so many stories of perseverance and courage, particularly in the face of adversity or rejection. Women have picked themselves up and used these opportunities to build a better life for themselves. From overcoming difficulties, we move on to Catalyst five – having a great idea.

CATALYST FIVE – HAVING A GREAT IDEA

This was a very common theme in our interviews, with many of our interviewees starting a business after identifying a great opportunity. However, we found a number of different versions of this that might inspire you when developing your great idea.

- Some saw a gap in an established market and created a new product or service to fill it.
- Some created a whole new product or service category (as opposed to filling a gap).
- Some couldn't find a solution to their lifestage issue and so invented it for themselves and subsequently for others.
- Some wanted to create a business with a strong social purpose.
- Some grabbed an opportunity and grew it into a successful business.

Seeing a gap in an established market and creating a new product or service to fill it

Amongst our cohort there are plenty of examples of people who spotted a gap in an established market and then took the initiative to fill that gap.

The first example is Rebekah Hall, founder of innovative drinks company Botanic Lab. She always knew that she wanted to be an entrepreneur and so looked for an opportunity in markets where she had some interest and knowledge. Rebekah recalls:

> As I went through my teens and into choosing my career, I knew I wanted to be the boss of something. I couldn't tell you what, but I was surrounded by a group of people who either encouraged that or showed me the way to do that.

After a stint in the corporate world, Rebekah resigned from her job and took some time out to find an opportunity that she could launch. She continues:

> I found a business partner who wanted to start a drinks business and I thought that sounds interesting. I know a bit about the market. The States is a good five years ahead of us, which we can bring to the U.K., and I have nothing to lose. I can raise money for the business as I can raise money for anything. And so I went very naively into starting a business. It could have been gin, trainers, anything really and it still could be anything to be honest. I'll do this again and I'll do it with something else, but I have no idea what it will be. When the business was launched, we were one of the few businesses experimenting with innovative healthy drinks. All of a sudden in six months there were lots of people doing the same thing – it just exploded. The partnership didn't pan out as planned but the business had flourished.
>
> What we did differently was to take ingredients that have a functional use in the body and marketed them in a way that's very different to Innocent. Innocent branding is very quirky, funny and jokey. We went right to the opposite end of the spectrum creating branding that is factual, functional, transparent and a bit masculine. It seemed to resonate with a generation of people who are interested in knowing where the ingredients have come from, how it's produced and how it's reached them.
>
> That journey has been at a million miles an hour. We're in a completely different space with consumers now than we were four years ago. We bat alongside the likes of Coca Cola in a way that I would never have thought possible. The whole drinks space is being redefined. And as with all business ideas we came to it at the right time as a stroke of luck – with an interesting concept and the entrepreneurial drive to push it through the difficult times.

Botanic Lab has enjoyed great growth since its inception in 2014 and is now available in many well-known retailers such as Sainsbury's, Waitrose, Wholefoods, Fortnum & Mason, Co-op, WHSmith and Planet Organic. A huge achievement.

Rebekah's story is an example of a market 'first mover'. It's also interesting that she had no personal crusade to pursue. The interest in drinks came from her business partner. But the fusion of his idea, her commercial nouse and their joint hard work paid off. Like many others it took time – four years to become profitable. Recall that Mumsnet took eight years to reach profitability. Whilst there are one or two examples of early commercial triumph, they are notable for their scarcity. The journey can take a while and be bumpy – so be warned.

Creating a whole new product or service category

The next story is also an example of a 'first mover', but this time creating a whole new product and service category.

In 2014, Sarah Turner created Angel Academe, the first angel network in the U.K. expressly designed to invest in female technology entrepreneurs. Sarah tells us:

> I wanted to create an angel network as opposed to a crowd funding platform. An angel network builds relationships between angel investors and between investors and entrepreneurs. Crowd funding is a 'no strings attached' financial transaction. They are very different.

> Entrepreneurs looking for investment need to figure out which of these (and other sources) will most suit their business and growth ambitions. When I first set this up, the ecosystem did such a poor job of supporting women, especially in technology, because it was so male-dominated. It didn't reflect the diversity of the population and increasingly the diversity of founders. It was a personal mission for me to create a community that started to level the playing field for women. I want women who are raising money to have access to both female and male investors. And I'm passionate about empowering women to be angel investors. It's a way to be entrepreneurial without being an entrepreneur, and to do something really interesting with a sensible portion of investible assets. And it may result in more women becoming entrepreneurs themselves.

When people think about how they can support female founders better, the automatic thing is to say: 'Oh, well, they need more training or mentoring or this or that'. I say no, they don't, they need a level playing field and money. Otherwise we reinforce the idea that women aren't as good as men in the first place. The other myths we need to de-bunk are that female entrepreneurs lack confidence, are risk averse and only build niche businesses. To me, that's nonsense. We're not at the same level as some of the bigger, more established angel groups, yet we're very ambitious and passionate about empowering women to be successful entrepreneurs as well as angel investors.

Couldn't find a solution to their own lifestage issue and so created a product to address it

Melanie Lawson (founder of Bare Biology) and Sian Sutherland (founder of Mama Mio) are two examples of people who couldn't find solutions to their own lifestage issues and so created products to fix them.

Melanie Lawson discovered that concentrated fish oil helped her through pre- and postnatal depression. This was her inspiration for Bare Biology – making high strength, good quality fish oil available to others with the same health issue. Melanie says:

> I didn't realise at the time but I had pre- and postnatal depression with my second child. Postnatal depression resulted in me setting very high standards for myself. The little voice kicks in: 'I should do better', which can be tough on a personal level because nothing's ever good enough. So I did some research into nutrition, and found that fish oil is really important in pregnancy and afterwards as a big chunk of our brain is made of a type of Omega 3, called DHA, as are our eyes. When you're pregnant and breastfeed, the mother's DHA goes to the baby and you end up with no DHA which can exacerbate anxiety and depression.
>
> U.K. medical professionals know little about nutrition. They confuse Cod Liver Oil, which you should not take in pregnancy because it's

high in vitamin A, with fish oil. So I started eating sardines pretty much every day and taking a high strength fish oil. I did lots of research and found that most fish oils available here were not powerful enough to make any difference. No guarantees of purity, so no transparency on their test results or levels of mercury. A lot of them taste horrible because they're rancid. So I bought one from Canada. I got really irritated by the lack of transparency and quality, and the more I researched it, the more I got irritated. But then I didn't give it much more thought until after I'd had my third child.

After four or five years of full-time motherhood I knew I wanted to get back into business. I just didn't know what to do. My husband and I were chatting about the start-up 'Graze' as it was really taking off. It was healthy snacks delivered to your home that fitted through your letterbox. It was really pioneering at the time. It made us think: 'Wow, what a great business model – a sort of money-while-you-sleep business'. So I said: 'Why not do something similar for vitamins because there aren't any good vitamins available, and you could tailor it to your needs?'. But in the end I kept it simple and specialised in Omega 3.

I didn't have a clue where to start. But whilst my youngest napped, I researched. And in the course of the research I came across a trade exhibition in Geneva. I went and found a Norwegian fish oil manufacturer. I rocked up looking as businesslike as I could, feeling a bit unsure as I hadn't had any business interaction for over seven years. I dusted off my advertising pitch mode and tried to sell my high concentration Omega 3 idea to their Head of Sales. She initially said: 'You're absolutely mad but I like it. We could work with you. Let's give it a go'.

I came home all excited. I thought I have to go and check them out in Norway. So I went to see them. They showed me how it was made and asked me what I thought my projected volumes would be. I didn't have a clue. So I just made a load of stuff up and said: 'Well, we're going to get it stocked in Wholefoods and blah di blah' – totally blagging it. I had to persuade them to sell me one barrel of raw fish oil – something I think they'd never done before. But they did. I came home and thought: 'Right, I've now got to find someone who'll bottle it'. Eventually I found a bottler who bottles other types of oil – rape-seed, olive and coconut oil. And I said: 'Would you bottle fish oil?'. And they said 'I don't see why not. Come up and we'll have a go'.

Bare Biology now has three employees as well as contractors that Melanie has worked with for a long time. And it's stocked in retailers such as Wholefoods, Liberty, Harrods, Planet Organic, John Bell Croydon and many more. A resounding success from very small roots.

That's Melanie's story of how she turned her personal challenge into a great business and expanded the category of the market by doing so.

Similarly, Sian Sutherland co-created a whole new product category for pregnant women including herself and her co-partners. Sian recalls:

My creative partner Kathy Miller and I were hitting thirty, and both about to get married and enter our baby-making years. We wanted to do something that gave us flexibility and enabled us to focus on projects that we had a personal connection with. And so we built this boutique brand creation agency which focussed on the two areas that interested us – beauty and drink – which was a lot of fun.

As a brand creation agency we thought: 'Why don't we create some brands for us?'. So we developed a bath and body brand called Mio with Lyn Harris and Tanya Kazeminy. At the beginning it was a complete indulgence for us. It was a brand that we wanted on our bathroom shelves but also something that we could propose for design awards. Mio became a *Vogue* 'It' brand of the year and sold in just two shops, Liberty and Harrods. We'd do the tiniest runs in the world. A few years later we also needed skincare products to help us through pregnancy. With no commercial intent, we made these little brown bottles of tummy rub oil just for ourselves and our pregnant friends.

Fast forward to the early 2000s. Kathy and I had done a lot in this brand creation space and had had our kids. My husband is also an entrepreneur and had built up the largest privately-operated U.K. bar chain of sixty-five bars called PoNaNa. It was when that business hit a tough time that I realised I could no longer keep my foot halfway on the gas pedal. This was the catalyst for me thinking: 'OK, I now need to do something really serious because our PoNaNa pension pot is no longer around'. We had Mio the brand on the back burner and this uncommercialised pregnancy range. We knew that in this massively saturated beauty market there was a niche that nobody else has spotted – the first genuine skincare product for a woman who is going to put thirty inches of stretch on her tummy. It's all about skin elasticity which is a genuine need. You could have driven a bus into that niche and yet nobody had. So I talked to my partners – Kathy and Tanya – and said I would love us to pull this brand out of the deep freeze and take it to the States where we have had a lot of experience with distribution. They said: 'Great, we're in'.

We went to the States, met the key buyers at Sephora and others who advised us to focus on the Mama Mio pregnancy range rather than the Mio line-up. We considered lots of different ways to raise smart money and finally met a fantastic woman based in California who had tremendous beauty experience. Jill Dunk gave us distribution potential on the ground which made the U.S. a no-brainer. Pregnancy is a numbers game and the large U.S. market was always going to be a big focus for us. It was only when Nicky Kinnaird, the founder of Space NK, saw our presentation and said 'Why don't you launch in Space NK?', that we even thought of launching in the U.K.

We launched the brand in September 2005 in the U.S. and the U.K. Genuine innovation often comes out of adversity and our retail launch was a great example of that. Something we initially thought was a disadvantage became one of our major advantages – having a very different distribution pattern to the usual beauty brands. Initially we went the traditional route – knocking on the doors of Barneys, Sephora and the beauty departments of John Lewis and department stores. Every buyer would say the same thing: 'I love it, I get it, but we don't know where to put you because your category doesn't exist'.

In the end we thought: 'Instead of going where all the beauty brands are, let's go where "our woman" is'. Our woman is not in the beauty department, she's in the John Lewis nursery on the fourth floor and in Pea in the Pod in the U.S. It felt much smarter to be the only skincare brand in a department where everybody who steps across the threshold is either pregnant or married to or buying a present for somebody who's pregnant. Being forced into the nursery and maternity wear areas turned out to be an entirely accidental stroke of genius!

The penny dropped going upstairs into John Lewis's nursery area and Destination Maternity in the U.S. We realised that they're selling pregnancy jeans at a hundred dollars a pop and everything that you need when you're pregnant, and there are no skincare brands there. Mama Mio was the perfect incremental purchase at a time when women need care and indulgences. Little things that are going to help nurture and understand them, rather than their baby. We were billing over a million dollars a year at our locations in 'Destination Maternity' in the U.S. in just eighty stores. Truly a light bulb moment. We wouldn't have been doing a fraction of that if we had been in a traditional beauty department.

Mama Mio ended up being launched into twelve countries by Sian and her team. It grew so successfully that it was acquired by The Hut Group in 2016 and is still considered to be one of the market-leading players in the global pregnancy skincare market, worth over $22 billion in 2017. Not bad for a brand that started out in Sian's own words as the 'most selfish brand in the world'.[1]

Sian's story, like others, stresses the importance of embracing a challenge to make it work to your advantage. In her case, selling her products in the nursery department where there were no competitors, rather than in the beauty department where they would have fought for attention.

Having a great idea for a business that also has a strong social purpose

We now have two examples of women who set up businesses with a strong social purpose – Lara Morgan, founder of Scentered, and Kate Andrews, founder of Loco2.

Whilst these two woman were inspired to set up a business with a strong social purpose, other interviewees mentioned that social purpose had had a bearing on the type of business they set up and how they operated. We frequently heard the desire to create a more flexible, collaborative, female-friendly working environment that would attract women (as well as men) needing more flexibility and control. More on this in Chapter Eleven.

To be clear, having a strong social purpose does not mean a business that purely operates for the greater good. The business must also be commercial and make sufficient returns for shareholders and backers. Let's see what some of them are doing.

Lara is in her second phase of entrepreneurship having already founded, grown and sold Pacific Direct. Now she invests in other people's businesses and runs Scentered with co-founder Fay Pottinger. The pair founded Scentered in 2011 – inspired by Lara's experience of using aromatherapy to keep her balance and sanity whilst she built Pacific Direct into a global business and raised a family. Frustrated by the impracticality of aromatherapy products available at the time, Lara wanted to create a 'solution-led, lifestyle-focussed brand' that delivered well-being benefits through a range of multitasking, easy-to-use, truly portable products. Scentered today offers a range of modern aromatherapy products that help people restore balance – by stopping the clock and literally 'smelling the roses' on a plane, in an airport lounge or a scruffy hotel ro___ or when under stress.

___ees, Lara had a challenging childhood, which later _ gap in the (aromatherapy) market. Lara says:

_ c child. I remember at five years old having to lie on _ Mum whacking my back to clear my lungs. In many ways Mum was the inspiration for Scentered. She had this saying: 'Don't forget to smell the roses'. At some level I realised that smell has a critical role in making the stress of modern living bearable. It did for me when I was a child, despite the paucity of the aromatherapy products then available. I figured I could do it better and make life not just bearable but better for the army of people out there battling to make a difference. And in turn I could make a decent living whilst also enjoying the calm our products induce. I am who I am because of the journey I had as a child, and the need to balance creating a global business with bringing up a family.

Lara continues:

People are running so hard today and forgetting to look after themselves. We need to be more considered about the way we're self-disciplined in our lifestyles – about stopping, really switching off and enjoying some downtime. Scent can help us take that rain check, as well as 'fake it and make it' when we might otherwise crack. Fay and I realised that scent could make the world a better place, and we believe we do.

We come away from all of these interviews and say: 'Why didn't we think of that?'. Brilliant!

The same is true for our second example of a business with a strong social purpose – Loco2 founded by Kate Andrews. Kate and her brother Jamie were brought up by environmentally aware parents, both of whom were entrepreneurs having set up an energy consultancy when their children were young. Both of these factors appear to have been a strong influence on her and her brother's decision to set up their own family-run business: Loco2.

In the early 2000s, their parents gave up airline travel. Not flying has the greatest carbon impact on any action an individual can make to tackle climate change and so every holiday was taken by train regardless of the distance. Soon Kate and her brother had abandoned aviation too.

Kate recalls:

> We started Loco2 because we have a passion for low-carbon travel, and a desire to make it easier for people to ditch planes and choose a lower-carbon journey by train. As the name, inspired by the word 'locomotive', suggests, our focus was on rail, but our environmental mission was present from the beginning as the name is also short-hand for 'low CO_2'. The motivation was completely selfish, rather than some lofty, noble ideology. I wanted to travel further afield in Europe without flying and I found it quite difficult to book online. For example, you could book Eurostar to Paris and travel within France. But to travel further afield by train took a huge amount of patience and a stiff drink to co-ordinate! There just weren't the tools or the necessary co-operation between rail operators to make it easy.
>
> Our mission was to build software that would enable travellers to buy tickets from different rail operators across Europe – hassle-free in one transaction. The online tool that we developed searches multiple rail operators at the same time, using logic to work out which operator to ask for what, enabling the user to book a complex itinerary very quickly. The passion wasn't for the trains themselves. It was for the positive environmental impact of making international train travel more accessible, whilst keeping the carbon footprint low. That was the inspiration for Loco2.

Grabbing an opportunity and growing it into a successful business

Our last example in this section is about someone who grabbed a small opportunity, which eventually morphed into a large standalone company. Claire Randall (founder of Claire Randall Consulting) doesn't think she qualifies as an entrepreneur as her business was originally set up to provide outsourced TV production consultancy to a large global advertiser, after learning her trade with Saatchi and Saatchi. For seven years she provided that exclusive service to them on a six-month rolling contract, until she won agreement to break away as a standalone firm and had permission to offer her services to other clients. It struck us that others could learn from her experience.

Claire takes up the story:

> My client couldn't hire me, they didn't have the headcount plus there was no career path for me in TV production there. It was a dream opportunity as they paid for everything and took all of the risk. But the problem was if I needed to give someone a pay increase or an air-conditioning unit broke, I had to ask them for money – which became increasingly untenable as we grew from a one-person band into a team. For the first seven years it was almost like we were a division of their business. After seven years of being exclusive, it became increasingly hard to deal with the financial side of it. I needed to pay my people the rates that they could get in agencies and each one required a separate negotiation with my client.

> I realised that the model had to change, so I went to them and asked to be freed from the exclusivity arrangement. I said: 'I love working with you, but you could share the overhead with others if you let me extend my services to other advertisers. At the moment you're paying for everything. Why don't you let me take on other business as long as it's not a direct competitor and then I can reduce the cost to you?'. They weren't keen at first and rightly made me repitch which took a year. This was awful because I knew I'd have to get rid of my team if I didn't win it. It was a lot of pressure. But in the end we won it back with the freedom to go non-exclusive.

> That's really when I think of the company as being properly Claire Randall Consulting. That was 2003/2004. Since then the business has grown, predominately due to people leaving that client and going to other companies and giving us a call. We have one individual who has followed us through five companies. Plus I still have some of my staff who joined right at the beginning. Now we have twenty-six staff, virtually all women, but it's not a deliberate gender bias. The job really suits female producers who want to work but need a good work–life

balance. Normally, production jobs mean travelling to shoots and working very long hours. But in our consultancy they work from 9:30 'til 6:00. It's the perfect job for a career mum who's been in production and has a lot of experience and expertise to offer to clients but doesn't want to go on the shoots anymore. Virtually all my staff are working mothers, some divorced or the main breadwinner, and what they need is stability and security. This gives them full employment with benefits such as a pension, healthcare and several weeks of holiday to cover the school holidays.

We now move onto our sixth and final catalyst – following a passion.

CATALYST SIX – FOLLOWING A PASSION

A number of our interviewees turned a passion into a business – interestingly both our oldest and youngest interviewees, but also others in between.

Stephanie Wray, Michaela Jedinak, Bridget Connell, Jane Mosley and Verity Drew Firth are five examples of women who turned a passion into a sustainable business.

Stephanie Wray, founder of Cresswell Associates and later Director of Biocensus, got the passion for her environmental consultancy at a very young age.

> I was interested in ecology from about the age of eight. I wasn't some Gerald Durrell running around the countryside catching bugs and starting my own zoo. I love animals but I grew up in Middlesbrough where we didn't have a lot of access to the countryside. But, as a slightly socially awkward child, I spent a lot of time in our local library where I came across a book on ecology.

> It was the logic that fascinated me at first. How you could look at complicated systems, break them down into chains or webs of inter-action, and see that if you change one thing it can have ramifications over thousands of miles away or perhaps even affect the whole planet.

Stephanie followed her passion by completing a degree in zoology and then a PhD in ecology, which resulted in her leading research trips in far-flung corners of the world. Once home, she joined a small environmental consultancy that taught her the first principles of business and marketing – which gave her the confidence to start up her own environmental consultancy three years later.

Michaela Jedinak is also someone who has followed her passion. Her mother taught her how to dress people from a young age, creating her passion for dress design. This in turn gave her the idea and impetus to create her clothing line, Michaela Jedinak. Michaela recalls:

> My mother taught me from a very early age the importance of strength. She said: 'You need to know yourself from the inside out. You need to know who you are so you can pick yourself up and rely on yourself – because in life there isn't always someone there who will help you or have your best interests at heart'.

Michaela continues:

> I didn't have a clear vision of becoming a fashion designer and an entrepreneur when I was young but dressing right was always part of my upbringing. My mother, who was a hardworking doctor and one of the most fashion-conscious women I know, dressed herself in minutes and made shopping decisions in split seconds. She put me in charge of her wardrobe from a very early age. I chose her outfits for important meetings, special occasions and holidays, as well as which accessories to add as 'icing on the cake'. She believed that fashion is there to empower and bring out the best in you. It was important to her that her look suited her, was comfortable to wear and fitted the occasion. Anything else would make her look like a 'fashion amateur' rather than a 'fashion pro'. Liking something is not reason enough to wear it. She believed that you need to know yourself and understand the rules of fashion before you can have fun with it. Early on, I had to understand that my mother and I were very different. We liked different things and I had to find the right clothes for her. So, I guess the skill set and knowledge was always there. It took a few turns before

> I followed my fashion vision and put it into action. But it eventually became the catalyst for my fashion idea which helps busy working women like my mother who don't have time to window shop.

After university, Michaela worked in companies that trained her in how to market luxury goods. And then she met her entrepreneurial husband who gave her the courage to follow her real passion of launching her own clothing label, Michaela Jedinak.

Bridget Connell worked in technology and IT for major corporates like DHL and O2 – helping to introduce the first Blackberry and the first Apple iPhone. This was at the beginning of the technology revolution and Bridget managed to put herself centre stage with no background in technology. Her degree was history. Her first test was in the IT department of DHL where male colleagues weren't initially impressed. One year in she was running the department (minus some of the early doubters!).

Bridget picks up the story:

> After thirty years working in IT and technology, my husband and I decided that life was too short and we were working too fast and too hard. I knew I didn't want to work in full-time corporate life any more and wanted to do something very different. I planned two new futures. One was to set up my own coaching consultancy which I've done. I now work for myself and I'm really pleased with the progress it's making. I like to work one to one with people who are working in tech businesses or who are tech entrepreneurs – mostly women. The second aspiration was to be an angel investor in companies founded by females. I'm a board member in Sarah Turner's Angel Academe and I invest through her syndicate which I'm really passionate about.

Our oldest interviewee was Jane Mosley, who is in her sixties. After a full career spent working around horses, Jane turned her lifelong hobby of cake baking into a business called Granny Olive's Kitchen. In her sixties, many others of a similar age are pondering retirement. In contrast, her business is now baking for local farmers' markets and rural shows in the English county of Hampshire and well beyond. It took courage, determination and a great deal of stamina. The baking hours are long and then she has to stand and serve all day for the duration of the event. Single-handedly she does the marketing, baking, deliveries to the shows and clients, serving and winding up at the end of busy days often in torrential English weather or sweltering heat. Sitting in her modest kitchen over a very English cuppa, her underlying steel, focus and resolution was evidently at the same octane levels of other interviewees half her age or younger. It's yet another interview that had a super humbling effect on us authors.

Our youngest interviewee was Verity Drew Firth aged twelve, who started her entrepreneurial career very early on:

> I started dancing when I was three or four and drama classes when I was four or five. I got signed up to an agent when I was about six and I got one of my first jobs when I was six or seven on TV, for a show called *Man Down* with Rik Mayall and Greg Davies. I then started appearing in adverts when I was around nine, and interviewing famous celebrities on the red carpet when I was ten. And I started writing, producing, directing and editing my own films when I was eleven.

At the age of twelve, Verity is already helping experienced vloggers produce their own films.

> A production company wanted to do a film on mental health. A film student and well-known vlogger who's twenty-two years old asked for me to work on it with him, because he'd seen what I'd done before and how passionate I am. So the oldest person on my film course asked me, the youngest person, to direct, produce and edit his film.

In the future, Verity is very keen to work for herself, combining her two passions of acting and filmmaking. As she says: 'I see myself as an actress and a filmmaker, and I will hopefully be successful at both'. For us authors meeting Verity was an electrifying experience. A non-stop show lasting one and a half hours. We'd love to fast forward ten years to see the heights she will doubtless climb. We'll have to be patient!

Readers might reflect on their hobbies and wonder: 'is there a business in sailing, flying, discos and the like?'. There probably is if you are motivated enough to try.

That concludes our analysis of the six main catalysts that our interviewees said had encouraged them to become entrepreneurs. Perhaps readers may identify with one or more of these catalysts, as many of our interviewees did.

But before we conclude Chapter Two, we'd like to say a few words on what our interviewees thought was the best age to start a new entrepreneurial venture.

When is the best age to start?

We interviewed fifty-two women who started their businesses between the ages of less than ten to over sixty years old. We found that you can start an entrepreneurial venture at any age or lifestage. It's never too late or too early to start. But the patterns of starting out are many and fascinatingly varied. In our interviews, we identified four life stages when people embarked on entrepreneurship.

First, those that started very young, often because they had an entrepreneurial parental role model or family member who made it seem the norm or a passion that they wanted to follow from an early age. Examples include Verity Drew Firth (our youngest entrepreneur, still only twelve years of age), Mursal Hedayat, Stephanie Wray, Phoebe Lebrecht, Naomi Sautter and Kate Andrews.

Second, those that started after some years of corporate experience, mostly in their late twenties and thirties, often borne out of a desire to break free from the constraints of corporate life or a desire to do something for themselves. Examples include Tamara Gillan, Rebekah Hall, Tash Walker and Aurée de Carbon.

Third, those that started when faced with having children or other family members to care for, driven by a desire to have a fulfilling career as well as the flexibility to be at home when needed. Examples include Dena McCallum and Liann Eden, Melanie Lawson, Elizabeth Cowper and Claire Randall.

Lastly, those that started much later in life, sometimes due to needing a second career or to earn money post-divorce and sometimes just to change direction. Examples include Jane Mosley (our oldest entrepreneur who started her business in her sixties), Bridget Connell, Etty Laniado and Sarah Ali Choudhury.

So what did our interviewees have to say about the best age to start? Whilst the maxim of any age holds, some interviewees who started their businesses young, when commitments, overheads and responsibilities are few, felt they had more time to experiment and hone their idea until they got it right.

Victoria Mellor, founder of Melcrum, says:

> I was twenty-six years old when I started my business and I was in the fortunate position of not having many commitments. I think that's one of the things that holds people back. I had a small mortgage on a flat in Notting Hill, but other than that I was quite independent and free to do what I wanted to do. I remember having a conversation with my family who thought I was absolutely crazy to quit a perfectly good job. But I didn't take a lot of financial risk. I set up the business at such a young age that I didn't understand what it was going to take to get to the point where it was self-sufficient. So for a few years there was just me and my partner trying things out. We were lucky as we hit on a great idea and built a healthy subscription base early on.

Mursal Hedayat, founder of Chatterbox, also talks about the benefits of starting young. She says:

> I guess it's different for someone that quits a very high paid job to start something up, that's probably a very different experience. For a recent graduate, it's easier. At the time I just thought you have nothing to lose. This is an idea that is worth trying because if it works, great. I think looking back I always accepted that it could fail and had

a contingency plan. So I feel like if you're going to do it, it's good to think about the worst thing that can happen, like the business failing, and have a contingency plan. It's just about managing the risks.

Michaela Jedinak, who started her clothing line Michaela Jedinak when she was in her forties, concurs. She says:

> When you start a business in your twenties and you put in fifteen years, you're still only thirty-five. Any company will hire you whether you were successful or not, because you know the answers when things don't work which saves time and money. And at thirty-five you still have time to reinvent yourself. But when you start in your forties, you need to change your lifestyle, and your body and concentration levels are not the same. Between twenty and thirty-five it doesn't matter, you're physically and mentally fitter, you can cope with the stress and you have a second chance. Starting out at fifty is much more difficult, as you're physically and mentally less fit. You have to adjust your lifestyle to the new reality, and you don't have the same time to reinvent yourself if it goes wrong.

Conversely, some entrepreneurs who started their business later in life talked about how their previous experiences had helped them to build their confidence and hone their business idea.

For example, Jane Mosley who started Granny Olive's Kitchen says:

> I didn't start until after I was sixty. In a way, it would have been lovely to do it earlier. But I could never have done it when the children were small, or when they were teenagers as they were both very involved with sport. I also don't think I had the confidence to do it at a younger age. It never occurred to me that I would be an entrepreneur. I never wanted to run my own business as I had always been happy working for someone else. The moment I left work was a big step for me. I didn't have a salary coming into my bank account, which was terrifying. But this is my new stage of life. And I've been very lucky, with great support and encouragement from my friends and family.

Encouragingly, when talking with our interviewees, it became apparent that there is never a right age or lifestage to start a business. And, conversely, no one is too young or too old to make the leap.

This concludes Chapter Two. We will now move onto Chapter Three where we will look at how to discover and hone your business idea, drawing again from our interviewees' stories.

NOTES

1 www.grandviewresearch.com/industry-analysis/pregnancy-care-products-market; www.standard.co.uk/business/mama-mio-selling-skincare-to-the-yummy-mummy-set-6524628.html.

Discovering and honing your business idea

Having crossed the line from 'I might do my own thing' to 'I will do my own thing', the question becomes 'what is your big idea?'. If you have it already, then this chapter will hopefully help to verify it. If not, then this chapter will hopefully give you some clues on how to find it. But don't despair if it takes time to land. It took some of our interviewees months, others years, to nail their business idea.

In this chapter we will review ways to:

1. *Discover your business idea.*
2. *Use your life's journey to hone your business idea.*
3. *Look externally for your business idea.*
4. *Validate your business idea.*

DISCOVERING YOUR BUSINESS IDEA

A s we saw in Chapter Two, the main predictor of entrepreneurial success is the desire to become an entrepreneur, even if you don't initially have the right proposition. That desire is burning in some and latent in others. As we have seen earlier, the appetite may emerge early in life, after having children, after working in the corporate world, after overcoming a personal challenge or just needing to pay the bills. Once it is clear that you have the appetite to be an entrepreneur, then you need to find a winning proposition.

When defining their business idea, we found that our interviewees fell into three broad camps – people who:

- Honed their skills within another company and then broke off on their own to do something similar for themselves.
- Didn't have a clear business idea but looked back over their life's journey to find one, for example by:
  - resolving a personal issue for themselves and then subsequently for others;
  - turning a passion or childhood experience into a viable commercial entity.

- Didn't have a clear business idea and so looked externally for one, for example by:
  - looking for a traditional market that was ripe for disruption;
  - researching new overseas technologies and trends that could be launched in the U.K.;
  - surrounding themselves with interesting people who they could learn from or combine complementary skills with to bring a new idea to market.

So, if you want to be an entrepreneur but it's not obvious what your new business idea is, then we suggest you ask yourself:

- From a 'personal life journey' perspective:
  - is there a personal issue that you have resolved or would like to resolve, firstly for yourself and subsequently for others?
  - do you have a passion that you can turn into a commercially viable business?
- From an 'external market' perspective:
  - is there a traditional market that is ripe for disruption?
  - are there new emerging technologies or trends being launched in other countries that the U.K. market is ready for?
  - are there entrepreneurial skills that you can bring to the table to partner with someone who has a strong business idea but lacks the entrepreneurial spirit or business acumen to launch it on their own?
  - can you surround yourself with interesting people who you can learn from or might know budding entrepreneurs who you could potentially partner with?

USING YOUR LIFE'S JOURNEY TO HONE YOUR BUSINESS IDEA

Hopefully the catalysts in Chapter Two will have stimulated your thinking. As we saw in Catalyst five, people like Melanie Lawson, Sian Sutherland, Lara Morgan and Kate Andrews started businesses to solve a personal problem that they then went on to market to others.

As you'll recall, Melanie Lawson wanted to find a high concentrate fish oil to help her during pregnancy, but she struggled to find it in the U.K. and so had to buy it from Canada. She thought no more about it until after having her third child, when she wanted to get back into business rather than be a full-time mother. But she didn't know what to do. So Melanie looked at brands with business models she admired, such as 'Graze' that delivered healthy snacks through letterboxes, and thought: 'Wow, what a great business model – a sort of money-while-you-sleep business'.

She tried to think of something she could launch that people would want delivered to their door. Given Melanie's difficulty in finding high concentrate fish oils, she thought about doing something similar for vitamins because 'there aren't any good vitamins available, and you could tailor it to people's needs'. But in the end she kept Bare Biology simple by creating a high concentrate Omega 3 fish oil that people could order online to be delivered to their door or could buy at good retail outlets.

Similarly, Sian Sutherland created what she calls the 'most selfish brand in the world', Mio, as a complete indulgence for herself and her fellow female business partners to use. It wasn't until some years later, when her husband's business (and consequently their pension) had hit hard times, that she really woke up to the market gap that these indulgent skincare products filled for pregnant mums. So Sian and her colleagues took these products out of the deep freezer and developed, launched and grew the Mama Mio pregnancy and new mum range in the U.S., the U.K. and beyond – taking something that they had started out as a skin saviour for themselves and making it widely available to others.

In Catalyst six, people like Stephanie Wray, Michaela Jedinak, Bridget Connell, Jane Mosley and Verity Firth turned a passion into a sustainable business.

For example Stephanie Wray, founder of Cresswell Associates, turned her childhood passion for ecology into a thriving business. She completed a degree in zoology and then a PhD in ecology, which resulted in her leading research trips in far-flung corners of the world. And then, once home, she joined a small environmental consultancy. As she recalls: 'I learned about marketing and business and really found it interesting. And I won a reasonable amount of work and thought: "I should be doing this for myself'". So, three years later, her newly acquired commercial skills gave her the drive and confidence to turn her passion for ecology into a successful environmental consultancy.

Our oldest entrepreneur, Jane Mosley, waited until after her children had left home to unleash her love of baking by setting up Granny Olive's Kitchen, providing home-baked cakes, biscuits, savoury and sweet pastries and desserts for events. Jane's confidence was boosted by two things. First, she replaced the catering manager at the charity she worked for when he retired, giving her much-needed experience in how to run a professional kitchen. And then she applied for the *Great British Bake Off*, where she got down to the last 160 applicants out of 12,000. An amazing achievement. This gave her the vision for how to make her passion commercially viable – as well as the confidence to take the entrepreneurial leap. Jane proves that it is never too late to turn a passion into a successful business.

So how can you similarly use your past life experiences to find your business idea? We are all influenced and shaped over time by family, interests, life challenges, friends, education, likes, dislikes, public figures and more. Aurée de Carbon even mentioned Elizabeth I as someone who gave her the courage to keep fighting when things got tough. Yet few of us pause to reflect on our life's journey and thus consider what we might do to set up a successful entrepreneurial business.

As we saw in Sian Sutherland's story above, it can often take a setback to trigger us into thinking about taking the leap into a new venture. But the financial pressure and low self-esteem that often accompany a setback can make it tough to see a positive way forward. It can be impossible to see the wood for the trees.

At times like these, many of our interviewees talked about taking time out to reflect in a positive and calm place. It takes planning and intent, and sometimes a new location. Interestingly, we noticed that when facilitating controversial corporate client workshops, a rural setting with a kitchen garden (or deserted art gallery) were the best environments to lower the temperature. When we reached sticking points, we'd send disagreeing board members out in trios into the kitchen garden to calm down and talk, and soon enough they'd return with a more positive and constructive mindset.

Taking time out in new locations is supported by psychologists who reason that solutions and new ideas emerge much more quickly when people are not obsessing about the issue or opportunity at hand. Good ideas may come to you in the shower or garden, or when travelling on a train, cooking at the end of the day, staring out of the window and the like. Even, it is said, in your sleep. Justification for a lie-in or a catnap at your desk.

To help power up the light bulb, we suggest you:

- Map your life journey from childhood to the present day, citing the people who have influenced you and why, and identifying your passions, hobbies and interests that your future business may lie within.
- Take some time out in a relaxed and calm location to ponder some of the questions below. If you have a collaborative home partner, friend or potential business partner, it may be good to do this together to identify differences and similarities from which a business idea might emerge.

Questions to consider include:

- What personal issues have you struggled to find solutions for?
  - Which ones have you found solutions for and how?
  - Which ones are still unresolved?
- What do you love doing at work?
  - What skills make you unique versus your peers? What are the strengths you can offer?
  - What are you doing on the days where time just flies by?
  - What motivates you to do a good job?
- What are you passionate about outside of work?
  - What did you love doing as a child? What were some of your memorable high points as a child?
  - What do you love doing when not at work? What are your passions and hobbies? And why do you enjoy them?

- Which brands inspire you and why?
  - What do they offer that is unique and different?
  - What is clever about their business model?
  - If you could only take one to a desert island, which would it be and why?
- Who do you admire and why?
  - Who were your childhood heroes and why?
  - Who are your present-day heroes and why?
  - Who would you love to have involved in your business? Why, what role would they play and what support would they provide?
- Reflecting five years out, what type of business would you like to have created?
  - What would make the 'seven-year-old you' proud?

Your reflections will hopefully help to inspire you and maybe even enable some emerging business idea(s) to crystallise.

LOOKING EXTERNALLY FOR YOUR BUSINESS IDEA

Some of our interviewees knew that they wanted to be an entrepreneur but didn't know what business they wanted to be in or what their business idea would be. So they:

- Looked for a traditional market that was ripe for disruption.
- Researched new overseas technologies and trends that could be launched in their home market.
- Took time out to become open to new opportunities and more comfortable with risk – often travelling, doing further education, taking a job working for an entrepreneur or a mixture of these.
- Partnered with someone who had a business idea, combining complementary skills to make it a success.

It often took them weeks or months rather than days to find their thing, as well as, in some cases, a change of location. So don't despair if it's taking time for you to find your business idea – it will come.

Rebekah Hall and Victoria Mellor are two examples of entrepreneurs who took time out and surrounded themselves with interesting people before finding their business idea.

Rebekah Hall, founder of Botanic Lab, is a great example of someone who always knew that she wanted to be an entrepreneur but didn't know in which business area or what her business idea would be. So she took time out to find her idea and ended up partnering with someone who knew what he wanted to do.

Rebekah recalls: 'As I went through my teens, I knew I wanted to be the boss of something. I couldn't tell you what, but I was surrounded by a group of people who encouraged me'. After a stint in the corporate world, Rebekah resigned from her job and took some time out to find an opportunity that she could launch.

She continues:

> I got to a point in my career where I was doing quite well but was restless. And so I made a choice to work for a client of mine who was a very creative entrepreneur. The people I worked with told me it was a huge mistake and I shouldn't do it as he was very unpredictable. And he was very unpredictable. But it was one of the best things I did because I got exposed to an environment and a world that were totally outside of the corporate box that I had been working in. It also exposed me to a group of individuals who are very entrepreneurial, several of whom invested in my business. I felt I wasn't an entrepreneur and needed to learn how to do it. And so I wanted to spend as much time with these people and soak up as much as possible. I wanted to understand how they had done it. Looking back, I wish I'd done it when I was twenty-two. But I needed to go on a journey to understand that I could do it.
>
> At thirty, I got to the point that: 'If I don't do this now I am never going to do it', but I still didn't know what that big idea was. A friend advised me to talk to a CEO about what kind of job I wanted to do. And he said to me: 'The only way you're ever going to do the job that

you want to do is to do something on your own'. And he didn't mean that in an encouraging way. But that was the final thing that made me think: 'You actually have to do this'. So I threw the baby out with the bath water, I gave up my job, finished with my boyfriend and thought: 'What am I going to do now?'.

It was a sort of crisis point. So I did some travelling, I learnt to teach yoga, I mixed with a group of people I'd never mixed with before – and after a year I was more open to opportunities as they came along and to taking risk. In the end, I fell blindly into a 'health and well-being' opportunity. I found a business partner who wanted to start a drinks business and I thought that sounds interesting. I know a bit about the market. The States is a good five years ahead of us which we can bring to the U.K., and I have nothing to lose. I can raise money for the business as I can raise money for anything. And so I went very naively into starting a business. It could have been gin, trainers, anything really and it still could be anything to be honest. I'll do this again and I'll do it with something else, but I have no idea what it will be. When the business was launched, we were one of the few businesses experimenting with innovative healthy drinks. All of a sudden in six months there were lots of people doing the same thing – it just exploded. The partnership didn't pan out as planned but the business had flourished.

Another example of someone who took time out and was inspired by interesting people was Victoria Mellor, founder of Melcrum, which she successfully sold in 2015. For her, working with an entrepreneur helped build her confidence, learn entrepreneurial techniques, increase her risk appetite, make great connections and hone her potential business ideas. She said:

I went to university and did a conventional economics degree. The idea of getting into the corporate world filled me with horror. I'd set up a couple of businesses whilst at university – a magazine and an alternative ball that lost money which was a lesson learned – and so I definitely had entrepreneurial flair.

After university I went to Spain and learned Spanish and trained to be a teacher. I had a desire to have a huge degree of independence in what I did. I was then very fortunate to work for the late Richard Armstrong in publishing. He was an unconventional character but someone who recognised entrepreneurial potential. His original team was the catalyst for four different start-ups.

At twenty-five years old, Victoria offered to open an office for Richard in the U.S., with her future husband as a fellow business partner. She goes on to say:

This gave me the opportunity to go on an incredible exploratory tour of America, learning about the business world and figuring out the connections. I travelled extensively to conferences and was stimulated by the new ideas I heard. I'm entrepreneurial and just wanted the freedom to continue – the freedom to be me and express my own ideas.

In 1996, she came back from the U.S. and set up her own publishing business, Melcrum, from the kitchen table in her Notting Hill flat, which grew into a thriving $10 million business.

In contrast, other interviewees looked externally for their business idea by looking for traditional markets that they could disrupt to make them fit for purpose for the 21st century. Liann Eden, Dena McCallum, Sherry Roberts and Sarah Turner are all examples of this.

As we saw in Chapter Two, Liann Eden and Dena McCallum decided that their corporate jobs were untenable now that they had young children, as they involved too much long-haul travel and a lack of control over decisions about when and how they worked. So they thought about starting their own business. They both loved consultancy but not the frequent business trips and so wondered if there was a different way to offer clients consulting work. When Dena wanted to hire McKinsey at Condé Nast, she knew that she didn't want a big consulting team with a big budget. She wanted to handpick individual consultants herself. But McKinsey couldn't offer her that. So Dena went through her rolodex to find ex-McKinsey consultants she could use instead. Based on this insight, Dena and Liann wondered if they could disrupt the management consulting market by setting up a strategy house resourced with self-employed associates around the world that could deliver McKinsey-style work with bespoke teams at a better price. This would give clients access to the best consultants for their particular business issue and give the consultants more control over their working lives because they opted into every project – a win–win.

Since their launch of Eden McCallum, Liann and Dena have received much praise for their foresight in being one of the first to surf the gig economy in professional services. Dena and Liann cleverly adjusted their business model over time to embrace and capitalise on the huge changes in how people want to work and view their careers, as well as how clients want to buy experienced bespoke consulting teams. So much so that strategy houses such as theirs have now become legitimised. Ten years ago, only one third of their consultants saw freelance consulting as a legitimate long-term career path – now that figure is over 60%. And headhunters now recognise Eden McCallum as a highly selective option for top strategy consultants.

Similarly, Sherry Roberts disrupted the furniture and home accessories market with her launch of The Longest Stay. After working in a number of industries, Sherry went into hospitality, helping a company launch their first boutique hotel in Rome. As part of this she attended 'hotel school' in Switzerland for two years to learn her trade. And whilst there, she realised that people want to recreate the style, look and furniture that they see in upmarket and boutique hotels in their own homes. In essence, they want to furnish their home with hotel furniture that they love, so that they never want to leave it – making their time at home their 'longest stay'.

So she decided to turn this insight into a big business idea to great success. The Longest Stay enables people who have stayed in luxury and quirky hotels to buy the furniture and artefacts they have seen in their rooms online at her website. She is creating the world's first chain of shoppable hotels.

Our third disruptor is Sarah Turner who disrupted the angel investing market by creating Angel Academe, the first angel network in the U.K. expressly designed to invest in female entrepreneurs. As we learned in Chapter Two, Sarah noticed that the current investment world did a poor job of supporting women, especially those building technology businesses, because it was so male-dominated. Sarah says:

> I got started as an angel investor and was often the only woman in the room at pitch events. Although women own 48% of the net wealth in the U.K., they are much less likely to invest in entrepreneurs. The barriers aren't financial, there are clearly other factors in play.

> Angel Academe started from quite a selfish thing. I wanted to develop a network of people that I would enjoy investing with, that were a bit more like-minded but at the same time brought complementary skills. So I made it my personal mission to create a much more diverse community that helped to level the playing field for women entrepreneurs, by giving them access to female investors, as well as introducing more women to angel investing.

The group's first angel investment was made in 2014 and they've doubled the amount invested every year since then. Over £2 million was invested by Angel Academe members in 2018 and they've backed more than twenty female-founded tech start-ups. As Sarah says: 'We're the largest, mainly female angel network in the U.K. and have helped to change the landscape. There are now far more women starting businesses, far more interest in supporting their businesses, and more women investing'. Which is quite an achievement and a great niche to own.

So how can you look externally for a great business idea? To help find a compelling business idea, we suggest you look for traditional markets that are yet to be disrupted. For example 'Bought By Many' disrupted the insurance market by enabling people to cost-efficiently buy insurance that has been traditionally expensive – such as insurance for extreme sports or exotic pets, or travel insurance for older people with medical conditions. They did this by harnessing the power of the internet to find communities that wanted similar types of hard-to-get insurance – and then brokering with an insurance company to get a good deal in bulk.

Similarly, Uber disrupted the taxi industry by harnessing the power of the internet to enable people to order cars that are close by online in real time, thus reducing response times and cost. A win–win for both taxi drivers and customers.

Additionally, it may be helpful to take a trip overseas (for example to the U.S. or China) to identify emerging technologies and trends that could be launched in your home market. Before doing so, we suggest you check out online which countries or areas are leading the way in developing the market, as the specific geographies will vary according to which industries you're interested in.

Those entrepreneurs who were brave enough to take time out to explore and let their idea come to them say that this experience was invaluable in helping them find and launch their business idea. Some of them surrounded themselves with interesting people with the aim of finding a great idea or someone to partner with, combining complementary skills to make the business a success. Some worked for entrepreneurs to learn what it takes to launch and grow a business successfully. Some worked a stint in a financial or commercial role to build their business skills. Others took time out travelling or doing further education to expand their horizons.

Hopefully the stories above will inspire you to keep looking for your big idea. In our experience, if you want to be an entrepreneur, it will come. It might take a while, as it did for some of our interviewees. But keep looking, it is out there.

VALIDATING YOUR BUSINESS IDEA

So once you've identified your business idea, it is important to validate it. In this section we look at how our entrepreneurs validated their idea before launching it.

Our advice is that these initial wispy ideas need to be quickly fleshed out into something tangible. One way to do that is to write a first draft proposition which can form the basis of a customer-facing website. If it stands up to your own scrutiny and that of family, friends, advisors and backers, you could be one step closer to realising your aims.

Many of our interviewees launched their business without any external research or validation, relying on face validity and a good dose of gut instinct to have the confidence to take the leap. The right stuff for an entrepreneur you might think. Co-author John Smythe did just that when he started both of his consultancies, being of the view that as the propositions were new, few people would have a view on them and that there was no time to lose. However some interviewees took the opposite view and validated or road-tested their propositions before launching.

Obviously those people who created products for themselves that they subsequently marketed to others (such as Melanie Lawson and her Bare Biology high concentrate fish oil or Sian Sutherland and her Mama Mio skincare range for pregnant women) were their own first guinea pigs. If it wasn't good enough for them, why would it be good enough for others?

Other entrepreneurs validated their ideas with potential clients they knew before launching. For example, co-author Ruth Saunders asked the advice of over twenty client contacts before taking the leap in starting her own strategy consultancy.

Similarly, having hypothesised that there was a gap in the strategy consultancy market, Eden McCallum's founders, Dena McCallum and Liann Eden, carefully road-tested their proposed model with both potential clients and freelance strategy consultants before launching. Potential clients liked the idea of working with more bespoke teams selected and supplied by Eden McCallum and the ability to retain more control of the process and ownership of the answer. Freelance strategy consultants confirmed that, like Dena and Liann, they loved the consulting work but wanted more control over their working lives. And so Eden McCallum was born. The gap they spotted may not have emerged if they had not taken client-side roles that enabled them to see the consulting world from the client's perspective or had not stepped back to look at the downsides of the consulting market and the opportunities that the dotcom era presented.

Conversely, some entrepreneurs validated their ideas with potential customers they didn't know before launching, using market research. For example, Kate Grussing, founder of recruitment firm Sapphire Partners, could not emphasise enough her belief in testing and honing her idea before launching. She presented the idea to key client segments in focus groups to assess their interest and get their feedback on how to optimise the offer. Interestingly, the focus groups made potential clients feel more ownership of Kate's success as they felt that they had been invited in early on to help shape the offer. As a result of this, one of the CEOs in the focus groups became their first client.

Other entrepreneurs identified, honed and validated their idea whilst working in another company. For example, as we saw in Chapter Two, Sandra Macleod, founder of Echo Research, was introduced to a media analysis company in the U.S. called CARMA International. She recalls: 'I thought it was dynamite at the time and believed in it 100%. And so when working at RWA I franchised it for the whole European jurisdiction, and brought it into the U.K. and then Europe'. Sandra was then ousted from RWA when pregnant, so she seized her opportunity.

> I wanted to continue working so I asked if I could take the media analysis franchise with me. My boss said 'Well it's not going to come to anything, so yes you're welcome to it'. I said thank you and hugged him and left. So I took on the franchise as no one was interested in it, rebranded it to Echo Research, and grew it into a eight million dollar company.

So Sandra found her big idea when working in another company that didn't see the enormous value in it.

When deciding whether to validate an idea pre-launch, you can either just go for it or take time validating it. If you choose to validate it first, then ways to do this include:

- Creating a first draft proposition that could be used to create a customer-facing website to ensure that the idea stacks up.
- Road-testing the product or service for yourself.
- Running it past potential customers you know.
- Conducting qualitative or quantitative market research among potential customers you don't know.
- Identifying and honing an idea whilst working in another company – and getting permission to take the idea with you when setting up on your own.

Interestingly, as Stephanie Wray of Cresswell Associates remarked: 'No one is going to steal your idea. No one will be able to do your unique thing better than you'. So there is probably little to lose by doing some research first.

By now you've hopefully discovered, honed and validated your business idea, at least to some degree. In Chapter Four we focus on how to take the leap and get your new business idea off the ground.

Building the confidence to take the first steps

Once you've discovered and honed your winning idea, it's time to take the next steps towards realising it. In this chapter we look at some of the early decisions you may have to take and the personal qualities that will be necessary to run the distance – with some words of advice and wisdom from our female entrepreneurs who are already on or have completed the journey.

Specifically, we cover:

- *The confidence dilemma and overcoming 'imposter syndrome'.*
- *Being determined yet patient.*
- *To partner or not to partner?*
- *To plan or not to plan, and how good is good enough?*
- *Events that encouraged our entrepreneurs to step up to the challenge.*

THE CONFIDENCE DILEMMA AND OVERCOMING 'IMPOSTER SYNDROME'

In this first section, we will cover:

- The sharp divide between those who feel confident as an entrepreneur versus those that don't, and why there is such a sharp divide.
- What the imposter syndrome is and how to overcome it.

Levels of confidence stem from a blend of intrinsic and extrinsic influences. Intrinsic influences include personality, values, self-image and personal qualities. Extrinsic influences include social background, social mores, family, role models and the ups and downs that come at every life stage.

Confidence is seen as an important attribute when starting up a new business – with a positive view of life being essential. Here we distil what our interviewees said about the importance of confidence and how to attain it.

Among our interviewees there was a polarisation between those that disclosed confidence issues (despite being successful) and those that reported few or no confidence issues, or at least didn't declare them to us.

Many of our interviewees talked about experiencing a lack of confidence or even the imposter syndrome when they started out. The imposter syndrome is defined as 'when a person doubts his or her accomplishments and has a persistent internalized fear of being exposed as a fraud'.[1] We will illustrate how a lack of confidence and imposter syndrome manifested in some of our interviewees' stories and how they coped with it.

Some interviewees reported few or no confidence issues. We will share some of their views to inspire others on how to overcome or at least mitigate or perhaps mask a lack of confidence. However, those with high levels of confidence struggled to offer advice about something that was a natural part of their persona and thus was not an issue that had crossed their minds – which was the polar opposite of those who disclosed confidence issues. Interestingly, the best advice on confidence came from those who had learned the hard way by developing coping tactics or outgrowing it.

Some expressed irritation that the issue gets so much airing, suggesting that it discourages other women from becoming entrepreneurs or forces them to 'bury their lack of confidence and blag it'.

So, first, let's listen to some of the interviewees who experienced a lack of confidence or suffered imposter syndrome.

In our interview with Martha Lane Fox, she shared how she has suffered from and overcome confidence issues day to day. She recalls:

> I think the strengths of true female entrepreneurs is that we bring a different set of skills. You shouldn't feel you have to copy the way men are in order to be successful. You just need to know your shit, be credible, work hard, and have confidence in who you are. I say that with vulnerability myself. I've joined boards where I'm one of the only women on the board and I have to flick a switch in my brain that says: 'Be confident'. Never feel that your voice isn't valid and you don't have credibility. It doesn't necessarily get easier and if you keep doing the 'be confident trick' people will hear you in a different way.

She also goes on to say that her desire to 'get stuff done' means she reprimands sexist behaviour in a friendly way.

> Recently, I was in a Board meeting and a man was sub-consciously calling me 'Martha, dear'. I started calling him 'darling' back. Someone said: 'Why are you calling each other dear and darling?'. I said: 'I'm calling him darling because he's calling me dear!'.

She adds: 'Small things, but they matter'.

Melanie Lawson also talked about how she suffered and overcame confidence issues. She says:

> Although I do have a crisis of confidence, I think, paradoxically, 'Oh, I could do that'. I've got the male blagging gene from my dad. I know what my strengths and weaknesses are, and I know how to play to my strengths and outsource or avoid the bits that I'm weak at. I think if you focus your energies on the things that really matter, and play to your strengths, you can be really successful.

Elizabeth Cowper has also overcome confidence issues. She says:

> I still have moments where I think 'Oh my god, I can't do this'. I have to talk myself out of them. I do have moments of lack of confidence but they're not that frequent anymore. I've been through some really tough times. For example, leaving my ex-husband when I had two small children, with a very difficult divorce at the beginning. Nothing can ever be as bad as that. In a way you have to go through the lowest lows in life to really experience that. I hardly slept for a year, I probably drank too much on occasion and was in self-destruct mode whilst trying to be a good mum and hold down a job. I just didn't know where to turn, I was all over the place.

> I look back now and I'm so grateful for that year – because I did keep going, I did survive it, I did put one foot in front of the other and I did keep building my career. I succeeded in the end. Now when I have a moment's lack of confidence I think back to that year and say: 'It can never be as bad as that, why are you doubting yourself? Look what you've achieved before'. So, I think an experience like that, requiring

true grit and not knowing how to keep going, totally kills off my fears now. Because I can do it.

Elizabeth, Melanie and Martha's disclosures show that if you know and focus on your strengths and past successes, you can draw on them to prevent a lack of underlying confidence from undermining your presence and self-belief.

Conversely, let's look at the mindset of some of our interviewees who claimed not to have suffered from confidence issues – to inspire budding female entrepreneurs on how to overcome or at least mitigate a lack of confidence.

Lara Morgan, founder originally of Pacific Direct and now well-being investor of Scentered, described becoming an entrepreneur because it was the only way to pay the bills in the 1990s' recession. She had learnt much from her parents about the vicissitudes and gruelling nature of building and running a global business whilst having a family.

She didn't mention confidence issues, but instead seemed sure-footed and winningly positive. She said:

> To some extent my parents failed because they were so wrapped up in surviving and paying the bills. As children we witnessed and learnt from their struggles. I thank god for my headmistress and public-school education, paid for out of the exertions of my hard-working parents. I learned that, with the all-important personal qualities of ambition and self-belief, anybody can do it provided they keep their ambition and belief uppermost in their minds especially in the tough times.

Claire Randall was another person for whom confidence was not an issue. She was bankrolled, as it were, by her first client for seven years as its outsourced production consultancy before becoming an independent entity. As with Lara, confidence was never an issue – it was evidently part of her DNA. Claire says:

> There was a real sense of self-belief and confidence which I believe stems from the way my parents brought me and my two older

brothers up. I always believed I could do anything I wanted to do or whatever I thought I wanted to do as long as I worked hard.

But she adds: 'I think I've been very lucky. But I also think that one makes one's own luck, at least to a certain extent'.

John recalls being sharply and memorably struck at the seemingly complete absence of doubt in the telling of Claire's story. It warrants mention as there may be others out there with this gift of unconscious confidence who just need a good idea and the life catalyst to get them started. John also recalls having had the good fortune of working for U.S. oil magnate Dr Armand Hammer in the dead zone that was 1970s Britain. Hammer would comment that 'he made his own luck by working 24/7'.

As Lara and Claire's stories show, the lucky few that are unconsciously confident need no coping tactics. Stepping back and being aware of your strengths can help to fire up your ambition and self-belief. The lesson for others starting out is to take time out to re-connect with their ambition and self-belief, rather than becoming blinded by the daily grind. Some do this with meditation, others with the aid of a coach, partner or friend, whilst others lose themselves in sports and activities that require undivided attention, such as horse riding, bridge, charity work, gardening, flying, coaching others and many more.

As Ronald Heifetz of the John F. Kennedy school of government at Harvard said:

> The difference between a manager and a leader is defined by whether they remain on the dance floor of day-to-day operations coping with immediate pressures, versus having the discipline to ascend from time to time into the tranquillity of the balcony above to reassert their direction.

Finally, let's hear from Sarah Turner of Angel Academe (the leading female investor in female entrepreneurs) who thinks that the 'female confidence issue' is used much too often as an excuse (by men) for not investing in female-owned businesses. She should know as she works with female entrepreneurs every day. She says:

I am constantly told (by men) that women don't invest as they're too risk averse, do due diligence to death and lack confidence. All of which I think is nonsense. We might do more due diligence, but that's because we're more thorough which makes us better investors. As time goes by and this is vindicated, male investors will follow their wallets rather than their prejudices.

A lack of confidence or ambition is often the reason given by men to explain why women don't raise as much money. Time after time, I go to these investor events where there are relatively young female entrepreneurs pitching to a room of older, more experienced men. Confidence comes with practice, experience and knowing your stuff. Entrepreneurs need to be well-prepared and have a well-honed 'elevator pitch'. Confidence is also contextual. People feel more confident when they're comfortable, which is more likely when some people in the room look like them. For many of us, being confronted by a sea of male faces doesn't inspire confidence. Few men have ever experienced being the only man in the room, and perhaps more should.

There's a huge amount of research that shows that women founders are treated quite differently from male founders by investors, particularly in the technology sector – they just don't conform to the norm of the young hoodied male geek. When it comes to raising either angel investment or venture capital money women typically receive a tiny proportion of what's given out, and that number has stayed stubbornly low over time. Ironically, there's another body of evidence that says that women when they get backing perform quite well, sometimes ahead of male counterparts. So, it's an illogical decision by male investors to discriminate in this way.

Whilst there is an increasing number of female investors, it will take time to level the playing field. Meanwhile female entrepreneurs need to show that investing in them pays off at the bottom line for everyone including male investors. Women can also develop confidence coping tactics that are built on female rather than male traits, thereby remaining true to themselves and their gender.

BEING DETERMINED YET PATIENT

There are other personal qualities that our interviewees said were important alongside confidence when building a successful business. Interestingly, these cover two sides of the same coin:

- On the one hand, determination, resilience and self-belief.
- On the other, patience and flexibility.

DETERMINATION, RESILIENCE AND SELF-BELIEF

Many women talked about how determination, resilience and self-belief had been critical to keeping going when faced with adversity. Di Burton, Verity Drew Firth, Tamara Gillan and Sherry Roberts are great examples.

Let's start with Di Burton, founder of Cicada Communications.

> I'm not scared of anything. What's there to be scared of? I don't see barriers or hierarchy. If I get knocked back, I think: 'So what?'. I put it in relation to the guy who put his finger on the atom bomb. I'm very resilient. My market researcher who I've worked with for many years said of me: 'Like many successful entrepreneurs I've seen Di negotiate the path from the garage to international stage with an unerring belief that she can do it. And with a pragmatism of being accompanied by a complementary team. She was not afraid to acknowledge that she needed people who were smarter than her in their specialist fields and was able to motivate and manage them.

> Successful entrepreneurs have a touch of the alchemist about them. They're able to conjure up a golden idea from a simple and basic premise – and they have the ability to take their internal team and clients with them. I would put Di in the class of real entrepreneurs and successful leaders. She's been helped by many personal traits – charm, resilience, never being afraid of hard work and expecting other people to work as hard as she does. And an absolute brass neck which allows her to shrug off things that don't go to plan. Her style is leading from the front'.

It seems that having insight about the qualities and attributes to be successful is not confined to those with years of experience. At the time of writing, Verity was just twelve years old with work experience already going back eight years. She has firm views on what qualities are required to make the running.

> If you're passionate about what you do, then pursue it relentlessly. You should never give up, but recognise that it's definitely 100% going to be hard. I constantly pester my mum asking her if she has any more work for me, because I love the work and I want to keep working as much as I can. If you're doing it just for fame or only for the money, then it's probably not going to work out. If you're doing it for the love of acting, or for any of your passions, then you're definitely going to get somewhere. You always have to believe in yourself. I know it's hard when you're not doing as much work as you'd like, but you always have to stay positive. That's one thing I always tell myself.

If you miss out the 'mum' bit, you'd be forgiven for thinking that this is the wise reflections of a successful forty-something looking back over a glittering period as an entrepreneur. As we said in Chapter Two, you can be successful at every age and lifestage.

Tamara Gillan, founder of Cherry London at age thirty, was determined to make her partnership marketing agency a success. She won her early clients such as Red Bull, P&G and Superdrug through sheer determination and resilience by conveying she was bigger than she really was.

> I faked it in the beginning. I had a separate email account for my fake assistant and fake finance director. I was trying to punch above my weight and win big accounts by saying that my system was set up. By doing this, we won Superdrug when we were only two people – and then very suddenly we became fifteen people overnight.

Sherry Roberts had many ups and downs on the way up and some forthright comments on the need for inner strength in the face of extreme circumstances.

> My wrist broke this year. I fell and tripped and broke it in fourteen places. I didn't feel sorry for myself. The day after surgery I bought a

new wardrobe so I could wear clothes that went over the cast. And the following day, I was at a networking event, meeting people that could add value to my business. It didn't stop me – even in the first twenty-four hours. And that's the kind of drive and determination you need to have. You don't get to do anything else but to focus, visualise, manifest, pray, and know that if you trust in something bigger than yourself and you're on the right path, you will get the miracles that you need to guide you.

The last word on this goes to Michaela Jedinak, founder of the fashion label Michaela Jedinak, who also talks about the need to be resilient even when it's tough. She says:

> People often ask me 'how do you motivate yourself?'. I've found it really helpful to read biographies on entrepreneurs who changed the world, whether it was Walt Disney who was fired from his job because he wasn't creative enough, or Oprah who was fired from her job because she didn't have a TV presence, or Steve Jobs who said you always need to stay foolish and hungry.

> We're living in a time where things are changing constantly so you need to adapt and refocus. It's like Darwin's law. The person who survives is not the strongest and fittest, but the one who adapts the most to his environment. Often things happen and you don't know what to do, you don't know how this is going to fall and you feel quite paralysed. But you have to keep moving. You can't stop, you can't give up. Winners never quit because quitters never win. It's all about per-severing and finding the strength to keep going. Entrepreneurs need to follow their heart in having a clear vision, but also take their brain with them to stay realistic.

She adds: 'I'm still standing – even if sometimes it's only on my toes'.

The spirit of determination, resilience and enterprise rings out from these stories. It's important to keep going even when facing adversity and setbacks. But, on the other hand, knowing when and how to be patient, as well as when to change course, is also important – a tough one for entrepreneurs who want to achieve their goals fast.

PATIENCE AND FLEXIBILITY

We expected some advice from our cohort of entrepreneurs on knowing how to be patient. However, looking back over our interviews, it was impossible to find anyone who deliberately chose the path of patience. Patience was imposed upon them by circumstances and the word itself was used rarely. The art of having to be patient is fitting as overnight success is rare. The time between having an idea and making adequate returns can take years. Recall that Mumsnet took eight years to become profitable.

Let's continue with Sherry Roberts' experience of entering the hospitality trade.

> I left Ecole Hotelier de Lausanne in 2008 but I didn't launch the website for my new business until 2013. It took a serious amount of time. That wasn't because I was focussed on anything else. It was just hard to get the idea off the ground due to having to learn four new industries – retail, ecommerce, journalism and furniture – and a new language to enable me to speak with suppliers in Italian.

Similarly, Rebekah Hall of Botanic Lab commented:

> Profitable? We're just about there. It's been a long four-year slog. Consumer product businesses are capital- and people-intensive. It's quite a milestone for me getting to this point. It's not been an easy journey. It took us a long time to find our niche, with probably close to thirty different products being launched. The pace of change in products and habits has been enormous. Brands that provide more information, more transparency and provide the consumer with the 'plus plus' beyond just the 'product in the bottle' are really starting to gain traction.

> Over time, we've had to better understand who our core consumer is, which products resonate with them best and which are commercially viable for us to create, and then focus on them. By the end of this year, we will have only five products in our range. A big turning point was being the first to innovate into the cannabis beverage space.

Finding that sweet spot took some time through trial and error and a process of evolution – not just in what our consumers are looking for, but also in how to grow and scale the business and make it work for us. You've got to learn as you go along, through trial and error. And the products that we are releasing now are very different to the ones that we started with, both in terms of product characteristics and how we take them to market. Finding that sweet spot has taken some time.

Whilst the word patience was not much mentioned, it's clear that it's needed in abundance to run the distances necessary to succeed. Patience is perhaps the engine of determination – flip sides of the same coin.

Both Rebekah and Sherry's stories illustrate the time and patience it takes to find your sweet spot. Sherry had to learn a vast array of new skills. Rebekah had to constantly adjust her product offer to find her creative and commercial sweet spot among the wealth of very well-known drinks competitors – not an easy feat.

That concludes the section on personal qualities necessary for success – and now we move on to the subject of whether to partner or not.

TO PARTNER OR NOT TO PARTNER?

As you start out, the question of whether to go solo or partner with others should be considered.

Partnership may be necessary in numerous circumstances including:

- The need for a broad set of skills at the top.
- The desire to share the risk of starting a new venture.
- The desire to share the responsibility of managing a large number of employees, especially when located across borders.

But partnership may not add value where:

- The founder has or can develop the necessary skills to lead on their own.
- Growth can be achieved with freelancers and associates rather than employees, such as Melanie Lawson's Bare Biology business, which (at

the time of writing) has just three employees supported by freelance contractors, and Mélanie Chevalier's Creative Culture business which has a handful of employees and over two thousand associates worldwide.

- A home partner provides the support that a business partner would otherwise provide.
- A founder has very high control needs which would prevent other partners from contributing and flourishing.

As with much else, the right way is the one that works for you – although we suggest considering other options which might at first feel alien. So in this section we will look at the pros and cons of:

- Having a joint founder and partner.
- Being the only partner and single leader and employing others.

First, let's look at some entrepreneurs who believed that having partner(s) was key to their success.

Martha Lane Fox partnered with Brent Hoberman when starting lastminute.com. She says:

> It's really hardcore being an entrepreneur. It's not for everyone. You have to be resilient, tenacious, optimistic, pessimistic and realistic, as the business goes up and down. I think that everything is better if you've got someone to share it with. If you can share that experience with someone, I believe that not only will you be happier but whatever you're trying to build is going to be more successful.
>
> I can't imagine not working with a partner. I think if you get the right partner, it's phenomenally helpful as it enables you to share some of the burden of responsibility. And if it helps with your confidence then it's an incredibly valuable thing to do. I'm a massive believer in partnerships and taking those opportunities when they present themselves. I don't think it's that complicated. You look for somebody who has the same values as you. When I met Brent, we were different but the same. We were focussing on different things, but we believed

in the same things, such as how to be a generous-spirited and kind human being. I think that wanting someone with real integrity is pretty much the defining feature.

Some of our interviewees partnered with their husband or wife, including Sophie Le Ray, Stephanie Wray and Michaela Jedinak.

Sophie Le Ray, founder of Naseba, describes:

> I work with my husband, who's also my best friend and business partner. He's very complementary to me. We balance each other. We used to fight a lot because doing family and the business together is not easy. I would not necessarily recommend it to everybody. But it works for us. If you don't partner with your husband, I would enrol a business partner you can trust. It's a huge, huge benefit. It's such a comfort to have somebody you completely know and trust to do business with, at least during the start-up phase.

Trust is a key ingredient but so are complementary skills. Stephanie Wray noted:

> When we started Cresswell Associates, my husband and I both worked on the technical side of the business. We were both ecologists. But over time I got more interested in the commercial side of the business and so we naturally split our roles. I focussed on the running of the business, whilst he focussed on being our technical guru which worked very well.

Michaela Jedinak, founder of the fashion label Michaela Jedinak, also started her business with her entrepreneurial husband David Lethbridge and concurs with both Sophie and Stephanie:

> My husband is my rock. I couldn't have done it without him. He's been an entrepreneur and so understands the emotional cycle. He gives me courage, puts things in perspective, and helps me understand what I need to do. He works partly in the business doing a lot of things that I'm not good at, like marketing, strategy, finances, technology and visioning. We complement each other.

We also encountered a number of sibling business partners including Alex and Nick Beer (founders of Feed the Soul vegan café) and Kate and Jamie Andrews (founders of Loco2).

Let's take a look at the sister and brother business partnership between Kate and Jamie Andrews who developed Loco2 and saw it through to a sale to France's SNCF. Their challenge lay in figuring out who should do what between them, particularly as the skills split was not neat. They resorted to using a coach to help them limit the bickering and learn to respect and accommodate each other. It worked.

Kate says:

> In the beginning, Jamie and I didn't know what we were good at and it turned out that there were skill crossovers between us. We both love to write which led to rows and treading on one another's toes. But over time we had a clearer division of responsibility. And with that came more respect for what the other person does well and a bit more self-knowledge of knowing what you're good at and where you need to rely on your business partner. We acknowledged that bickering was interfering with our decision making and hired a counsellor really early on. We were recommended someone who took a holistic approach with us, looking at our emotional maturity and how we communicated. It's probably one of the hardest relationships you'll ever navigate in your life, and we still go and see her every three months.
>
> I'm comfortable that we went through some hardcore counselling with her because you have to be so honest with your business partner about how you feel. I would say having the idea was one thing and having the courage to pursue it was another. But I don't think that we would have had the lasting power if we hadn't had the courage to have those very difficult conversations because it made us more like a leadership unit rather than two individuals. We really learnt to know our own feelings and the impact they have on each other and on the kind of organisation we wanted to build. Our mum also encouraged us to get some counselling because we were both ringing her up

bitching about one another over the phone. She said: 'You know this is exhausting, you're going to tear each other apart'. So, we did, and it worked. We highly recommend it to everyone with a business partner regardless of whether they are family.

Conversely, some of our interviewees preferred to go it alone, but recognised the need to have a strong team around them. For example, Rebekah Hall has built her business, Botanic Lab, with the help of investors and advisors rather than a fellow partner. She says:

I decide most things. I'm a bit of a control freak and I've built this business with no management team until now. I just hired the first person in my management team about nine months ago and the second person about two weeks ago. So, I've made most of the decisions, albeit with the help and support of a group of investors and an advisory board who I listen to. But, ultimately, it's me who's made those decisions day to day.

It can't stay that way because we've got to the point in the business where I've realised that my hands are too full, and I've become a blocker. There's a lot of opportunity available for us. But I've noticed more and more over the last nine months that there are opportunities I've not followed up on in the way I could have done. Opportunities lost if you like, simply through lack of available resource.

The business is too big to be just me anymore. And it's not healthy, as you don't make good decisions when it's just you. Businesses that manage to scale well do so not off the back of one person. There needs to be breadth and depth in the team. I now recognise that it's important that we build a strong team, yet it's still quite difficult to let go.

Julia Hobsbawm and Claire Randall are also women who are comfortable being the sole owner and leader of their business – but cited close support from home partners. Julia Hobsbawm, founder of Editorial Intelligence, says:

Generally speaking, behind every high-achieving person is someone propping them up. I'm very lucky that my husband has been the backstop at home and the best counsel for my business. He is one of the very small number of people that I run everything by. There is something quintessentially lonely about being an entrepreneur. In the end, the ideas come from your head and the creativity and the drive, push and innovation is led by me too. There's absolutely no doubt that I would not have been able to build and stay in business on my own without my partner.

Similarly, Claire Randall says of husband Robert, her informal business partner:

He's a highly intelligent businessman and ex-lawyer who has helped me tremendously with the business, dealing with all of the legal contracts and providing advice and support. I own the business 100% which can be quite lonely. I don't have a business partner to bounce things off, and so he's always played that role. I don't think I could have achieved what I have without his support.

Having listened to our interviewees, it seems that there is no right answer to the question 'to partner or not to partner'. Some people are comfortable doing their own thing. Others want a partner to share the journey with. Our advice is to think through the rationale for partnership and make the choice to partner (or not) a conscious one early on, rather than going semi-consciously with your initial gut instinct. We will talk more about how to select the right partners and teams in Chapter Five.

TO PLAN OR NOT TO PLAN AND HOW GOOD IS GOOD ENOUGH?

Another topic that was much referenced in our interviews was whether or not to plan. There were those in favour of 'organising the future' and others that 'made it up as they went along'. Again, there's no right way but it is a choice that merits conscious consideration at the outset.

In this section we will cover:

- What is meant by 'planning'.
- The contrasting virtues of highly detailed plans with contingencies versus 'making it up as you go along'.
- How good is 'good enough'? When does perfectionism become destructive?

So, what is planning? In corporate environments, planning (and organising) implies the setting of targets designed to deliver shareholder promises or owner's (and occasionally employees') aspirations – and in turn the allocation of resources to deliver the plan over time periods ranging from a few months to years. For some, this attempt to tame the future is seen as 'policy' to be adhered to, whilst others see it as 'loose guidelines' to follow.

Start-ups that need the investment of other people's money need a plan showing how the money will be used and when a return might be expected – with progress reviewed and reported on at regular intervals. In contrast, 'resource-lean' start-ups often survive at the beginning by putting one foot in front of the other without much of a plan. As many interviewees said, in the early days the first steps are often taken in the dark until a pattern emerges.

At first we thought that there would be a clear distinction between the planners and those that made it up as they went along. But, in reviewing the data, it became apparent that the two concepts were much messier than that. Some of our interviewees felt that highly detailed plans with risk contingencies were very important to success. Others preferred a more organic, iterative approach to 'planning' where they 'made it up as they went along'. And the majority fell somewhere in the middle. This in turn led us to think that 'planning' is often less of a cold, rational exercise and more a reflection of personality and desire for control. So, it's important to ask yourself where you are on the pendulum between being an absolutist planner and adopting a 'take it as it comes' approach.

Take one of the planners – Di Burton of Cicada Communications:

> I'm a huge planner. I'm always looking forward. Where's the next deal? What's coming up? I never live in the moment. That's something

I need to work on. If and when I retire, I will need to live more in the moment. I'd work a full day and then I'd go out networking night after night. Planning ahead provides me with control over my day (and evenings and weekends). It means I can squeeze more into my days in an organised and predictable way. It gives me more certainty over the allocation of my time – my most precious resource. I can't leave things to chance. Plus, it enables me to make time for my home responsibilities.

Know thyself. Di had insight about her psychological needs and her need to be in near complete control of her calendar, leaving little to chance. Is that really planning or is it organising ahead meticulously? The learning for others is to have insight about your psychological need to be in control (or not) and, if so, of what. Di surrounded herself with people who understood and signed up to Di's leadership style, so it worked for her and them.

Stephanie Wray is also a planner. Sudden redundancy forced Stephanie and her husband to set up their first business, Cresswell Associates. But their breakthrough idea didn't fit any potential banker's list of approved new business ideas and so they, like many entrepreneurs, were unable to get external funding. Stephanie recounts the story.

> We didn't have money to pay the mortgage because we didn't get our last salary, and we didn't have anyone to borrow from. So, I wrote a business plan. We got agreement from the insolvency practitioner dealing with our old employer to contact all of the clients Warren and I had been working with, and we were allowed to pick up the projects that we were currently working on. So, we started with no money or assets, but we did have work.

> I went to see the bank with my shiny, much-researched business plan. We didn't want to borrow much because consultancy is not a high capital investment business. We just wanted a short-term overdraft facility to tide us over. They let us open a business account but wouldn't let us have an overdraft facility because they didn't have a box on their form for ecological consultancy and didn't know what

it was. The next day the bank manager phoned me up and said that he ran training courses at their bank for other business bankers, and asked if he could use my business plan as the best example he'd ever been presented with.

Much as that satisfied my nerdy need to do things right, we still had no loan or overdraft. Super! So, we warned our clients that we would be invoicing them quickly. We weren't exactly hiding behind the sofa when people came knocking at the door to collect money, but we certainly didn't open any letters from the mortgage company until we'd become cash positive after four months. We ran that business together for twelve years, entirely in credit and self-funded. We never borrowed a penny from anybody. I'd say don't let your lack of money stop you. There are ways around it.

There are a number of salient points here. Stephanie and Warren had to act fast to meet living costs in the face of sudden redundancy. They had some work in progress, which meant potential cashflow if they could get Cresswell Associates up and running. So, they developed a business plan (based on some known truths) to make their idea real very quickly and give them the confidence to go ahead, as well as provide a practical map to follow. 'Planning' served a psychological as well as a practical purpose. Sadly, the bank didn't have the commercial nouse to back them – but even that turned out to be a blessing as, with belt tightening, determination and courage, they managed without the bank's money and thus reaped all of the rewards.

Interestingly, the Creative Industries Council researched 18,000 small and medium-sized businesses and found that 27% relied on family and friends for funding compared with only 9% of larger enterprises. The Council also notes that creative entrepreneurs in businesses like fashion have the hardest time being financed by other people's money, as backers are concerned that they may be good at the creative but not at the commercial. So, it's not just about gender bias but also about industry bias.

Others, like Sophie Le Ray of Naseba, had a more organic, iterative approach to 'planning and organising'. She says:

> I'm a big believer in iteration. You have an idea, you try it, you fail, and you do it again until you perfect it. I'm not into big business plans with a lot of Excel projections because it never really happens the way you were expecting it to happen. Stuff happens that no-one can predict with a fancy plan. I use a lot of mind mapping because it helps me to 'ideate' and then I go out there and just make it happen. Sometimes you need a little bit of Excel. I don't say I'm against it. I just say that you have to have some form of flexibility in the way you project. You need to execute immediately after ideating and accept that it's not going to be perfect. That you're going to have to tweak it here and there until it gets perfect. And it rarely gets perfect, but it gets done which is great.

> Another thing that I do is mood shooting, which is looking out ten years from now and having a crazy idea to future build a plan back to today. So instead of doing it from today to the future, I do it from the future to today. Back to front.

Sophie talks to the dilemma of 'just how perfect does it need to be', arguing that iterations of an idea should be tested quickly rather than one option being constantly refined in the search for perfection.

Tash Walker of The Mix presents what seems at first to be an apparent contradiction in her approach to 'planning'. She says:

> At the outset, there wasn't a great design or a year's worth of business planning. I had no plans, no investors, just an idea and a kind of sense of 'Why not?'. For me, the biggest thing was the risk of not doing it, which was so much greater than the risk of trying and failing.

> Now I have a five-year plan. I met somebody the other day who had a fifty-year plan. I felt very jealous! Our five-year plan involves creating a picture of how to deliver our aspiration of building a bigger

business. For us, bigger doesn't mean more and more people. The plan's real purpose is to be our guide to staying at the cutting edge of what we do, which requires us to make bigger and bolder decisions. We use the plan directionally. But when it comes to execution mostly everything we do is definitely not on plan. We're pragmatists holding to the direction but executing using our gut instinct.

In fact, Tash's approach is less a contradiction and more an example of using a plan to paint an iterative picture of the future without it dictating operational decisions. She says: 'The plan is no substitute for pragmatic operational management'.

The last words on planning and organisation go to Lindsay Levin of Leaders' Quest who talks about the need to not over-plan:

You need planning, but you can be paralysed by over-planning. Women are usually pretty thorough and careful anyway, especially in small businesses. I've started a number of businesses and I've never had a five-year plan. Right now, our focus for our next decade is on our ethos and what we stand for and direction of travel. It's not asking where we'll be in month twelve. Well, that's my way of working. It's not everybody's way of working. Having a directional plan helps us to be open to the right opportunities when they pop up and to know which ones to ignore. And it helps us get over what's the worst thing that can happen, and recognise that it's nowhere near as risky as some of the other things in our lives.

Listening to our interviewees, the choice of whether to plan or not seems to primarily mirror personality. Some like to be buttoned down, to squeeze as much into their day as possible. Some like to plan to give them confidence to take the next leap. And others believe that 'planning' should be used to paint a future picture of the direction to take that can help to guide future decision making. But it shouldn't become a straight-jacket that over-influences daily operational decisions. There seems to be no right way, just the one that best suits your preferred working style.

EVENTS THAT ENCOURAGED OUR ENTREPRENEURS TO STEP UP TO THE CHALLENGE

In this last section we'll look at some of the self-imposed or external events and circumstances where the 'rubber hit the road' and caused our female entrepreneurs to step up to the challenge. These include:

- Self-imposed events and circumstances such as:
  - hiring their first employee(s);
  - declaring visible goals and targets;
  - using other people's money.
- Unpredictable external events and circumstances such as 9/11, the anthrax scare, the London 7/7 bus bombs and recessions.

Some of our interviewees talked about how taking on more responsibility (such as new employees or outside investment) or setting themselves tough targets had forced them to step up their game.

For example, Tash Walker, founder of The Mix, recalls having spent the first year in business 'dossing around' and going nowhere. She says:

> The best decision I made was to employ someone at the end of year one. That was really galvanising, because when you've got somebody working for you, you've suddenly got responsibility. You've got to pay someone's wage, and that's a 'growing up' moment of inflection. It gave me a kick up the backside and forced me to question why I was getting so much rejection.

> I tinkered with the business model which had been too broad, aimed at everyone and anyone. I decided that Nestlé was going to be my first client and so we pursued Nestlé. We had endless meetings and we eventually got a project from their U.K. team. That was one of those galvanising moments where I learned that you need to decide you want to do something and then work really hard and do it. The act of deciding is the most important thing, not the act of doing.

Mursal Hedayat, founder of Chatterbox, talks about the importance of setting herself visible targets to drive her forward. She says:

> I measure the successful progress we're making by setting ourselves targets. For the next few months my biggest target is raising £300,000. Almost every time up until now I've set a target and achieved it. I've said that we're going to hire this person in February, and it happens. We're going to win this contract, it happens. We're going to have more university clients, we don't just double or triple it, we quintuple it. They were the big ones.

Similarly, Ellena Ophira of Weddingly talks about the importance of setting tangible milestones that lead to increased investment. She says:

> It's all about milestones. You need to have big dreams. For us, we want to disrupt the wedding market and make Weddingly the number one go-to resource for people planning their wedding. But dreams are not reality without goals. And for goals to exist you need tangible steps. Otherwise it's just vacuous, empty and destructive. You can get lost in a dream but if you have goals with real tasks you have structure to move forward. For us, it's about living in a twelve-month period. So right now, we're raising £250,000 for our Seed Round and that's going to take us to x, y, z. When we hit those milestones, we'll have further proof points and data which will support my ask for a more substantial Series A raise and make my investor conversations easier. Then I'll lay out our plans and milestones for growth and each day we'll get a little bit closer to the dream.

Other interviewees talked about how external negative world events had led them to shape their business to be more successful. For example, Victoria Mellor, founder of Melcrum, recalls how the impact of external world events changed the course of her publishing business.

> Our first lesson was to learn from the crises that you go through. Many of the big moves in our business were borne out of major external events. During the financial crisis, we lost three major

training accounts with banks, worth about £750,000. Keeping a dialogue going with your customers during challenging times fuels innovation and new ideas and ultimately business growth. As soon as you lose sight of your customers, things go quickly off track.

By the time 9/11 happened, we had about ten employees and had launched a new publication which involved heavy investment in direct mail. Then came the anthrax scare which resulted in most of this marketing being destroyed and a twelve-week period with very little money coming in. This was a turning point for us, as we realised that we had to radically rethink our product mix.

So we started a research business. I'd always been driven by talking to customers, understanding their needs and turning data into new ideas. This discipline led to a series of successful product launches and helped us to adapt to new market conditions.

Victoria went on to sell her business for multi-millions to Washington-based CEB in 2015. Her story illustrates that a crisis led to them changing course with a successful move away from publishing to research.

As we can see with Victoria's story, whilst the initial impact of big external events may be negative, they can often be turned to advantage. A skill which distinguishes entrepreneurs even though it may also scar them. Unlike in larger businesses, with a broader ownership base, there is no dodging the dangers. Entrepreneurs should not waste time in planning for the unplannable with 'paper' plans. Instead they should maintain maximum flexibility when negative events strike. And they should identify events and circumstances in their personal and business lives that they have already had to react to – and reflect on what worked well and what they should do differently this time.

This section concludes Chapter Four. In Chapter Five we look at how to surround yourself with the right people.

NOTES

1 Wikipedia, https://en.wikipedia.org/wiki/Impostor_syndrome.

Surrounding yourself with the right people

Once you've taken the first steps in getting your business off the ground it's important to surround yourself with the right people. In Chapter One we noted that entrepreneurs work with, through and around others. Typically, they are sociable and enjoy good teamwork. Rarely are they solo artists.

Advisors may be people who have already taken a similar journey and can give great advice, accelerate progress, fill in for your weaknesses and introduce you to people who might want to invest. They are people who get to know you well and support you through the ups and downs.

In this chapter we will cover:

1. *Building the right inner circle.*
2. *Building the right day-to-day team.*
3. *Playing to your strengths and minimising your weaknesses.*
4. *Building the right support network.*
5. *Whether to bring in other people's money.*

BUILDING THE RIGHT INNER CIRCLE

Despite being sociable, many interviewees talked about entrepreneurship being a lonely business, particularly when making tough commercial decisions or working through fraught situations. To counter this, they sought out advisors to be part of their inner circle. Some of these advisors had taken a similar entrepreneur journey and thus could talk from experience. Others were keen to invest in the business and so were incentivised to help it succeed. Others became part of a more formal advisory network.

Tamara Gillan, founder of Cherry London, talks about her advisor, 'Uncle Nick'. She recalls:

> Someone in the industry recommended him when I was just starting out. He's a serial entrepreneur and non-exec chairman in my industry, has sold a big media network and has worked with a lot of female

entrepreneurs. I said: 'That'd be great'. He's my Chairman and he's been amazing and spectacular at pushing me. Sometimes he has been really tough, telling me to stop running the business like a family business. Sometimes he's helped me when I've been frustrated about people issues or at really fractious moments. And sometimes he holds me to account which I also like because no one else does.

Similarly, Victoria Mellor, founder of Melcrum, talks about the value that her Chairman brought to her business. She says:

Between 2005 and 2010, I built the management team around me, putting into practice a lot of the things that I'd learnt on the Cranfield Business Growth Programme. We brought in an investor, James, who became our Chairman. He was incredibly useful and added that all-important grey hair to a relatively young team. He created a formal board and helped us to professionalise the business, improving financial reporting, holding the management team to account and improving the quality of our decision-making. He also helped us to attract great people by showing them we were well managed.

If you're thinking of building an inner circle, the first question to ask yourself is: 'do you need advisors in a more informal capacity or would a more formal advisory board be better?'. Be very clear with candidates about their roles and your expectations. Do you want to surround yourself with people who have taken a similar journey and so can give you great advice and speed you up? Or people who can give you the investment money and support needed to build your business up? Or people who have great connections and so can open doors for you?

You then need to identify people in your network who can play these roles and would be happy to do so. Our interviewees advised entrepreneurs to ask the people they wanted most, even if they seem very senior or out of reach. Most people are flattered to be asked and want to help and be part of the journey, especially if they have succeeded themselves. Co-author John Smythe managed to attract Rick Grogan, formerly a senior figure at strategy consulting firm Bain, in the run up to the sale of SmytheDorwardLambert to Omnicom in the 1990s. John commented that it was good to have an outsider to air tough internal political agendas with, especially when partners could see a sale pending.

Bridget Connell, founder of Thinking Partnerships and an investor in female start-ups, adds:

> I don't think women are very good at asking for help. Make it clear what you want and people can only say no. I'm always amazed at how much help I get when I ask for it. Also, get your own advisory board. When I invest in very early stage businesses, I always look to see which advisors the entrepreneurs have got around them. Who have they surrounded themselves with? Have they thought to ask well-respected industry experts to mentor them? Have they got enough about them that an experienced industry expert is interested in and would make the time to do something with them? That tells you so much. When you work for yourself, get yourself your own board.

Rebekah Hall of Botanic Lab echoes this, saying:

> I would advise entrepreneurs to pinpoint what they're good at, and then by default what they're not good at. That's not an admission of failure. No one is good at everything. Spending my time on the things that I'm really good at is where I am most effective. Then, I need to know what I don't know and find a person who can fill the gap. If you're seeking a partner or an investor, define what you need and pinpoint exactly what you want from them rather than just taking the first offer that comes along. That helps you be much more focussed on what you're looking for. Early on, I was reticent to ask for help and maybe that was due to a lack of confidence. But now I'm quite persistent. I think it's an interesting business. I think people like to know their value. And when people have helped me, it's been a huge value to me, and I think people get something out of that. Especially quite senior people who want to impart their knowledge.

BUILDING THE RIGHT DAY-TO-DAY TEAM

When building the right day-to-day team, our interviewees talked about the importance of knowing yourself – both your strengths that you can play to and your weaknesses or gaps that other people around you will need to fill.

For example, Tamara Gillan of Cherry London advises budding entrepreneurs to:

> Get to know yourself, your strengths and your weaknesses. Then focus your time on the things that only you can do that you're really good at. And stop doing the things that don't add any value to the business and are a waste of your prime time.

Consequently, it's important not to hire people who are in your own likeness – but rather people who are different and thereby complementary to you, as well as people who are better than you. For example:

- If you're great at raising capital but poor at marketing, hire in an expert marketer to drive that part of the business.
- If you're more free-spirited and laissez faire, and less buttoned down or good at planning, then hire in an expert planner who can ensure that the business stays on track.

Martha Lane Fox advises entrepreneurs to what she calls 'hire in your own shadow'. She believes that it's important to work with a diverse network of people, with differing views and skill sets to each other. So, her advice is to think about what you as the entrepreneur want to focus on and build the team to support you in the areas where you're weak. She also believes that people shouldn't be shy of recruiting people who are better than them. It's important to build a team that is as good as it can be and can thrive without you in the event that illness or worse removes you from office.

Mélanie Chevalier, founder of Creative Culture, talked about how she brought in a Non-Executive Director to focus on new business, but over time realised that that was where her real strengths lay and thus where she needed to focus. She says:

> I brought a Non-Executive Director in to help support the new business effort, as I was adamant that this is what the business needed, and the rest I could figure out myself. But I now do every single piece of new business myself, as I've realized that I'm the best one to sell. I am best placed to anticipate what my clients' needs are going to be and be one step ahead of them because I know where they're coming from. So, I've prioritised new business over the last year and left some of the other tasks behind. The Non-Executive Director is now helping with other growth areas such as marketing and strategy.

Liann Eden and Dena McCallum talked about how their hire of a Finance Manager two months after starting their business was 'the best thing they ever did'. They recall:

> Many people warned us that cashflow is king and that having some-one focussed on it was important for survival. Many companies fail as the faster they grow the more cash they need, and so the less cash they have and they run out. We were determined that the faster we grew the more cash we had.

> We hired our part-time Finance Manager in October 2000 just two months after starting our business. She was at our accounting firm and we really liked her. She totally focussed on our P&L and cash flow, to ensure we stayed afloat. For example, she chased our clients for cash so that we didn't have to, as well as helped with a lot of the office administration such as IT, contracts and desks – enabling us to focus on what we loved best, which was our clients and the consulting work.

That said, a number of our interviewees talked about the importance of never stepping away from the P&L. Cashflow is the lifeblood of the business and without it the business will go under. Tamara Gillan, founder of Cherry London, knows this better than anyone. She took her eye off the cashflow ball which resulted in the failure of her first business.

> In my naivety I didn't run the business well. I didn't look at the cashflow or who owed us money – and one of our clients went out of business owing us a lot of money.

> It caused us to falter and was one of the most painful learnings of my life. I just believed I would succeed and it shook my confidence to the core. My dad said: 'Do you have it in you to get back up?'. And I went away for four days and came back and said: 'I can't lie down because I'd never be able to look myself in the mirror'. So I put the company into voluntary liquidation, restructured it, found new investors and started again in a much more focussed way as Cherry London. I then paid back everyone that we owed because my word is my word and I couldn't hold my head up if I didn't do the right thing. Since then, I have founded The WealthiHer Network to help make the finance sector more relevant to women.

Interestingly, for many of our female entrepreneurs, the right day-to-day team goes beyond the commercial into the personal. Many talked about the importance of investing in a great nanny who can run the household smoothly, enabling them to have the flexibility to focus on the business when needed.

Single mum Tamara Gillan of Cherry London says:

> I'm so lucky. I call Dhari, our nanny, our mum. She's my full-time nanny and housekeeper – and she's amazing. She's also got a child and is divorced. In the holidays we all have breakfast together every morning. It's like I've got my family all around me. If I didn't do that, I don't think I'd have any quality time with my son. I think I would go mad. Recently I had an emergency hospital visit dash, and she came over in the middle of the night, because what else can you do? We don't have any family here. I don't want to ring my friends at three in the morning saying I'm in big trouble. But Dhari's like 'I'll be there' and I'm so thankful.

PLAYING TO YOUR STRENGTHS AND MINIMISING YOUR WEAKNESSES

Our entrepreneurs talked about using a variety of ways to identify their strengths and weaknesses when defining what their role should be – including reviewing their childhood experiences as well as their past work experiences with a self-critical eye.

Some recalled how their strengths today have been shaped and honed by their childhood experiences. For example, Aurée de Carbon, founder of CARRHURE, a French search firm focussed on NGO recruitment in developing countries, told us how influential her father had been in developing her skills. She said:

> He was a teacher involved in the developing world and we used to have students coming into our home for their PhD. When I was six, I saw my father talking with Indians and Africans in our home. I couldn't understand what they were talking about but the fact that they were there, it's as if it was in my DNA.

> He was deeply committed to the developing world, so when he died, I wanted to continue what he'd done. It's like a legacy. He was very informal, supportive and nice, and his students were very respectful. I have lovely pictures of those people coming in our house and listening to their discussions.

Aurée's consultants are now based all around the world, most notably in Africa, Asia, Europe and the United States. Her story reminds us that sometimes thinking through what our departed loved ones might do can help guide us to the right ideas and decisions.

Others recalled how their skills and networks had been shaped by their past work experiences. Some worked in corporates, others in big consultancies, some in government and party politics, others in not-for-profit NGOs and some alongside other entrepreneurs. All talked about the importance of recognising the skills that they had learned in past roles which could help to equip them in their journey into entrepreneurship.

For example, Rebekah Hall talked about the skills she learned in corporate finance that she has used to good effect in the growth and investment of her own business, Botanic Lab. She says:

> I fell into a career in corporate finance that, with hindsight, gave me a good grounding for being an entrepreneur. It led me to work with entrepreneurs who'd started their own businesses. I would go in, understand their business, and tell them what they should be doing. And it taught me how to raise money which is a very useful skill for what I do now.

Additionally, she talked about how working for an entrepreneur before starting up her own business was

> one of the best things I ever did, as I got exposed to an entrepreneurial world and group of people that were totally outside of the corporate box I knew – which gave me an entrepreneurial lens, mindset, skills and confidence to set up my own business.

Similarly, Kate Grussing, co-founder of Sapphire Partners, cites her time at Dartmouth College and McKinsey as being pivotal in building the skills she needed to become an entrepreneur. Whilst at Dartmouth College she analysed dozens of case studies and realised that she had the 'right tools' to start her own business. Additionally, her time at McKinsey in New York and London taught her to look at companies holistically. And so, for her, it was only a matter of time before she started her own business, which she did just after her fortieth birthday.

Stephanie Wray, founder of Cresswell Associates, talked about how both her PhD field trip work and her stint in a small environmental consultancy gave her the skills and confidence to set up her own environmental consultancy.

For her PhD, Stephanie led a research expedition to the Comoro Islands, a small archipelago in the western Indian Ocean between Mozambique and Madagascar. She says:

> It was a major research project, so I had to convince grant bodies to fund us, get major international conservation bodies to believe in us, and pull a research team and equipment together. It was then

that I started to see myself as a leader – independent, self-reliant and accountable to ensure that the things that need to happen do – a side of myself I'd never known was there before.

After her PhD, Stephanie worked for a small environmental consultancy which gave her the confidence to set up on her own. She said: 'I learned about marketing and business and really found it interesting. And I won a reasonable amount of work and thought: "I should be doing this for myself"'. She did.

Bridget Connell of Thinking Partnerships talked about the need to build and maintain your corporate network whilst working for others, as it will become useful later on when setting up your own business. She said:

> I don't think women are particularly good at building and looking after their network. If you've worked in corporate life for a long time, your external network can be very small. People don't think about the need to invest in it. I noticed that when a number of people I knew were made redundant after twenty or thirty years in a company, they would want to meet for a coffee with me and sometimes seemed a bit like a rabbit in headlights. What do I do now, where do I go? And I'd ask: 'Where is your network?'. If you're in a corporate company, waste no time in maximising your network, concentrating on those that will be most valuable when you start out.

The important thing is to play to your strengths and minimise your weaknesses. Recognise what you loved doing in your childhood and past working life and incorporate those things in your day-to-day entrepreneurial role.

Additionally, recognise the professional or personal skills that you have that you can leverage in your life as an entrepreneur. As someone once said to co-author Ruth: 'You always make money out of the thing you're third best at in life, as you take the things that you're first and second best at for granted, assuming that everyone can do them'. The important thing is to recognise and play to all of your top skills and delegate the things you're less good at to others.

BUILDING THE RIGHT SUPPORT NETWORK

Many of our interviewees talked about the importance of also having a broader, more informal network of people who they could go to for advice. For example, people who may have helpful contacts as the business grows and changes. Or people who have taken a similar entrepreneurial journey and so can empathise with issues and challenges. Or people who know the entrepreneur well and so can offer empathy, support, advice and confidence during the highs and lows.

Elizabeth Cowper, founder of WoMo, says:

> Build your wolf pack. Think about the people you need by your side who are going to be your advisors and support and will play different roles. On the WoMo platform we say: 'Who do you go to when you're sad, or when you want to celebrate something, or when you want to have a whinge?'. They are likely to be different people. We naturally have them as women in our girlfriends. But there's still the mate that you always call when you want to have a rant, and the mate you call when you're crying.

Similarly, Sophie Le Ray, founder of Naseba, says:

> When you start a business you have so many naysayers, so you have to be super protective of the people around you. You need people who can lift you up and encourage you when you feel terrible because it's not going the way you want. I realise now that I was very lucky because I had people around me who were extremely positive and very present for me. And I now understand how valuable it is to have that support system.

Ellena Ophira at Weddingly says:

> I think it's really important when you embark on something new like this that you are supported by people who love and believe in you. Whether that be the love of a family, partner, best friend, teammates or even a dog. Having people around you who can pick you up and

are prepared to pick you up numerous times is priceless. For me, it's been the key to my survival.

Tamara Gillan at Cherry London says:

> I have a huge network of very trusted female connections – both clients and partners we work with – and I regularly see them and know about their lives. They are deep personal connections that I respect greatly. I honour them, protect them, promote them, and advise them if things are not going well for them.

When thinking about the right support team, the first question to ask yourself is: 'what are the circumstances where you might need help?'. Would you like someone to celebrate with you in the highs? Or build your confidence in the lows? Or help you with the commercial side? Or the recruitment side? Or on the marketing side? Or in how to take your next steps in your entrepreneurial journey?

You will then need to identify people in your network who can help you in these circumstances and ask for their help. In our experience, people love being asked their opinion and advice and people love helping people. So it's rare to be turned down.

As Rebekah Hall of Botanic Lab says:

> I've asked more favours than I ever thought it was possible to ask, from people who know me and care for me and who I've worked with in the past. And I've got quite good at asking for them unashamedly. I've been very lucky that I've had good people who have helped me. I think everyone needs help but sometimes it can be quite difficult to ask for it. I've got a friend who I used to work with a long time ago in banking. She was in HR and is now working for us for nothing sorting out our HR. I'm very lucky that people have come in and helped us. And I continue to ask people to help and they continue to say yes. I hope they've got something out of it as well. It's not something I was comfortable doing at first, but I've got quite good at asking now. You should too.

But when thinking about your networks, be warned. You may need to be prepared to change your circle of friends as your funds are diverted to the business and your income lessens. As Michaela Jedinak, founder of the fashion label Michaela Jedinak, remarked:

> Starting out as a self-funded entrepreneur in your forties, in a new career with no outside funding, is difficult. You can't maintain your lifestyle in terms of holidays, weekends, parties and expensive dinners, which means that you're removing yourself more and more from your old life. I had to change my lifestyle and my friends because I could no longer afford them – and had to find new like-minded people with the same mindset to hang out with.

Having looked at building the right support team, let's move on to the subject of funding, namely whether to bring in other people's money.

WHETHER TO BRING IN OTHER PEOPLE'S MONEY

Some of our interviewees self-funded their business. For example, Liann Eden and Dena McCallum believe that one of the key reasons they are successful is because they put their own money in. In their view:

> If you have investors then you spend a third of your time managing the investors rather than building the business, which slows down the business growth. We self-funded to avoid this by increasing our mortgages so that we could both invest a six-figure sum each, and then not paying ourselves a salary until year three. We both have very supportive partners who enabled us to do this. They supported the business venture and were prepared to forego income for a while.

Obviously not everyone has this advantage but it's worth sounding out partners, family and close friends.

Others needed to bring in outside investment. As Rebekah Hall, founder of Botanic Lab says:

> One of the best decisions I made was to bring in smart money not dumb money. My first raise wasn't necessarily focussed on smart

money. It came from a group of individuals who invested and then had nothing to do with the business. And that's fine because it serves a purpose, if it's capital you need to get going.

My second raise, however, was smart money from investors with a unique and valuable set of relationships and skills. In my case, I have had quite a longstanding relationship with these individuals, so I know how to work with them. Having someone who's done it and has seen those lows is very helpful. Not only do they give you moral support, but they can also advise on where you might be going wrong. If there's a specific issue, for example a contract negotiation you're going through, they can give you advice on how to look at it slightly differently. And I use them as sounding boards when I've made important hires.

It's very lonely being an entrepreneur having to make all of the decisions. Knowing that there are a group of individuals who have your back and who are invested alongside you has given me more confidence along the way. They believed in me and have spent a lot of time with me, mentoring me. You don't make good decisions when it's just you. And I think I need to be challenged by people with knowledge outside of my sphere.

Similarly, Ellena Ophira, founder of Weddingly, talks about the additional value her investors have brought her.

I bumped into our office neighbour who happened to have experience in raising start-up capital. He's a CFO and I joked: 'If you've got time on your hands could you look at my business plan as I'm thinking about raising some money?'. Amazingly, he said yes. I popped into his kitchen with my business plan and cashflows, and after a quick chat he said that he would like to support me and could help me get funded.

I'd never raised capital before. So he introduced me to people in his network and showed me how to put together a pitch deck and present cashflows. He also introduced me to a very smart guy who was raising money for his own start-up, just to ask for his advice. He was really tough to get hold of but, when I finally did, it was amazing. He gave me an hour of his time and told me about the different ways of raising money and which might be suitable for me. I learned a huge amount. At the end of the call he said: 'I think I might like to invest'. I said: 'You're joking?'. He replied, 'No, I love the proposition, I love your passion, I'll give you some money'. A great example of why it's so important to follow up every opportunity, as you just don't know where it will lead. He ended up investing £50,000 which is more money than I had anticipated, and with that we were able to launch.

Again, the refrain is don't be afraid to ask.

Sian Sutherland of Mama Mio fame also took her time to find the right investors. She says:

We went out there through lots of different connections to look for smart money. And we ended up meeting this fantastic woman based in California who had tremendous beauty experience. Jill Dunk was involved in this start-up called Urban Decay which broke the mould in make-up and was then sold to LVMH. This gave us distribution feet on the ground in the U.S. which I knew, just on a numbers game, had to be our biggest opportunity.

But not all investor decisions end well. Let's listen to Sophie Le Ray's experience of building her company Naseba with external investment:

We had a lot of fun growing really fast and completely on our own cashflow, and so avoided a lot of the usual teething pains. We were passionate and resilient and kept growing without much of a business plan in mind. Just a big idea and a lot of work to execute it.

Four years into the business we decided to bring some investors into the mix, and then it became a whole different business. We grew a lot, we learned a lot, we made a lot of mistakes. Every single mistake you can think of making, we did it. Like going public too soon. Like bringing in the wrong investors who were not aligned to our values and didn't want the same things from the business. Like doing a bunch of acquisitions, two or three in the same year, and trying to merge all of them together. Like opening five or six offices in the space of sixteen months, going from one hundred to four hundred staff in a year and a half. And expecting all of this to work out with all the plates spinning. It was a huge learning experience. When you're growing super-fast, you tend to not see the dangers, you feel invincible.

Now, looking back, I would do it as passionately but differently. I would keep the same ambition and growth. But I would choose the people I get into bed with professionally more wisely, and not be blinded by the 'heat of the moment' excitement of getting funded. Because when you don't have the same agenda, it's very risky. You get the funding, but you also get someone else's agenda.

Similarly, Maria Kempinska, founder of Jongleurs Comedy Clubs, also made investment mistakes early on. She says:

My big mistake was that I gave away my business very early. I gave away half of my business to my first investor and then I gave away another chunk to another new investor, making us equal partners. Never ever, ever do that, never have equal partners. If you're the creator of the business, you have to have the majority stake. Even if they are financially your equal, make sure that you have the last say. I made that big mistake and will never ever, ever do that again.

So, when it comes to investment, first ask yourself if you really need the money and, if not, then try to self-fund. Then you will reap all of the benefits of the hard work as well as spend less time managing the investors and more time doing what you love.

If you do need outside money, our entrepreneurs advise you to:

- Raise smart money by assessing what else your investors could offer you in terms of commercial expertise, distribution opportunities or door-opening introductions.
- Always retain a majority share so that you retain control of your business.

- Select your investors wisely, bringing in people who have a shared vision and values and who will support you in your growth every step of the way. Ensure that you have the same perspectives on time frames. Many financial partnerships fracture because time frames were not negotiated clearly enough upfront. And watch how your potential investors behave when negotiating with you. As Professor David Guest said: 'Past behaviours are the best predictor of future behaviours'.[1]

This concludes Chapter Five. In Chapter Six we look at how to grow and scale up a successful business.

NOTES

1 *The Velvet Revolution at Work, The CEO: The Chief EngagementOfficer by* John Smythe.

Scaling up a business to be successful

There comes a time in all entrepreneurial businesses when the start-up phase is over. You need to decide if you want to scale up and, if so, whether you have the necessary capabilities to do so.

Plenty of people are happy not scaling up. For example, as we saw in Chapter One, one of our interviewees built a successful artisan business employing no others. She then hatched a plan to grow. But when thinking through the plan, she realised that growth would mean her having to step into managerial shoes away from her loved artisanship, which wasn't attractive.

But for others it's a must. Victoria Mellor at Melcrum recognised that there was a real opportunity to scale the research arm of her business. But she recalls: 'For us, getting a business off the ground or having a new idea wasn't the hard part. Scaling the business was. I was so young that I didn't really understand what it took to build a self-sufficient business'.

In this chapter we move beyond the start-up phase to look at some of the qualities that it takes to scale up a successful business. Notably:

1. *The leadership qualities required to grow a business.*
2. *Changing your and others' roles as the business grows.*
3. *Taking your business to the next stage.*
4. *Staying true to your entrepreneurial roots.*
5. *Managing the end game.*

THE LEADERSHIP QUALITIES REQUIRED TO GROW A BUSINESS

Many of our entrepreneurs talked about the different leadership qualities they needed to scale and grow a successful business after the start-up phase. In this section we will look at some of these, including:

- Building a more well-rounded leadership style.
- Treating your people and those with whom you do business with respect.

Tamara Gillan, Melina Jacovou and Sian Sutherland are entrepreneurs who have changed and developed their leadership styles as their businesses grew.

Tamara Gillan, founder of Cherry London, says:

> As your company grows, from one where you are pretending to be an assistant to ten people to becoming a leader and manager of say fifty, you have to adapt at pace. You can't just be a 'flouncy pouncy' with great ideas. You have to manage a team and a structure. I and my team have had a lot of coaching, which has been a cornerstone of our success and growth. I had this more matriarchal, positive and protective leadership style. As a female entrepreneur I've struggled to find that more steely side of leadership, the one where you need to have tough conversations with people, even clients.
>
> An authentic leader has to be able to talk about the positive feedback, as well as the areas for development or improvement. I never used to be able to talk about money. I hated talking about money with clients. But now I can. I've had to find that balance between being direct, fair and tough rather than needing to be liked. I did some coaching and practised having direct, honest feedback sessions. I learned how to raise stressful issues earlier, so that I don't go silent and get frustrated. We all have leadership traits that we need to offset. But I have learned through feedback and coaching that you can adapt and change which is essential.

Melina Jacovou of Propel talked about the importance of creating a clear vision and strategy that the team can follow. She says:

> The best decision I ever made was setting up Propel. The worst decision I ever made is not defining its purpose a lot sooner. Your vision has to be reinvented all of the time, because the world changes. But it's good to have a purpose and focus quite soon, because you'll be everywhere if you don't. You can be so busy running around trying to do the day job that sometimes you don't get the opportunity to strategise.

Don't underestimate the value of being strategic and taking time out to consider what the future might look like. Last week we redid our mission and vision statements with the leadership team. It's important to redo them from time to time as things move on and people change. We have a Propel playbook which outlines how to treat clients and candidates to ensure that our messaging is current and consistent throughout the whole business. We give it to anybody who joins, so that they know what's expected of them whatever team they're in. For example, how do you treat your clients, how do you treat the candidates, what does good look like? Because if you're going to scale a business there needs to be some sort of code of conduct that everyone adheres to.

Sian Sutherland, co-founder of Mama Mio, beautifully sums up her leadership challenge when scaling up. She says:

As the business grew, we became a very widespread team. We had an events team in New York, a marketing director in Florida, our U.S. sales office headed up by our U.S. partner in California, our U.K. sales team out on the road, a warehouse in South London and our head office in east London. And all of our distributors in the countries that they represented. So, this was a real example of a 21st-century company. We had a maximum of fifty people but rarely more than ten people in one place at any one time. As CEO, my toughest job was to drive the bus. But I also had to make sure that everybody was on the bus, knew where the bus was going, and felt great about being on the bus.

As these examples illustrate, to successfully scale up there comes a stage where entrepreneurs need to transcend being the 'chief bottle washer, mother and CEO' (as Rebekah Hall called her initial role). Instead they need to put in place the team and structure needed to scale up, as well as to keep the team motivated and aligned around a clear vision, strategy, goals and plan.

A second leadership trait that our female entrepreneurs believed is important is treating those you do business with and those who work for you with respect, celebrating their achievements and success.

Vicki Willden-Lebrecht, founder of Bright, believes that it's very important to focus on the people and share in their success. She says:

> I'm most proud of how happy Bright has made both our employees and artists. There's been moments when artists have said they've bought a house which they would never have been able to do, and won awards that they never even dreamed of. It's an incredible feeling that you've got artists working with amazing art directors and pub-lishers and film makers, and that you exceed people's dreams in what you can deliver for them. It's so rewarding.

She goes on to talk about the importance of treating people with respect:

> I think good manners and loyalty are incredibly important. Treat people how you want to be treated. Don't do bad business. Don't be a shark. Be fair – and when I say that I mean be fair to yourself too. When you think someone is taking advantage of you say: 'No, that's not right'. One of the things the London *Times* asked me was: 'What's your biggest investment been?'. And I replied: 'On myself'. I've done Ashrams in India, twelve-day detoxes to clear my mind, deep business coaching where you are the person in your business and role play, really trying to be as compassionate as possible and looking at it from other people's perspectives. If you help others achieve their goals, you get closer to your own.

On motivating her employees, Vicki mentions the importance of creating a listening culture where there is genuine freedom of expression, although she readily and refreshingly admits that this is hard to do when you have a clear view. She advises:

> Make sure everyone in your team feels appreciated. When things are moving at a hundred miles an hour this can be hard to do. Most issues I ever have with anyone comes down to: 'What about me? Am I important? Am I doing a good job?'. Everyone wants to do a good job. No one wants to do bad work. You need to give people the opportu-nity to achieve in your organisation and to praise them when they've done a good job. When your team are not delivering, look at how

you're communicating with them. Have you given them clear roles and responsibilities? Do they know what's expected of them? Are their wins being acknowledged? We all want to feel loved and appreciated. To know that our work matters and that we matter. Most issues come down to that.

Vicki demonstrates the importance of creating a work culture where people feel able to speak up and be listened to. She also has the self-knowledge to admit that this runs counter to one aspect of her personality. Believing it is one thing, doing it every day is another. Vicki's reflections also illustrate a paradox of being an entrepreneur. On the one hand, you've taken all the risk and made all the early decisions. On the other, to grow, you have to trust in others when devolving risk and decision making. And that's hard and maybe explains why growth can be elusive.

Melina Jacovou of Propel agrees with Vicki: 'One thing that really helped me is honest relationships in life and business. Supporting others and being supported at every stage. Invest in that support and the rewards are incredible'.

Di Burton, founder of the very successful Cicada Communications, also echoes Vicki's advice by talking about how her behaviour towards others has been her biggest regret. She says:

> I probably shouldn't have made as many enemies along the way. I should have been nicer. I have incredibly high standards and so am highly critical. But I think it's because I'm highly critical of myself. I've learnt that some of the most successful people aren't the brightest or hardest workers, but they're such nice people. And that's what I'm not. So, I have a fridge magnet now which says: 'It's a really good idea to be nice to people'.

We end this section with some very wise words from Lara Morgan, founder originally of Pacific Direct and now well-being investor of Scentered:

> There are so many different varieties of human beings who run businesses, and there's no preconceived style of leadership. You don't have

to be noisy or bossy or loud or overconfident. You can be calm and well refined and deeply civilised and steady eddie and still achieve different but equally important stuff.

CHANGING YOUR AND OTHERS' ROLES AS THE BUSINESS GROWS

As the business grows, your team structure may need to change. For example, you and your partner may have increasingly different visions and need to go your different ways. Or you may need to build a strong management team around you. Or you may need to let someone who doesn't fit go. In this section we look at what our entrepreneurs said about:

- When a business partnership is past its sell-by date.
- How to broaden and deepen your team.
- How to let someone go.

Some of our entrepreneurs have split from their original business partner due to a clash of visions or a difficulty in working together as the business scaled.

Let's look at Kate Grussing who co-founded her business, Sapphire Partners, with a partner that she later split from. Kate decided that she wanted to take the plunge at the time of her fortieth birthday, which was partly triggered by being passed over for promotion at a well-known American investment bank.

She felt that she had the capital, technical knowledge and personal skills, so all she needed was the right business idea. Kate left the bank and considered creating a magazine for working women 'which, happily, was shot down by my group of sense checkers'. But then she touched on the right idea – a high-level search firm with a focus on diversity. As someone who had waited until forty before jumping ship, she had experienced plenty of recruitment processes where gender diversity did not seem to be a key focus. And this idea passed the sense check when one CEO asked if he could be their first client. She wanted a business partner and found one with complementary skills. They worked hard, but after two and a half years her business partner decided to leave.

Unfortunately, they had put off doing a shareholder's agreement which hugely complicated the exit and required Kate to rebuild the business from the ground up, which she has done spectacularly well. Her strong advice to others is to tie up legal arrangements early on in case you and partners decide to split. But, as she says: 'Not so tightly that it becomes an overly bureaucratic affair'.

Echoing advice from others she also advises talking through the reality of how long it will take to get the business off the ground with potential partners, rather than fantasising that you will be one of the few businesses that will make it quick. As she advises: 'avoid marrying in haste and repenting at leisure'.

Other entrepreneurs found that, as their business grew, they needed to bring a strong management team on-board to share the responsibility and broaden the skill set. This is especially true if teams are spread out geographically, which, technology enabled, many are.

For example, we saw in Chapter Four that Rebekah Hall built the business as a sole partner but increasingly realised that the business had become too big for her as the lone leader. To address this, she set about recruiting a strong team around her with the necessary skill sets and values to form a solid leadership team.

Similarly, Victoria Mellor, founder of Melcrum, went to business school eight years after starting her business because she realised that she lacked the financial and planning skills to scale her business. She says:

> There's a critical point where you go from sitting in a room together having fun, to getting serious about building your management team around you. The people who don't manage to scale up their businesses never get through the stage of building a management team with complementary skill sets, and the ability to set up the right processes and focus on all of the 'behind the scenes' stuff.

Between 2005 and 2010, I built a management team around me by putting into practice a lot of things I'd learnt on the Cranfield programme. I hired the management team on the basis that we were going to grow and exit the business, whether that was selling it to the management team or an outright sale, by offering share options. I had to get out of the way of my own business and let the management team take up the reins.

One word of caution. If you have disrupted a sector then beware of hiring people with the old sector's DNA. Go outside of your sector to find people who have alternative attributes and skills to create a truly disruptive business. Tash Walker of The Mix talks about the value she found in doing this.

At the beginning we tried to get bigger by hiring from traditional agencies. But that didn't work as we simply re-created a traditional agency with no differentiation. So we decided to go back to a disruptive model.

Instead of hiring from the old agency model we hired an event producer as a junior designer because her different background had nothing to do with anything we did. She brought a whole new energy and creativity into the agency which has taken us in a different direction and put us much more in that disruptive space again. That's been one of the things that has allowed us to grow really quickly in the last year. So she has moved through the ranks quite quickly and is now our MD.

Many of our entrepreneurs also talked about the difficulty of letting people go. Sandra Macleod of Echo Research sums it up well.

When I left Echo, one of the things I missed most was hiring, growing and developing people. I also learned that markets wax and wane. When things are tough and you've overextended, you have to make people redundant. I don't care what anyone says, I get sleepless nights over this. If someone isn't right for the business, then you need to deal with it as quickly and as professionally and as kindly as you can.

It's easy to hang on to people for too long. Well, I certainly did as I always found firing people difficult. But it's important not to let those things linger. I don't think it's anyone's fault, either theirs or ours. But when you know it's not going to work you need to move fast. As most people say, it's the people issues that are always so tricky, because you're dealing with people's livelihoods. Unless you are completely disconnected, it's a very emotional and challenging time and one that is difficult to navigate well.

So, as you move out of a start-up into a growth phase, ensure that you have the right partners at the top, a strong management team to set up the processes and structure needed to scale up and the right day-to-day teams with the skills, capabilities and mindsets needed to deliver your proposition. But, most importantly to be successful in the scale-up phase, as Victoria Mellor so wisely said: 'Get out of the way of your business and let your management team take up the reins'.

TAKING YOUR BUSINESS TO THE NEXT STAGE

If you have identified a great commercial opportunity, competitors will have most likely noticed and followed or even tried to leapfrog you. So, it is imperative to keep refreshing your business idea once launched to keep it ahead of the competition. To do this, it's important to put your head above the day-to-day parapet from time to time – by taking the time to step back to see where you're at and be insightful and mindful about where you would like to go next.

Some of our interviewees have successfully kept their businesses ahead of the game by finding new sources of income.

Victoria Mellor set up Melcrum in 1996. As we saw in Chapter Four, in 2001 Melcrum lost a lot of business in the U.S. due to the anthrax scare after 9/11. So she set up a research business as an alternative way forward. She says:

We started a research business because I'd always been driven by talking to people, understanding their needs and turning them into good ideas. This skill is part of the reason why we were able to launch successful products and adapt to new market conditions.

In 2010, Victoria changed tack again by focussing on a new product that they could get a competitive advantage in – an enterprise membership for large global corporations to access intellectual property, know-how, research, tools and training IP. She moved the business away from publishing into research and then into training and consultancy, following lucrative veins that enabled her to scale.

By 2015, she had grown a global business with fifty employees and a network of associate trainers – which was successfully sold for millions of pounds to Washington-based CEB.

Claire Randall set up her outsourced production consultancy for one client seven years before opening her company up to new clients. She recalls:

> After seven years of being exclusive, it became increasingly hard to deal with the financial side of it. I needed to pay my staff the rates that they could get in agencies, and each one required a separate negotiation with my client.
>
> I realised that the model had to change. So I went to my client and said, 'I love working with you, but you could share the overhead with others if you let me extend my services to other advertisers. At the moment you're paying for everything. Why don't you let me take on other business as long as it's not a direct competitor and then I can reduce the cost to you?'. They weren't keen at first and rightly made me repitch which took a year. This was awful because I knew I'd have to get rid of my team if I didn't win it. It was a lot of pressure. But in the end we won it back with the freedom to go non-exclusive. That's really when I think of the company as being properly Claire Randall Consulting.

Other interviewees, such as Melina Jacovou, founder of talent agency Propel, talked about the importance of continually reinventing your business to keep it ahead of the competitors and relevant for the next stage. She says:

> Propel has been going for seventeen years and been through various stages of growth. We've been changing and evolving. We've been agile and flexible. Not just for the clients that we work with but also for the people who work here.
>
> Reinventing ourselves was really important because we're a service provider. It's all about keeping ourselves relevant for the latest trends. We initially started building teams for creative and media agencies because that was what my client base wanted. Then we started to build teams for clients in performance marketing, such as SEO and PPC, with organisations like Yahoo and Overture. Now we build strong leadership teams for a wide range of companies, all of which are in technology in some shape or form.
>
> The journey has not been easy, we've gone through three recessions. Recruitment is a people business and people move on. We constantly have to attract and retain the right people – and build a strong culture where people can deliver our vision, mission and values. You should always be evolving and changing and never become complacent. Keep learning, keep reinventing yourself to ensure you're relevant in this competitive market.

Melina has adapted her business to different industries over time, but the constant theme that she says gives her the biggest high is 'helping a business to grow from a people aspect, and helping people build their career until they reach the top positions'.

These stories show the importance of stepping back from the day-to-day operations to think: 'where am I on this journey and where could or must the business go next?'.

For Victoria Mellor, stepping back helped her to identify new profitable growth veins resulting in the sale of a multimillion-pound business. For Claire Randall, it gave her the momentum and confidence to make the transition from a single client company to Claire Randall Consulting. For Melina, it helped her to survive and grow through three recessions.

STAYING TRUE TO YOUR ENTREPRENEURIAL ROOTS

As you start out, it's important to behave cost-efficiently as an entrepreneur, working with a small team to hone and optimise your business idea. But some of our entrepreneurs talked about how, over time as their business scaled and attracted high levels of investment, they made the mistake of moving away from their more cost-efficient entrepreneurial roots and behaving more like big brands, to their detriment.

Tash Walker, founder of creative agency The Mix, made this mistake. She says:

> 2015 was tumultuous. We'd been in business for a few years and we'd hired account managers and set up new departments to try to be more like a big company, and we were becoming reasonably success-ful. But we were becoming like any other classic agency. The intention was always to be disruptive and work with great purpose, producing genuinely awesome work.

> But the more you become beholden to driving the revenue stream, the more you become process driven and lose that. I could feel us being sucked into that rat race hamster mentality you get in agencies, where you churn out projects and the quality of the work becomes quite stand-ardised. There was a moment after a particularly tough quarter where we turned over more than we'd ever turned over. I felt really shattered. But not in an 'I'm exhausted but rewarded' way, but in a drained 'I can see the future and it wasn't something I wanted to be in' way.

> It was really tough. I had to look at what we were doing and admit that if we wanted to disrupt the industry in a bigger way then we had to stop and readjust our course. Otherwise, we'd end up being stuck with a small to medium-sized agency just churning out work. So, in 2016, I got rid of the whole account management team, which was challenging because we had ruffled our own feathers and taken a bit of a bruising. But, the last two years have been quite different. We are back in the disruptive space that we originally started in again, which has helped us grow really quickly over the last year.

Sian Sutherland, co-founder of Mama Mio, also got sucked into moving away from her entrepreneurial roots and behaving like a big brand. She recalls:

> So three years into the development of Mama Mio, we were introduced to the ex-president of Estée Lauder, Bob Nielsen, who is a legend in the beauty world. He created many iconic brands such as Clinique, Aveda and Origins and brought Joe Malone and MAC into the Estée Lauder stable. We met him, and he invested in the business. I understand that we were the first beauty business that he had invested in out of his own pocket.

> But we got a bit giddy. We believed we had so much to learn from the big guys. We were listening to people telling us to build a beauty brand this way or that way, resulting in us spending a year behaving like a big brand. We burnt through a lot of money in the year running up to the 2008 crash including opening a New York office in September 2008. But the world then imploded, so we closed it in October of the same year.

> I remember Bob Nielsen calling me up saying everybody needed to take a 25% pay cut. And I thought 'We're not going to do it that way. We're going to go back to rolling our sleeves up and doing it the way that we know how to do it. We're going to stop behaving like a big brand and start behaving like the scrappy entrepreneurial brand that we know how to do'.

> The one thing about entrepreneurs is that they know how to make shit happen with very little money and how to pivot. So, we quickly lost any non-essentials, such as our external New York marketing agency, lots of external people and our new U.S. FD, and we went back to being true entrepreneurs and doing it our way. Nobody had to take a pay cut and that year we turned around our loss-making business into a million dollars profit. It was such a validation for everybody in the team that we rediscovered what to do and how to do it.

Melina Jacovou, founder of Propel, also took her eye off her original proposition. She recalls:

> Seven or eight years after launch, we started to build management and day-to-day teams, supported by a proper structure and processes. We

got to fifty-six people when it all fell apart. Our culture was all over the shop. We were hiring the wrong people, and all the things that we tell our clients not to do, we were doing. It was horrendous. So, over a period of six months we stripped it back. We needed to make sure that our people were right and would stay – and we needed to put in place the right processes, values and culture. So, we redefined the business as a leadership team. Now the business is rebirthed, and I'm the happiest I've ever been here.

That's due to the people who work here, the innovative companies that we're working with, the fact that this market is amazing, and that we're building and changing the future.

As these examples show, it's important to stay true to who you are and what you know by staying true to your vision as well as remaining lean and cost-efficient. As you scale, you may be offered high levels of investment which makes it tempting to behave like a big brand. But, as we saw in these examples, burning through 'cash-chasing grandeur' is rarely a good strategy.

We end this section with some wise words from Melina Jacovou:

Never believe your own hype. Always learn and grow from those that work with you and for you. Never get too egotistic. Always do stuff. Never ask anyone to do anything you wouldn't do. And most importantly, enjoy the journey and be grateful for it. Because one thing that will definitely happen is that we will all die.

MANAGING THE END GAME

In this last section, we glean words of advice from our entrepreneurs who have successfully sold their businesses on how to manage the end game. We touch on:

- Building the business with the end in mind.
- The art of good negotiation.
- Capitalising on the exit opportunities when they come along.

We start with Victoria Mellor who built her business Melcrum with the end game in mind and who successfully sold it to Washington-based CEB in 2015.

She says:

> During the pre-sale period, we recognised that CEB had an attractive business model that they had successfully scaled. They were located close to our U.S. team in Washington D.C. and inevitably you start talking. It became clear that they could be a potential acquirer for our business. A lot of our decision-making at this time was based on the fact that CEB could be a potential exit for us.
>
> Consequently, I incentivised the management team on varying levels of share options. And when looking at systems and processes that we needed to invest in we'd ask ourselves: 'What does CEB use?'. We wanted to make it as easy as possible for them to recognise at due diligence stage that we would be easy to integrate into their own business.
>
> When we went to market with the business, we had advisors in New York who helped to create a lot of competitive tension, resulting in a couple of people bidding for it. But very early on in the process CEB said that they wanted an exclusive due diligence period – and were happy to let me and my partner walk away with no earnout, which was fairly unusual. At that point I'd also stepped away from being CEO to Chairman and so I didn't really have any day-to-day responsibilities. I was easy to let go.

Victoria goes on to talk about the art of negotiation.

> It's very easy to get anxious and stressed, as there's a lot going on. But none of these behaviours are productive. I think in hindsight I would have negotiated things differently. I would have had a better sense of where the other party is coming from, how they are feeling and what they're going through, rather than just being engrossed in my feelings and emotions. I think maybe that's just age and wisdom. I'm not saying I don't get cross now, but I look at things with a much longer arc and try not to react to things immediately.

Lara Morgan also sold her first business, Pacific Direct, a luxury toiletries business, and is now running her new business, Scentered. Like Victoria, she built Pacific Direct with the aim of selling it, although missed out twice before finally making a good deal. She explains:

> I learned recently that only 7% of British businesses exit, leaving 93% of people never realising their wealth or assets, and needing greater education or more ambition. I suspect there are more people that realise their wealth in America, but that the numbers are still very low. That makes me very sad. I exited my first business in April 2008 with 476 people working in nine countries. It sold for £20 million and I was a 99% shareholder. I sold 80% of the business because I'd become bitten by the business education bug at Stamford and London Business School.

> I'd failed to exit the business in 2004 and almost lost the business in 2002 because of September 11th. Ironically, I was actually writing my exit plan in a hotel room in Los Angeles on September 11th. But then I had to go into business survival mode for three years because if you don't have hotel and airline customers, my products don't sell. I put the house up as a personal guarantee to get through these tough times with enough cashflow. It was a pretty big baptism, but every business has its moments.

She goes on to say:

> I would never build a family company because I've seen such misery caused by 'Auntie Mavis' never working a day in the business but still being granted part of the dividends. I've got a friend running a business today whose three sisters depend on her for their children's private education. What angst and anxiety to carry all that. People are increasingly realising that the hierarchy of family genes doesn't owe you a living – and that it should no longer be the tradition to pass the business onto the family. I think it's more powerful to bring in an outside professional to build the business.

The advice from our more successful entrepreneurs who have sold their businesses is to build the business with an exit strategy in mind. For them, creating the management and day-to-day teams, structure, processes and succession plan during the scale-up phase made it easier for them to sell their business and exit because every decision was serving the purpose of building and selling.

That concludes Chapter Six. In Chapter Seven we will look at the importance of embracing failure and using it to your advantage.

CHAPTER SEVEN

Failure comes with the territory

Failure, as well as success, is an inherent part of our natural world – and a huge learning opportunity for those who embrace it. Yet failure can be seen as negative and something to avoid. On the one hand, we recognise that everyone fails and that failure is a natural part of the learning process. Yet, on the other hand, we are conditioned from a young age that failure is 'bad' and a sign of weakness. It signifies that we have screwed up or are stupid.

So, to avoid failure, we typically do one of two things. We either deny failure – we ignore it, bury it or see it as a one-off anomaly. Many people can't admit their mistakes to themselves let alone to others. Or, we avoid failure – we put our head in the sand rather than take a risk – to the point that we are so scared of messing up that we don't even try.

Human nature can make failure feel, at best, uncomfortable and, at worst, unacceptable. Yet, successful entrepreneurs embrace failure alongside success. They understand that they can learn at least as much when they get it wrong as when they get it right. And they use failure to find new, bigger, bolder ways to grow their business.

In Chapter Seven we look at what our female entrepreneurs had to say about failure, including:

1. Embracing failure and learning from it.
2. Using failure to drive you forwards.
3. Overcoming fear of failure.
4. Overcoming adversity.

EMBRACING FAILURE AND LEARNING FROM IT

Failure can be seen by many as negative. Some people talk about not starting a business as they are frightened that they will fail. And many of our female entrepreneurs have experienced failure, often repeatedly, along the way.

Some of these set-backs can be caused by external events, which had to be responded to fast. For example, as we saw in Chapter Six, the very successful entrepreneur Victoria Mellor lost a lot of her U.S. publishing business due to the anthrax scare that happened after 9/11. This led her to look for new lucrative avenues to mine, leading to the launch of successful research, training and consultancy arms.

Other set-backs can be caused by internal issues, such as over-extending the business in the quest to grow quickly. For example, as we saw in Chapter Six, seven to eight years after launch Melina Jacovou over-extended her talent agency, Propel, by bringing in too many people, many of whom didn't fit the company culture. To enable it to survive, she had to stop, diagnose and admit the issue, and then strip the company back to basics, which in turn meant letting a lot of people go. This resulted in her leadership team redefining the business back to its core, which in turn enabled Propel to get back to doing innovative work with innovative clients.

Similarly, Tash Walker over-extended her creative agency, The Mix. She wanted to build it into a big agency, but this resulted in her bringing in too many people and setting up too many teams. In her words:

> In 2016, I got rid of the whole account management team which was challenging because we had ruffled our own feathers and taken a bit of a bruising. But, the last two years have been quite different. We are back in the disruptive space that we originally started in again, which has helped us grow really quickly over the last year.

Paradoxically, slimming down the company made it much leaner and customer-driven, which resulted in strong business growth.

Sian Sutherland, co-founder of Mama Mio, also got sucked into moving away from her entrepreneurial roots and behaving like a big brand. She recalls: 'We burnt through a lot of money in the year running up to the 2008 crash including opening a New York office in September 2008. But the world then imploded, so we closed it in October of the same year'. But rather than see it as failure, Sian saw it as an opportunity to take the business back to what they knew best – namely being a 'scrappy entrepreneurial brand'. This resulted in the business being turned around from loss-making into a million-dollar profit, which was a huge validation for Sian and her top team.

Many of our female entrepreneurs have experienced failure, or 'course corrections' (as many preferred to frame set-backs), during the launch and growth of their business. Some failures may only require small course corrections – such as getting out of a weak product line or marketing channel. Others may need full-on surgery – such as closing down business arms, shedding people who are surplus to requirements or changing the company direction into a new area.

In the short term, failure may cause a temporary blip or set-back. But, with the benefit of hindsight, many of our female entrepreneurs now see failure as an important part of their growth journey, enabling them to put in the key building blocks that grew their businesses to new heights. In fact, they agree that without it they wouldn't have got to where they are today.

Vicki Willden-Lebrecht is one of these people. She talks about how important failure has been in the growth of her business, Bright Agency. She says:

> I've had so many big failings and I don't regret any of them. I've always recovered from them. I've always bounced back better and learned a lot. Some of the lessons have been huge. I remember we had some holes in our financial planning. We were increasing our costs over and above our income, so much so that the company was potentially heading for trouble if we didn't pull back. It was a really worrying time as I had to make six people redundant. Interestingly, by month three, we had made more money than we were making before. The extra costs had created a lot of internal pressure which stopped us being outward-focussed. It taught me that we had started to look inwards. If a company's talking to each other they're not talk-ing to artists and clients. There needs to be good internal processes but not meetings about meetings about meetings. You can become too obsessed with your own business and stop listening to your

customers. Everyone in your business needs to be looking outward. So what was a huge problem became a big opportunity. Actually, that's been true for all of our mistakes, it's how you learn.

Sophie Le Ray, founder of Naseba, talks about the importance of entrepreneurs expecting and embracing failure as a natural part of their growth journey. She says:

Many of us don't stay entrepreneurs because, let's face it, most of the time it's very painful before it gets rewarding. It's one of those things that you fall into and swim as you go. I started like everybody else, naively thinking that I could do better than what I was doing for my company. But failure and pain are a big part of my story. I had to learn how to use failure to grow, both personally and for my business. The failure I experienced was to be unable to sustain the growth I was going through and get to the destination I wanted to get to. It took me some self-reflection to understand that the destination was not meant to be. And that didn't necessarily mean failure, it was part of the process. I wouldn't take the failure away as it was so important to the growth of the business and my personal role within it. It was failure that made me reconsider my business and my personal purpose. At the time it felt like failure, but looking back it was a growth spurt. It was painful, but necessary. It sometimes meant that we had to do painful stuff like reducing the number of projects or decreasing some of the investment or even letting go of people, because it just hadn't worked the way we were expecting. But, at the end of the day, the result was learning and often material growth as well. It really depends on the perspective you're taking.

She has some very wise words for budding entrepreneurs.

Entrepreneurship is not for the faint-hearted. If you start out being fearful or limited by external or internal factors, then you really need to think long and hard about whether you want to do this, because this is what the life of an entrepreneur is all about. See the failures and mishaps as necessary developmental steps – rather than frame them as 'out and out failures'. If it goes well, it goes well, but it's not because you're a genius. If it doesn't go well, it doesn't go well, but it's not because you're a failure. You need some sanity, a clear sense of your identity outside of the business and a super tough mindset, especially at the beginning.

As we can see, failure isn't necessarily bad or something to be scared of. It's a natural part of any entrepreneurial growth story. Moreover, it is something to embrace and learn from, recognising that it will most probably lead to the next growth spurt.

USING FAILURE TO DRIVE YOU FORWARDS

For some of our entrepreneurs, fear has been a helpful force in driving them to launch, grow and stick with their businesses even in the tough times. Tash Walker and Etty Laniado both talk about how fear gave them the impetus to start their businesses.

As we saw in Chapter Four, it was the fear of not taking the risk of starting her business that gave Tash Walker the impetus to launch her creative agency, the Mix. Tash says:

At the outset, there wasn't a great design or a year's worth of business planning. I had no plans, no investors, just an idea and a kind of sense of 'Why not?'. For me, the biggest thing was the risk of not doing it, which was so much greater than the risk of trying and failing. That was six years ago and it has most certainly not been plain sailing. But, that simple decision to try and have a go has led me to where I am today.

As we saw in Chapter Two, a fear of failure gained from her childhood was instrumental in encouraging Etty Laniado to launch her catering company, Chef Laniado. Etty says:

I'm a positive person who has always loved to cook and always been into cooking. I can look at life in such an optimistic way that sometimes it can seem a bit naive. But that's what drives me into carrying on, even when I'm failing. I can thank my father and his love of food for where I am today. I have dyslexia which adversely affected my grades. I was growing up in a time when dyslexia wasn't recognised. If you were dyslexic you were considered stupid or slow or lazy. These were the words that I heard, which damaged my self-confidence. Dyslexia can be worked on and it's something that I have worked on all of my life, especially when I was young. But at that age I didn't know that other people suffered from it and that I wasn't alone. It was tough to see the disappointment on my father's face when I got the reports at the end of every term.

She goes on to say:

My father was the figure I most wanted to impress, yet the person I felt I had disappointed most. But, on reflection, it's thanks to him that I'm where I am today. It galvanised me to get on and succeed in something he loved – food. I can thank him for that even if it was hard to bear at the time as I wanted so much to please him. I visited him in hospital when he was fading away from us. He opened his eyes and woke up for a moment. I told him that I had won a place on MasterChef and that my business was taking off. He smiled and I knew that he was proud of me. It was a memorable moment. I felt a surge of self-confidence and got some peace from closing the circle.

Some of our entrepreneurs, such as Lindsay Levin and Mursal Hedayat, also talk about the importance of keeping moving forward when the going gets tough, by recognising and accepting the worst that can happen.

Lindsay Levin, founder of Leaders' Quest, says:

When creating something, like a business or project, keep walking forwards. You can't second guess it. You need to get over what's the worst thing that can happen. The worst thing that can happen is not usually that bad – you fail and lose some money or have to get another job. I still have lots of self-doubt. I have it all the time within the context of what we're doing. But you need to keep looking back and after a period of time notice your achievements and successes. Take time to stop and smell the roses.

Mursal Hedayat, founder of Chatterbox, concurs with Lindsay.

If I hadn't trusted my gut, I wouldn't have launched Chatterbox. If Chatterbox doesn't trust its gut to make big decisions, then we will theorise until our money runs out. So trust your gut, go with it. You might fail but then what? Get a job. That's the worst that can happen. And people will respect you for trying.

For some of our entrepreneurs, fear has been a helpful force in driving the launch and growth of their businesses even when the going gets tough. They advise others to think through and accept the worst that could happen and thereby free themselves up to give their venture the best shot.

OVERCOMING FEAR OF FAILURE

Now we get onto the tricky subject of overcoming the fear of failure. Some of our interviewees found coping with failure tough and have had to learn over time how to overcome their fear of failing. Let's see what they had to say.

Rebekah Hall of Botanic Lab talks about how tough she found coping with failure. She says:

I'm very hard on myself. I've always taken failures quite badly. But if you do anything on your own you have to get used to it. There are times when it feels hopeless. You lose a contract, you fall out with a supplier, your staff are on your case and you haven't left work until 12 o'clock for five weeks or been on holiday for three years. You feel like you're running to go backwards. It's a very up and down journey. Sometimes it can be all-consuming, but the hits keep on coming. When it goes wrong, you need to pick yourself up, learn from the mistakes and not do them a second time. As time's gone on, I've got better at picking myself up and moving on from the failures and not beating myself up. It's something I work on, but I'm not there yet. I find it difficult not getting it right because ultimately it's my responsibility. There isn't anyone else to blame. So I take any failure personally. But that's part of what owning and building a business is all about.

Rebekah goes on to talk about how she has overcome her fear of failure by not trying to be great at everything. She says:

I would advise entrepreneurs to pinpoint what they're good at, and then by default what they're not good at. That's not an admission of failure. No one is good at everything. Spending my time on the things that I'm really good at is where I am most effective. Then, I need to know what I don't know and find a person who can fill the gap. I used to feel like asking for help was an admission you'd failed or that you're not good enough or you're burdening people. I've now realised that people want to help.

Emma Hill, owner of Redefine hair salon, concurs with Rebekah. She says:

Everyone will make mistakes. There's nothing wrong with making mistakes, provided you take responsibility for those mistakes, acknowledge them and learn from them. I never use the word fail, even in our salon training. I always frame feedback as 'This is what you need to do next time in order to become successful'. 'Fail' is quite a negative word. I think you can invite negativity in if you use it.

Sophie Le Ray also learned how to overcome her fear of failure. For her, the trick was to separate who she is from what she did. By doing this she has been able to keep some much-needed distance and perspective between her and her business, thus enabling her to make better commercial decisions when things needed to change. She says:

Initially I was completely identifying myself with my business – and my business was fun and easy to do. When it started to not go the way I wanted it to, I kept identifying myself with the business – as if it and I were one entity joined at the hip. Then I realised this is super unhealthy because my business needed to change. I needed to separate 'me' from 'the business' and that's frighteningly hard to do. I am not my business. I am an individual who runs a business. Knowing the reason why you're doing what you're doing is crucial. Knowing helps to prevent you over-identifying with your business. It helps you put in adequate separation between who you are, your identity and your business. Going through this process of establishing the right level of separation from the business freed me to feel at one with myself and growth followed. I wouldn't be where we are today without that challenging period of re-alignment between me and the business.

Claire Randall also offers some sage advice to budding entrepreneurs who are fearful of failing.

I would say to people to go for it. Don't be afraid to fail. I think our generation were generally afraid of failure. We were brought up to decide what we wanted to do, get a job and stick with it. You couldn't just bail. We didn't chop and change careers as much as the millennials expect to do now. They are encouraged to try things and fail. They want a good work–life balance and are perhaps less materialistic. They believe strongly in equality and they want to have a job that they enjoy. Unlike us, they're really encouraged to try things and create start-ups. It doesn't matter if it doesn't work. You just try something else.

We finish this section with some research on how more successful people tend to view failure from Dr Carol Dweck's book *Mindset*. She shows that successful people tend to act in a counter-intuitive way, by embracing rather than shying away from failure.[1] For example, she tracked the two-year performance of students after they transitioned up into junior high school – a notoriously tougher learning environment. By doing this, she showed that students with what they call a 'fixed mindset' – a belief that their basic qualities such as character, talent and intelligence are largely fixed – view failure as proof that they don't have the characteristics needed to succeed and never will and so they avoid situations in which they might fail. In her experiment, students with a 'fixed mindset' showed an immediate drop-off in grades when they transitioned up into the new school and these grades slowly but surely dropped further over the next two years.

In contrast, those with what they call a 'growth mindset' – a belief that most basic qualities can be developed through hard work – embrace failure as a learning opportunity and are more likely to keep trying until they succeed. In her experiment, those with a 'growth mindset' showed an increase in grades over the next two years. In her words:

> When the two groups had entered junior high, their past records were indistinguishable. In the more benign environment of grade school, they'd earned the same grades and achievement test scores. Only when they hit the challenge of junior high did they begin to pull apart.

If you're frightened of failing then you're in good company. Many of our interviewees were too. They advise others not to be overly hard on themselves or take the failure personally. If the business fails, it doesn't mean you've failed. Instead, see failure as a learning opportunity along your entrepreneurial growth journey. And when you inevitably fail, pick yourself up, learn from your mistakes and don't repeat them a second time.

OVERCOMING ADVERSITY

Sometimes life can throw unexpected curveballs at us. These events are often out of our control and can cause us to have to course-correct our vision and plans. In this section we look at how to cope with adversity when it comes your way.

As we saw in Chapter Two, Sherry Roberts built the very successful business The Longest Stay enabling people who stay in luxury hotels to buy the furniture and artefacts they see in their rooms online at her website. Her 'first mover' idea was way ahead of other hotel chains aiming to create shoppable hotels.

Sherry built her business against the odds – with her entrepreneurial journey containing many precipitous turns. Her story illustrates the strains of supporting a sick home partner and scrambling to stay afloat, paradoxically worsened by the extraordinary growth of The Longest Stay. Hers was a capital-needy project and she went through gruelling money-raising rounds, each requiring steadily more than the last at an accelerating pace. Fast growth from nothing is a glorious but utterly unforgiving mistress.

When Sherry started her business she was encouraged and supported by her husband and champion Giovanni. They had met some years before, fallen madly in love, married and lived a fabulous life in Rome. Then one day it all came tumbling down. Sherry takes up the story.

> He came back from work and crashed the car into our house wall. I ran out and opened the car door, but he couldn't walk or talk. So I rushed him to hospital and was shocked to learn that he had been addicted to hard drugs for many years. I had no idea. After a period in hospital I tried to get him the help he needed in Rome but couldn't. So I got him into a rehab clinic in London, where he went through an eight-week detox programme with support group therapy. We then moved back to Rome but sadly the cash and drugs were too easy to come by. I felt that being in Italy was not helping him. I decided that the best way to support my husband's condition was to move him back to London.

> To get my business off the ground I needed to raise £350,000 of angel investment money. I was a green novice going into this as I'd only worked in corporates and so had no clue how to raise money. It was endless meetings and scams and people trying to take advantage of me. I even remember being in a Brussels bank vault discussing finance with people who became increasingly threatening. I was lucky to get out of there alive. But I successfully raised £350,000 from

British angel investors. One who I knew personally who brought in a friend and another who I'd never met before.

Then tragedy struck.

> I took a call from Giovanni in Rome that turned out to be our last because he died unexpectedly the next day of a heart attack at the young age of forty-five. I had a bad feeling the night before he died and woke up feeling nauseous. It reminded me of the feeling I had when my grandfather died. I called my housekeeper and she said: 'I can't get into the house. I can hear the dog barking but the door's double bolted'. I said: 'The door's only double bolted at night. Call the police and ask them to knock down the door'. Giovanni had sadly died, which at the time was very tough. You just want to be hit by a bus and die. It's only later that you can start to accept and find peace with it.

But that was just the start of the next chapter in Sherry's life. She goes on to say:

> When I lost Giovanni, I no longer had money. Even though I had been with him for almost nine years, his financial situation was blocked and locked in Rome as he hadn't written a will. In Italy, if you don't have children, items such as private pensions get equally divided between all family members, which can take years to work through. So, I no longer had my rent or mortgage paid, or a husband to cry on every night when investors weren't good or customers didn't pay their bills. I was on my own. I went back to Rome, buried him, packed the car, put my two cats and my dog in my Fiat 500 and moved back to London. I got myself a rental flat in South Kensington next to the office and said to myself: 'OK, it's time for a reboot'.

> At this time, the only thing I had was credit cards, lots of them. I'd paid off my MBA credit card debt in twelve months by buying two properties on credit cards and flipping them. So, I had a good credit history. I started to live life on the edge, by borrowing on credit cards to get my business up and running – to rent offices, pay my staff or even refund a customer. I also raised some money but, even though

I had some sales coming in, it'd soon run out. To get real traction, I needed to educate the world to buy luxury furniture online. And that meant spending a lot on marketing which I couldn't afford. Being first is very expensive. Thankfully Made.com launched and other brands like Loaf followed. They taught the world that they could now buy furniture online, which got the market moving.

I ended up meeting a business angel, Safeer Bashir, at a charity event. He really got behind the business, helped me raise money and became my rock. He would also do small things like pay for the team to go out on a team outing or bridge me if I needed it. Over the past five years he's helped me raise over one million pounds of investment to fund trade worldwide, shipping to places like Norway, Iceland, France, Spain, Croatia, the U.S., Australia and many others. He also nominated me to speak at the United Nations in front of ninety-eight diplomats and two million people online about what it's like to be a woman in technology. Amazing! I told the women in the audience: 'It's not fair for women. It's harder. You have to go into engineering, science, mathematics or technology. If you don't, it won't get better for the next generation. You need to help make it a little bit better for them'.

She goes on to say:

I don't really know what failure is. I don't feel I've ever failed and I don't look at anything as failure. I look at it as experience, deepening your soul, making you smarter and wiser. Without a doubt, I've had a very difficult journey. We all have things thrown at us that are difficult. But I'm succeeding. I've run a trading business in one of the most expensive cities for five years. Deep inside, I know that I'm going to own a successful global business. And one day I'll do a lot of charitable work – as well as inspire men and women to carry on doing whatever it is they're doing and to never give up on their goals even if they've hit rock bottom. As long as you see signs that you are on the right path, don't give up on the slightest blip. Be brave, keep going, you're tougher than you think you are. If there are no signs, then get off the path and do something else. And recognise that if you want to succeed in building a business from nothing, then you need to have serious patience and resilience. You need to be prepared to give it your all.

Sherry's is a tough yet admirable story. She has faced repeated adversity in her entrepreneurial growth journey. And she has survived by altering her course professionally at short notice whilst grieving, as well as living hand to mouth to keep the business alive as it grew. The lesson here is to keep going when adversity strikes – and to always stay flexible enough to cope with any surprises that are thrown at you. None of us knows what's around the next corner.

IN SUMMARY

Failure, as well as success, is an inherent part of our natural world – and a huge learning opportunity for those who embrace it. Many successful people have failed many times before they have succeeded.

Take Thomas Edison who failed nearly 10,000 times to create a commercially viable electric light bulb. In his view, it was the accumulated knowledge developed from nearly 10,000 failed attempts that ultimately led to his success. As he famously said: 'I have not failed. I've just found 10,000 ways that won't work'.

J. K. Rowling's first Harry Potter book was sent to and rejected by 12 publishers before the eight-year-old daughter of the editor of Bloomsbury Publishing read it and convinced her Dad that it had potential. Even then J. K. Rowling was warned to 'get a day job as she would never make any money writing children's books'.[2]

Similarly, Michael Jordan said of his years as a professional basketball player:

> I've missed more than 9000 shots in my career. I've lost almost 300 games. 26 times, I've been trusted to take the game winning shot and missed. I've failed over and over and over again in my life. And that is why I succeed.[3]

Learning from failure is key to our growth. As Matthew Syed writes in his book *Black Box Thinking*:

> Failure is rich in learning opportunities – it is showing us that the world is in a sense some way different to the way that we imagined. These failures are inevitable because the world is complex and we will never fully understand its subtleties.[4]

Similarly, our entrepreneurs talked about failure as an inevitable part of their growth curve. It isn't necessarily bad or something to be scared of. Moreover, it is something to embrace and learn from, recognising that it will most probably lead to the next growth spurt.

They advised others to identify and accept the worst thing that could happen. And when failing, to not take the failure personally, but to instead pick themselves up, learn from their mistakes and not repeat them a second time. Similarly, they should stay flexible enough to cope with any surprises that life throws at them.

We hope that Chapter Seven helps to inspire people who are frightened of failing to give the entrepreneurial life a go. We now move on to the next two chapters, where we look at our entrepreneurs' views on

- Embracing the natural advantages that women have.
- Overcoming the natural disadvantages that women face.

NOTES

1 Dr Carol S. Dweck, *Mindset*, pages 6, 7 and 57, first published in the U.S. in 2006 by Random House Inc. New York and in Great Britain in 2012 by Robinson, London.
2 'Best Sellers Initially Rejected', article sourced at www.litrejections.com, October 2016; www.litrejections.com/best-sellers-initially-rejected/.
3 www.forbes.com; October 2016; www.forbes.com/quotes/11194/.
4 Matthew Syed, *Black Box Thinking*, page 33, first published in Great Britain in 2015 by John Murray (Publishers), London.

CHAPTER EIGHT

Embracing the natural advantages that women have

In our interviews, our female entrepreneurs told us that there are some natural advantages that they enjoy that can help them build a more successful business. Perhaps these help contribute to the statistic we saw in Chapter One which suggests that businesses run by women deliver a higher Return on Investment (ROI). For example:

- In the U.S., First Round Capital's review of their own holdings found that female-run businesses deliver a 63% better ROI than male-run ones.[1]
- A Barclays Bank report states: 'When they do secure investment, women's businesses show returns of 20% more revenue with 50% less money invested'.[2]
- An RBS Report states: 'When firm characteristics (size, sector, age, funding) are controlled for, women-owned firms outperform those by their male counterparts'.[3]
- Chief Executive of the Small Business Service in the U.S., Martin Wyn Griffith, said that: 'A pound invested in developing women's enterprise provides a greater return on investment than a pound invested in developing male owned enterprise'.[4]

In this chapter we look at some of the characteristics that our female entrepreneurs felt gave them a competitive advantage in the workplace, including:

1. Ability to multitask.
2. Leveraging the power of part-time, flexible workforces.
3. Taking people with them by keeping their ego in check.
4. Tapping into intuition and lateral thinking.
5. Knowing when to stop.

Of course, male entrepreneurs will exhibit these characteristics as well, but they were much cited by our cohort of female entrepreneurs.

ABILITY TO MULTITASK

Whether true or false, it has long been said that women can multitask in a way that men can only wish for. That hypothesis tested positive in our fifty-two interviews – with many of our female entrepreneurs running a start-up, raising a family and in some cases managing pro bono work as well. Ours is a qualitative validation that women can successfully manage multiple roles at any one time – although we are reasonably sure that many readers including men will also resonate with these traits. Let's see what some of our female entrepreneurs had to say.

Elizabeth Cowper started her business WoMo, an online support service for working mothers, whilst successfully holding down a full-time employee role and bringing up her young children. Hers was a rollercoaster ride, a story of extraordinary resilience and determination. Elizabeth takes up the story:

> Minty (Araminta), my second child, was born when I was twenty-nine. There's two years and four months between the two children, so they were quite a handful. When I was on maternity leave with her, I got a job as Head of HR at Fenn Wright Manson, the women's fashion brand. I loved the transition back into Fenn Wright Manson. It was a textbook case of successfully having a baby and going back to work. Providing my own children with a good experience meant that I could do a better job, be a good parent and hold my head high.
>
> Despite this good experience, life was about to throw me a curveball. When my children were four and almost two, I left my husband and moved out of our family house into a little flat. My whole life turned upside down. All of a sudden I was a single mother. I was earning a bit more by then so I was just about able to pay my way in life. But it was not a good situation. It was a catch twenty-two. I had these two little girls but I was not going to quit work. I had to work to pay my way and, because it was critical to my self-esteem, I was determined to have

a successful career as well as be a great mum. I couldn't do it alone though. Happily, my nanny was amazing. She stuck with us working between two houses (mine and my ex's) and we got through it.

It was a very tough two years. I had to pay the rent and make do on very little. But somehow I managed to keep working, be a good enough mother and stay afloat. I made work work for me when the kids were with my ex-husband, by working like a nutcase in the office early until late. Awful though it was, the experience of multi-tasking later became the catalyst for my business idea – a support website for working mothers trying to keep the plates spinning. I knew I had something to offer because I had been through it and survived.

During that period I truly experienced the best and the worst. And one thing is for sure – if you treat women with respect and give them flexibility and control over their lives, they will, as I did, work their socks off to make work and home work side by side. Conversely, if you don't, you will prevent them from performing either roles well and nobody will be happy. Soon enough, female talent will head for the door to other employers or their own set-up where they can shape the work culture.

Elizabeth, at the time of writing, is still successfully multitasking. She is the Vice President of HR Europe and Global Wellness Lead for a multi-brand fashion house in the U.S., although by now with a third child and the ongoing scale-up of her online support business for other working mothers, WoMo.

A second example is Gemma Greaves who is CEO of The Marketing Society, mother of her three-year-old son and founder of her own business, Cabal. She says:

In 2009, I was about to become Marketing Director at the Marketing Society. I went on our Marketing Leader training programme and met a brilliant chap called Dom Grounsell who was Marketing Director at Capital One.

Dom and I benefitted so much from meeting each other that we realised that if you bring like-minded people together with a similar mindset, shared values and ambition and a desire to make a difference, you can make great things happen. So, in 2013, I launched Cabal, a private members club of extraordinary people, because I genuinely believe if you bring good people together, magic happens. I knew I'd only ever get the freedom, creativity and autonomy to make real change if I set up my own business. So I told my boss at the Marketing Society, the Chief Executive, that at some point I would leave to start my own business. He said to me: 'I think you'd be an amazing entrepreneur but give me another year'. I said: 'OK, but on four days a week. I'm going to do my business one day a week'. So we did that for a year and, at the end of it, my boss said to me: 'So another year and I think you're ready for Managing Director because you're now running the global business'. I said: 'OK, this is working. I think I can have a big job as well as follow my passion'. That was six years ago. Things didn't quite work out to plan. I'm now Chief Executive of The Marketing Society, a big job with a lot of travel, as well as mother of a toddler and Founder of Cabal, my special side hustle.

That said, the one thing I won't compromise on is Cabal because I am never working for another company again and because I genuinely believe in what we're doing. It's a handpicked club of like-minded people who do good for each other, good together and good for others. And we have fun, enjoy unforgettable experiences together and learn from each other along the way.

Gemma goes on to say:

The thing I find most difficult in life is time. Time is the most precious resource you have and there's not enough of it to do all the things that you want to do. There is so much going on that you've got to prioritise the things that you really want and need to do. You have to be a little bit selfish. Life for me pivots around nursery pick-up and drop-off of Joshie, with the big things in life like global travel for the

Marketing Society and my own business Cabal squeezed in-between. My advice is to take some of the stress out of being a mother and running a business by planning the week ahead with the people who are affected and making decisions together. It's about compromise and talking and accepting you can't do everything. Also, if you can combine what you love with what you do day-to-day, it's easier and more rewarding.

These and many other similar stories illustrate how women are adept at fulfilling multiple roles in a way that (perhaps) few men can emulate. These stories need to be told so that other women fighting similar odds, or keen to have it all, know that they are not alone. They too can draw on their inner strength to make it through tough times and come out the other end smiling.

However, before ending this section, we have one word of caution. Women should be careful not to take on too much. As Terri Tierney Clark says in her article 'Women's Advantages in the Workplace':

> When I was a young investment banker, my boss would brag about me to clients. 'She has two children in diapers, goes to the gym before work and is carrying more deals than any of her peers'. Guilty as charged. I didn't say no, which is a common problem with women. In my case, I started to see my work product slide because I didn't have enough time to do the projects I took on. And it was my fault.
>
> Of course my boss was happy to give me work. I needed to be the one to say: 'enough'. It turns out my experience was somewhat typical, at least according to research reported in the *Wall Street Journal*. In a study involving undergraduates, females were 50% more likely to comply with an implicit request for a favour than male students. Females were reportedly more concerned with the consequences of saying no. So when you start your career, leverage those assets that you've had since birth. But don't let the female tendency to agree to help, bury you.[5]

LEVERAGING THE POWER OF PART-TIME, FLEXIBLE WORKFORCES

Part-time and flexible working is a hot topic for many of our female entrepreneurs, with many leaving corporate environments to create a working life that works both professionally and personally. It's interesting that many of our stories feature women either preferring to employ other women or just winding up doing so.

Victoria Mellor of Melcrum says:

> We had a woman-friendly culture, particularly as our workforce has always been over 60% women. For example, when I was hiring, I could say: 'If you've got children and you want to drop them off at daycare in the morning that's fine with us'. In the U.S. that was a huge offering which enabled us to pick up very good people. We were focussed on results rather than presenteeism because I had to be flexible too given I was a mother of two children. I would always employ working mothers because they're very good with their time. They've got the edge on time management and they get stuff done efficiently because they have to. We had a lot of people with young children who had a lot to contribute and that profile worked very well for us. We let people know that we trusted them to do their best work and evaluated them on the output of their work, based on a very clear plan and targets.

Rebekah Hall, founder of Botanic Lab, also tapped into the power of part-time working women. She says:

> A lot of the people who have worked in my business have worked part-time for me. They're women who have a really strong set of skills but also have children to look after. They've given me a lot in terms of time, energy and effort. So I look at it with a different set of eyes now. Children seem to be a big stumbling point that excludes a large part of the workforce from working. So it strikes me that it's good business sense to find a way to get the best people in your business. Hiring people who want to work flexibly actually works quite well for me because I don't have to pay a full-time salary. And I get access to

a group of people who are hugely skilled and also have children and other priorities as well.

As we saw in Chapter Two, Claire Randall Consulting employs almost exclusively women, with Claire enjoying phenomenal retention by virtue of her family-friendly policies. She says:

> We employ mostly women, not as a policy, but because the women like the flexibility we offer. A lot of them are working four days a week instead of five. They can do the job from home if they need to and the hours are more manageable than those in production. I've only had four people leave in twenty-three years so we must be doing something right!

She goes on to say:

> Working women with children struggle in conventional work environments. Virtually all my staff are working mothers, some divorced or the main breadwinner, and what they need is stability and security. This gives them full employment with benefits such as a pension, healthcare and several weeks of holiday to cover the school holidays. I think it's true that if they were in production they might earn a bit more but they would have a worse work–life balance. They would be working much longer hours and it would be freelance which is harder to manage. We give working mothers more of the flexibility they need.

Tash Walker of The Mix has gone one stage further. She says:

> About nine months ago, we decided to go to a four-day week. Our people are the most important thing to us. So getting a life balance for our employees, including me, is another way to show how we are disrupting ourselves and the market – and demonstrates how we are staying true to our business purpose which is being interested in human behaviour. We're quite female-dominated at the moment, with two females at the top, five guys and ten other females. It's not intentional. In a way I'd want more balance. But regardless of who we

employ, our values are clear in the sense that we're people-orientated. So going to a four-day week was imperative. We wanted our people to get some balance in their lives. To enjoy life and be happy, and to turn up and give us their all. I really believe in that. Additionally, bringing women into the business is important to me. I speak most months at events about flexible working and equality in the workplace – and the need to develop more empathy both as business owners and market-ers. We can all be more empathetic in the way that we treat the people around us.

Susie Watson, founder of Susie Watson Designs, has just three men in a workforce of 130. Susie feels strongly about providing flexible working conditions given so many of her employees are mothers. And given most of her team work in her shops, she's found that cooperation between colleagues is key. She says:

> In the shops, women want to work in teams. Women respond very well to other women – and are at their best when they get on well and are supportive, which women naturally are. I think in every shop now we have a good team. They like each other and if one of them has a problem, like their child is ill or their mother has just died, the others will step in and cover for them as much as they can. You have to accept that people have lives. As long as they're not trying to take from you unfairly, then you should trust them. And if you do trust and respect them, you get a lot more out of them.

Female entrepreneurs are getting a competitive advantage by leveraging a highly talented workforce who are keen to work but feel disenfranchised by the less flexible corporate world. As one of the co-authors overheard a senior man say at an industry event this week: 'Mothers with children are by far the best employees as they are so productive. They focus on what really needs to happen and get it done quickly, to be able to leave on time to look after their children'. Isn't it about time that corporations embraced more of these highly talented, highly productive people by making their working environments more flexible?

TAKING PEOPLE WITH YOU BY KEEPING YOUR EGO IN CHECK

Like Susie Watson of Susie Watson Designs, many of our interviewees talked about creating a working environment where people are encouraged to work 'collaboratively, collegially and courteously'. To achieve this, they commented on taking people with them by keeping their egos in check. As one interviewee said: 'A leader who tries to control everything and take all the decisions will soon be alone or left with the flotsam and jetsam who can't find alternative employment'. Victoria Mellor, Lindsay Levin, Sarah Turner and Melina Jacovou all had much to say on this.

Victoria Mellor, founder of Melcrum, commented:

> I don't have a huge ego and I think generally a lot of women entre-preneurs don't. They're comfortable sharing power with others. I was always conscious that I didn't want to be the figurehead of the business nor for the business to be synonymous with me. Even though my name is out there, the business had to be more than me.

> In my experience, it's critical to not be the most important or most vocal person in the room. Being comfortable with sharing power and nurturing relationships was a really important part of the way we developed. We had a reputation for attracting good people because of our culture. As a founder who had been in the business for twenty years, I let people know that I didn't have all of the answers, which I think was very empowering for people.

> I also spent time talking about the business with our employees. I had a quarterly one-on-one with every single employee in our business, like it or not, which I think is quite unusual. I would tell them what was on my mind, what I cared about and what I was worried about. I think creating open and honest communication and trust was a very important part of what we did. By not having a huge ego, I created a shared responsibility and the expectation that everyone should contribute new ideas. This enabled us to stay innovative in how we

operated and what we launched onto the market, and enabled the business to grow.

Lindsay Levin of Leaders' Quest said:

> If you do Leaders' Quest work, you're signed up to a real deep personal growth path because that's what we're doing with other people. I think we're really honest. None of us get away with bad behaviour. If something's not working we talk about it, it's very open. At the end of every programme we all give feedback to every-body. We sit in lots of circles round a campfire. If you join us at fifty-five years of age, you get used to a twenty-five year old giving you feedback. We've got a very transparent culture. It's a pretty extraordinary team. The culture's special – very strong, very loving, very empowering.

Angel Academe's Sarah Turner has wide exposure to female entrepreneurs as she has created one of the first angel investor groups that invests in females. She says:

> I've noticed our female investors have some distinct characteristics. Most people in our network of angel investors have earned their money as entrepreneurs or in the corporate world or both. So they're very smart and mostly very modest. Unlike some of the other angel networks I've tried, ego doesn't come into it. They want to support other people's businesses rather than promote themselves. They also collaborate and are quite happy to say: 'Oh, I've never done this before, I don't know how it works, so please talk me through it'. Whereas I suspect that men feel less comfortable saying that kind of thing. We also have great fun. We learn about new technology and how the world's changing from inspiring entrepreneurs who are 'unreasonable optimists', which in itself is inspirational, entertaining and stimulating.

But ego works both ways. As we saw in Chapter Six, Vicki Willden-Lebrecht knows this when motivating the people around her. She says:

> Most issues I ever have with anyone come down to: 'What about me? Am I important? Am I doing a good job?' Everyone wants to do a

good job. No one wants to do bad work. You need to give people the opportunity to achieve in your organisation and to praise them when they've done a good job. When your team are not delivering, look at how you're communicating with them. Have you given them clear roles and responsibilities? Do they know what's expected of them? Are their wins being acknowledged? We all want to feel loved and appreciated. To know that our work matters and that we matter. Most issues come down to that.

Similarly, as we also saw in Chapter Six, Melina Jacovou of Propel offers some wise words:

Never believe your own hype. Always learn and grow from those that work with you and for you. Never get too egotistic. Always do stuff. Never ask anyone to do anything you wouldn't do. And most importantly, enjoy the journey and be grateful for it. Because one thing that will definitely happen is that we will all die.

TAPPING INTO INTUITION AND LATERAL THINKING

There's much said about 'female intuition' in the wider world. For example, Sigma Clique's article 'Advantages Women Bring to the Workplace' says that:

Females are perceptive, intuitive and sensitive, so they often pick up on non-verbal cues, making them effective problem solvers … Research shows that most women understand body language and perceive signs of unhappiness, frustration, stress, insecurity and confusion much better than men. As a result, they offer the advantage of being able to address workplace concerns, problems and issues before they escalate.[6]

Similarly, a survey by the executive search firm RSA found that 'women bring empathy and intuition to leadership'. The findings include almost two-thirds of respondents agreeing that women contribute differently in the boardroom compared with their male colleagues. Three quarters rate women higher than men for intuition and possessing greater awareness of the motivations and concerns of other people. A similar proportion rate women as more empathetic, with better insight into how decisions play out in the wider organisation. And over half rate women as better on communications and effective collaboration.[7]

Lindsay Levin, founder of Leaders' Quest, agrees with this. She says:

> Very successful men tend to be extremely focussed. You think about what it's taken for Jeff Bezos to build his business or Zuckerberg or Elon Musk. They're interested in many things and they're innovating over time. But they have an extraordinary focus on whatever it is they're going after. They ruthlessly focus on their mission. Women, myself included, tend to be equally hardworking but look more to the left and right. We are more naturally lateral thinkers who integrate different things, which ends up being a bit more of a diffused focus. I think women tend to see and experience their whole life in a more integrated way.

Ellena Ophira of Weddingly talks about the importance of listening closely to her customers to create something distinctive and creative. She says:

> Our proposition is so different. When we launched, we had very little capital so we had to be really smart with our money. That forced us to be really inventive, finding creative ways to get people on board and to market our platform. We've really listened to our customers to ensure that we're developing something useful and different. We're not remotely on a vanity kick. We only want to make a product that people really want to use.

Tamara Gillan of Cherry London added:

> As a leader and woman you've got so many more tools in your toolkit than men have. I can be quite challenging with some of my clients, whereas if I was a man it could come across as aggressive

rather than constructive. We have to use our female gifts as rigorously as males use theirs. I have a client who's a FTSE 250 CEO. She's fierce but also warm, often wearing bright blues and pinks. She totally embraces her femininity in her leadership within a FTSE 250. She's amazing.

We encourage entrepreneurs to trust their instincts and follow their intuition – as well as bring empathy to everything they do. As many of our female entrepreneurs told us: 'your first instinct is usually right'.

KNOWING WHEN TO STOP

Finally, some of our female entrepreneurs talked about the need to switch off after work – both those with children who need to spend time with them at home and those without who are keen to create a healthy work–life balance – and the greater ability of women to do so, for some of out of necessity and others out of choice. Tamara Gillan and Rebekah Hall both talked about the huge influence of children on this.

Tamara Gillan of Cherry London tries to switch out of work mode before going home to her young son. She says:

> You have to look after your health and your energy through wellness and good food. Emotionally and physically. It's the only way I can cope with this kind of extreme pressure. I go to the gym before my son gets up and the day gets started. I also do a quick twenty-minute workout on the way home and it helps me go from my work world to having quality time with my son. It's like: 'Wow, that was quite liberating'.

Rebekah Hall, founder of Botanic Lab, doesn't have children but says:

> The entrepreneurs I know who've got children have said to me that it can be a really good thing. It's quite tough to turn off at the end of the day. And when you've got kids you have to turn off because

you have to focus your attention on them. So in some ways it's quite valuable.

Susie Watson of Susie Watson Designs is very supportive of women coming back into work after having children. She says:

> Employers need to better understand the difficulty of combining work commitments with looking after children. Mothers can make a huge contribution if companies are sympathetic to their childcare responsibilities. A more open discourse would be helpful. If one of my staff is about to have a baby, I say: 'We need to think about what will work for you when you come back'. I don't want to put them under huge pressure to come back to work, too much or too quickly. They've got to think about what will work for them and the child. There are almost always solutions that will work for everyone. I think this business of nobody's allowed to talk about this kind of thing is wrong. We're all trying to pretend that something that is clearly going to have a huge impact on their lives doesn't matter. It's much better that we all talk about it and work together to find what's best. We need a national debate on this issue.

The authors thoroughly agree.

But it's not just about children. Sophie Le Ray of Naseba caps her working week by deliberately spending time helping others. She says:

> I try to focus at least 20% of my week on serving others. Whether it is mentoring, doing community service or whatever it is. Something else that isn't related to my business or my family – just so I have a counterbalance to my life.

So being able to juggle multiple roles may be a blessing in disguise. Being the primary family carer requires female entrepreneurs to switch off from work at the end of each day to focus on their family – thus creating more balance in life. That said, society needs to do more to encourage everyone, including men, to have a good work–life balance, as well as to help women juggle multiple roles when working in less flexible corporate working environments.

In this chapter we looked at some of the natural advantages that our female entrepreneurs feel they have in the workplace. In the next chapter we will look at some of the disadvantages that our female entrepreneurs feel they've faced and how they've overcome them.

But, before then, we end with the importance of retaining your femininity, rather than trying to build more masculine qualities that aren't true to who you are. As Tamara Gillan of Cherry London said:

> I want to embrace the bits about me that are feminine. I went to see a talk by Lynne Franks and she said: 'I like what you're wearing, it's very feminine. Do more feminine, embrace your feminine powers'. And it was one of those moments where I was like: 'Yes!'.

NOTES

1 http://10years.firstround.com.
2 'Untapped Unicorns', Female Founders Forum, Barclays, 2017.
3 'Women In Enterprise: A Different Perspective', RBS Group, 2012.
4 Martin Wyn Griffith speaking at the National Dialogue for Entrepreneurship, Washington DC, March 2005, www.prowess.org.uk/facts.
5 'Women's Advantages in the Workplace' by Terri Tierney Clark; www.ttierneyclark.com/womens-advantages-in-the-workplace.
6 'Advantages Women Bring to the Workplace' by Sigma Clique, http://sigmaclique.com/advantages-women-bring-to-the-workplace.
7 'Women and the Workplace. The Benefits of Gender Diversity Put To The Test' by Dina Medland, *Financial Times*, 17 October 2012; www.ft.com/content/1fc8a3dc-0d65-11e2-97a1-00144feabdc0.

CHAPTER NINE

Overcoming the natural challenges that women face

As we saw in Chapter One, U.K. female entrepreneurship is still struggling to match the level of its male counterparts. Women at almost every stage are less likely to become entrepreneurs, with much lower levels of females starting and scaling up a business. Research and data suggest that the primary reasons for the lower levels of female entrepreneurship are three-fold:

- *The continued struggle that women have to get funding versus their male counterparts.*
- *The ongoing role of women as the primary care giver for children and ageing parents, making it difficult to focus on building a new business as well.*
- *A perceived lack of confidence and fear of failure among females versus their male counterparts.*

Our female interviewees had much to say on this subject. So, in this chapter, we look at the barriers and challenges that they believe female entrepreneurs face versus their male counterparts based on their real-life experience, including:

1. *It's a male-dominated world.*
2. *Lack of funding.*
3. *Less brazen salesmanship and less time for networking.*
4. *Lack of confidence and lower risk mindset.*
5. *Greater reticence to be famous or celebrate success.*

IT'S A MALE-DOMINATED WORLD

Many of our female entrepreneurs commented on business still being a male-dominated world. One that has been subconsciously designed by men for men and that has been slow to embrace more feminine characteristics, and thus is tougher for women to navigate. Maria Kempinska, Di Burton and Victoria Mellor all commented on the differences in how men and women do business and the dominance of male values in the work culture.

Maria Kempinska, founder of Jongleurs comedy clubs, says:

> I think it's still incredibly difficult. It's a patriarchal system, not a
> feminine one. A philosophical creation. When women are in the
> boardroom, many think: 'what can I do to make the business better?'.
> In contrast, others, very often men, think: 'What's in it for me? If I
> ditch this job or get to that level, I can get a job in another company'.
> Men are always on the move looking for the next step up. Do men fit
> into that world? Yes, because it's their paradigm. It's a very big, old,
> rusty system but it works. To recreate and transform a system we
> have to prove that a new one has value. So how do women accom-
> modate not wanting to be in that system with needing to be effective
> within it? I think they need to work out and focus on the value they
> can bring. So say my value is making sure the shows are great. Then
> I need to find out what it is that makes people come back over and
> over again, and deliver that. In my view, make your product unique,
> make sure people know you exist and make sure they know you're
> valuable.

Di Burton of Cicada Communications concurs:

> When I started out it was a very male-dominated world. I remember
> going into a board meeting and saying to my partner afterwards:
> 'They'd made all the decisions beforehand'. And he said: 'Don't you
> realise that's how men work? Everything is done before you get in
> the boardroom'. I found out that men operate in a very different way
> to women and that was a salutary lesson to me. Nothing is nailed
> down in the boardroom, everything is discussed beforehand before
> you go in.

Victoria Mellor of Melcrum Publishing also talked about the prevalence
of male values and ways of working in the workplace. She says:

> I've had a number of conversations recently about female entre-
> preneurs feeling uncomfortable in corporate finance environments
> because their values and way of working are very different. There's a
> real opportunity for more women-led initiatives to support businesses
> in raising money. A lot of women are now taking matters into their

own hands with less tolerance of inappropriate behaviour towards female entrepreneurs, whether it comes to fundraising or just ignoring them. But it's still an old boys' network.

Rebekah Hall, founder of Botanic Lab, talks about how women are still not taken seriously in the corporate world. She says:

> Taking women seriously is a problem. I think I've done something interesting. I've built a successful business. I thought that that would be the first thing that people would ask me about. But no, they ask: 'How old are you? Are you married? Are you going to have children?'. Those are more often the first questions that I get asked in a business and a social context. But those certainly wouldn't be the questions that would be asked of a man.

As Tori Gerbig, a millennial mum and a successful entrepreneur, says:

> As the mother of two young children, I'm not afraid to say that I love work. But these words don't exactly roll off the tongue. Sure, work may be necessary. It may be a chore and a duty. But, if it takes you from the responsibilities and joys of home and family, how could a woman possibly love it …? In ways direct and indirect, I encounter this attitude on a regular basis. The often-implied subtext is that mothers who are ambitious and passionate about their full-time careers are somehow less invested in their family's well-being.

> This sentiment is a seemingly unshakable vestige of decades past. We see glimpses of this thinking in the questions we ask of successful, business-minded women who also happen to be mothers. One of the most common is 'How do you manage it all?'. This question is meant to determine how in the world these powerful women are managing to juggle their work, marriage, home and family responsibilities simultaneously. The trouble is, we rarely ask our male leaders and fathers the same question. How different would this conversation be if we stopped quietly judging our ambitious young women and successful female business leaders, but instead started asking them what

they love about work? What gets you excited about work each day? Which of your professional accomplishments most shifted the trajectory of your career? Why do you do what you do? Perhaps before we can reach the point where we embrace our ambitious working mothers, we need to better understand their points of view.[1]

Sadly, our interviewees confirmed that for them the workplace is still primarily run by men for men. Women are at a disadvantage as they have to learn and play by male values and rules – with industry being slow and reluctant to change. As we'll see later in Chapter Eleven, there's a long way to go in making the workplace work for all genders. But many of our female entrepreneurs are paving the way in creating more gender-neutral cultures that attract and engage both male and female top talent.

LACK OF FUNDING

As Victoria Mellor alluded to above, female entrepreneurs can feel very uncomfortable when seeking funding in male-dominated corporate finance environments. The data in Chapter One confirmed that the gender bias is still very prevalent in the entrepreneurial world. Just 1% of VC capital goes to businesses founded by all-female teams, 9% to businesses with at least one female founder and 91% to businesses founded by all-male teams. [2]

Many of our female entrepreneurs have experienced this in person when trying to raise investment capital – including Rebekah Hall, founder of Botanic Lab. She started out in corporate finance and so had a natural advantage when seeking funding for her business. Yet, even she with her corporate finance background found that women have a tougher time. She says:

> There are barriers in the way for women when raising money. I was part of a piece that the *Telegraph* did recently about access to capital

for women entrepreneurs. I think women bring something different to entrepreneurship than men do. Not 'different better' or 'different worse' but different.

There are a lot of skilled and talented female entrepreneurs out there who never have the same access to money that men do. That's not good for the economy or for our country wanting to build small businesses. I've come from a background of raising money, so I had access to that world. But most women don't because they haven't been in those careers. Banking, money raising and private equity still tend to be very male and inherently sexist in the way that they work with women.

Rebekah goes on to talk about the importance of female owners not being put off by the corporate finance world. In her view, they need to run the funding and commercial side of the business, rather than delegate this to others, often men. She says:

The money bit is often the area that women are afraid of, just because of lack of experience and exposure to it. The default tends to be: 'I'll bring in a partner, usually a man, and they can run the money side of the business'. But the reality of any business is that unless you run the funding and money side of your business you don't run your business. I get really frustrated when I see women founders who say that someone else deals with that. What they don't realise is that actually that's the person who's making decisions about what's happening in the business and there's no reason why women shouldn't be doing that piece.

Sophie Le Ray, Martha Lane Fox, Sarah Turner and Bridget Connell all talk about the statistics that show how much more difficult it is for female entrepreneurs to get funded and why this is so – as well as their own personal experience of the issue.

Sophie Le Ray, founder of Naseba, kicks us off.

Access to finances and funding is much, much, much more limited for women entrepreneurs than it is for men. It's going to change.

You already see more and more women funds in the venture capital ecosystem. But they're still a rarity compared to funding for men. That's why there are so many venture capital firms being launched by women. Last year, a woman launched a very successful tech company in the U.S. and she literally pitched to every single venture capital firm in Silicon Valley. That's something like fifty or sixty pitches. She finally got funded by a VC firm where there was one female partner. It was the only time there was a female partner at the table. Initially, I didn't believe the gender bias, I thought it was an exaggeration. But it's not, it's actually happening.

Martha Lane Fox concurs:

When you look at the numbers, especially in the technology sector, I think it's only 7% or even less of venture capital funding that goes to female founders. If they're not getting the funding, it's no wonder that there aren't very many female entrepreneurs. This is caused by a whole load of factors. In part, it's due to men making investments in products that they feel are for them. It's the classic case of: 'If I'm going to risk my money then will I risk it on a product that I don't understand or will use, or on a product that I do understand and will use?'. The fact that investors are primarily men is kind of a self-fulfilling prophecy. Not that they're bad people, but because it might be more scary to think about investing in something that is outside of their comfort zone.

Sarah Turner, founder of Angel Academe which invests in companies with at least one female founder, has experienced the same thing.

When it comes to raising angel investment or venture capital, women typically receive a tiny proportion of what's given out, and that number has stayed stubbornly low over time. Yet, there's another body of evidence that shows that when women do get the backing, they perform quite well. It's not necessarily a logical decision on behalf of the investors. The percentage of U.K. angel investors that are women is only about 8% or 9%, so it's very low. And women who do invest, invest less money and less often. So the percentage of capital coming from women is probably even less than that. You have this very strange situation where U.K. women own 48% of the net wealth, but only invest a tiny percentage of the money going into start-ups. There are certainly more women investing now but probably still in the same proportion as the men as the market has grown.

Interestingly, a study conducted by researchers from Harvard, MIT and the Wharton School confirms the bias towards male over female entrepreneurs. Even if the businesses are identical, investors are more likely to invest in men. The study had three parts:

- The first part looked at entrepreneurial pitches in the U.S. over three years and found that male entrepreneurs were 60% more likely to win a pitch than female entrepreneurs.
- In the second part, the researchers showed images of the ventures being pitched, but not the entrepreneur themselves. Instead, investors heard the person's voice over the slides they were viewing. This allowed the researchers to swap out a male voice and a female voice on the same exact presentation. When investors were asked to choose a project, 68% of them chose to fund ventures voiced by men. Only 31% chose those voiced by women.
- A third part found that the pro-male bias is even stronger if the male entrepreneur is attractive, with more attractive males being 36% more likely to receive funding than less attractive ones. However, high physical attractiveness did not significantly influence female entrepreneurs' likelihood of success.

It's clear, from this work, that men have a quantifiable advantage over women when pitching their businesses, which puts female entrepreneurs at a significant disadvantage.[3]

Another study conducted by Dana Kanze, a doctoral fellow at Columbia Business School, showed that male and female entrepreneurs are treated differently when pitching. When she and her male co-founder tried to raise money for their mobile tech company at TechCrunch Disrupt, they were asked different questions from potential investors – even though they had similar titles, went to the same school and both had ten years of experience in finance. Kanze was mainly asked questions about what could possibly go wrong, which she calls 'prevention' questions. Her male co-founder was mainly asked questions about how fabulous everything could be, which she calls 'promotion' questions. Kanze and her team dissected the videos of 189 company presentations at TechCrunch Disrupt from 2010 to 2016. They found that 67% of the questions posed to male entrepreneurs were so-called promotion questions, on subjects such as the total addressable market. By contrast, some 66% of the questions asked of female entrepreneurs were prevention-focussed, for example on how to defend market share. The entrepreneurs, not surprisingly, reacted in kind. Ask a man how big his market is and he'll tell you. Ask a woman how she'll defend her market share and she'll answer. The net result is that the women look defensive, while the men look visionary.

Kanze's research found that for every additional prevention question an entrepreneur is asked, he or she raised $3.8 million less in aggregate funding. She outlines two ways to fix this. The first is to get investors to ask similar questions to both men and women. The second is to get entrepreneurs to reframe prevention-focussed questions so that they can deliver a promotion-focussed answer. So, for example, when entrepreneurs are asked how they are going to defend their market share, they might point out that they're in a large and growing market which they expect to win an increasing share of by leveraging their unique assets.[4]

For the co-authors, the lack of female funding is one of the big issues that still needs to be tackled. The growth of female VC investors who are more likely to understand and invest in ideas created by females is a huge step forward. But clearly there is still much to do.

LESS BRAZEN SALESMANSHIP AND LESS TIME FOR NETWORKING

Many of our interviewees talked about the natural disadvantage women face when selling, pitching and networking. Women often lack the commercial training needed to pitch successfully, or the time in the evenings to network, or even the network itself when they've taken time out of the commercial world to bring up a family. Rebekah Hall, Bridget Connell, Melanie Lawson and Di Burton all had much to say about this.

As we saw in the last section, Rebekah Hall of Botanic Lab started out in corporate finance and so learned how to raise money and pitch. In contrast, most women lack sales training which puts them at a disadvantage when they're trying to raise money. She says:

> Knowing how to pitch, knowing what someone's looking for, is so important. I know how to do those things because I've sat in a lot of pitches and have been exposed to what works. But as a woman I'm in the minority, as private equity and banking is heavily skewed male. It could be educated out. There are organisations like AllBright with female-focussed funds that not only give money to women entrepreneurs but also provide access to experts in areas where women don't feel they traditionally excel, such as how to access capital or pitch. But there is still a long way to go.

Bridget Connell, Melanie Lawson and Di Burton go on to talk about the difficulties that women face when networking and how that puts female entrepreneurs at a disadvantage. For example, in Chapter Five, Bridget Connell of Thinking Partnerships talked about how women are not so good at building and maintaining their corporate network whilst working. She said:

> I don't think women are particularly good at building and looking after their network. If you've worked in corporate life for a long time, your external network can be very small. People don't think about the need to invest in it. I noticed that when a number of people I knew were made redundant after twenty or thirty years in a company, they would want to meet for a coffee with me and sometimes seemed a bit like a rabbit in headlights. What do I do now, where do I go? And I'd ask: 'Where is your network?'.

Melanie Lawson, founder of Bare Biology, took seven years out to be a full-time mother when her children were very young. She talks from experience about what it's like to drop out of the workforce and the difficulties of trying to get back in some years later. She says:

> Women tend not to have the networks that men have because they've been off work with children and have lost those contacts. I am a member of the All Party Parliamentary Group for Women in Enterprise. The group looks at ways to shape Government policy to encourage more women to become entrepreneurs, including helping them get the support they need both emotionally and practically.

Di Burton of Cicada Communications talks about how hard it is for women to network in the evening, given they are often the primary care giver as well. She recalls:

> I'm always looking forward. Where's the next deal? What's coming up? I've also worked so hard, I can't tell you how hard. I'd work a full day and then I'd go out networking night after night. It's harder for women. Men have wives. Women also take the brunt of the housework. And no matter how supportive the partner might be, we really do the bulk of it. Within the first year of me being here, my partner had gone off to work and I had to wait for the chimney sweep to arrive and I said 'Will you hurry up? I've got to get to work'. This old Yorkshire boy looked at me and said 'You modern women make me laugh, now you've got two jobs instead of one'. And he was so right!

Women's lack of training in selling and pitching in the financial world puts female entrepreneurs at a disadvantage. And whilst men continue to delegate the lion's share of the housework and family care to their female partner, out-of-hours networking will remain tricky for women. Supportive partners as well as support groups such as the one that Melanie Lawson is working in will undoubtedly be helpful, but, like the funding issue, there is still a long way to go.

LACK OF CONFIDENCE AND LOWER RISK MINDSET

W omen's lack of confidence is a controversial subject. As we saw in Chapter Four, some of our female entrepreneurs felt that they lacked the confidence and risk-taking mindset that their male counterparts seem to more naturally have. Some claimed to have few or no confidence issues and positively vibrated with confidence, and thus struggled to speak about the subject. And others thought that the idea of females lacking confidence is a myth that perpetuates male investors' reluctance to invest in them – and so wanted to discourage the idea from being aired.

Even so, as we saw in Chapter Four, some of our female entrepreneurs felt that they lacked the confidence of their male peers, such as Maya Magal, founder of Maya Magal Jewellery. She says:

> My husband works in private equity. He invests in large businesses with the majority of them run by men. I think men naturally have more confidence. I struggle with confidence. For example, when opening a store I'm like: 'How are we going to make this work?'. Whereas my husband is more like: 'Of course it will work, you've got a good product, you've got customers, it's just going to take time'. Women also have the family aspect which doesn't fall as much on the man. I've got a sixteen-month old and I'm hoping to have more children. Maybe that makes it harder for women to be confident about going to work. It's not just the practicality of it all, or the money or the time. It's the emotional side of it too. You've got this business you've built up and you're employing people and you're trying to make the best of it. But you're torn because you want to spend time at home with your child. And she doesn't want you to go to work. She cries when you leave in the morning! My child is a girl so it's nice for her to see that women work and that it's not always women who stay at home. That's how I manage my guilt.

Melanie Lawson of Bare Biology also talked about how she has suffered from and overcome confidence issues. She recalls:

> There's that statistic that if men look at a job description and can do 20% of the role they'll apply for it, and if women look at the job description and can't do 20% of it they won't apply. Women think they've got to be good at all those things before they take the leap.

She goes on to say:

> Although I do have a crisis of confidence, I think paradoxically: 'Oh, I could do that'. I've got the male blagging gene from my dad. I know what my strengths and weaknesses are, and I know how to play to my strengths and outsource or avoid the bits that I'm weak at. I think if you focus your energies on the things that really matter, and play to your strengths, you can be really successful.

Victoria Mellor of Melcrum gives some very sage advice to those who suffer from a lack of confidence or the Imposter Syndrome. She says:

> The Imposter Syndrome often comes from thinking you need to know all of the answers. A lot of women feel that they have to be fully qualified to do a job and that's not necessarily the case. You don't have to be the smartest person in the room or know all of the answers. You just need to be able to ask very good questions of the people around you. It's about getting the right support in areas that aren't your strengths. So, for example, I had a great Finance Director who was an incredibly supportive person for me. I knew the right questions to ask him and he knew how to counsel me. But I would never think 'I need to learn how to analyse our balance sheet' because I knew that he could do that. Why go through that pain? Instead focus on what you're good at and deliver the value you bring to your business.

As we heard in Chapter Four, Sarah Turner of Angel Academe (the leading female investor in female entrepreneurs) also gives some sage words of advice to those lacking confidence. She thinks that the 'female confidence issue' is used much too often as an excuse (by men) for not investing in female-owned businesses. She says:

> I am constantly told (by men) that women don't invest as they're too risk averse, do due diligence to death and lack confidence. All of which I think is nonsense. We might do more due diligence, but that's because we're more thorough which makes us better investors. As time goes by and this is vindicated, male investors will follow their wallets rather than their prejudices.

> A lack of confidence or ambition is often the reason given by men to explain why women don't raise as much money. Time after time, I go to these investor events where there are relatively young women entrepreneurs pitching to a room of older, more experienced men. Confidence comes with practice, experience and knowing your stuff. Entrepreneurs need to be well-prepared and have a well-honed 'elevator pitch'. Confidence is also contextual. People feel more confident when they're comfortable, which is more likely when some people in the room look like them. For many of us, being confronted by a sea of male faces doesn't inspire confidence. Few men have ever experienced being the only man in the room, and perhaps more should.

> There's a huge amount of research that shows that women founders are treated quite differently from male founders by investors, particularly in the technology sector – they just don't conform to the norm of the young hoodied male geek. When it comes to raising either angel investment or venture capital money, women typically receive a tiny proportion of what's given out, and that number has stayed stubbornly low over time. Ironically, there's another body of evidence that says that women when they get backing perform quite well, sometimes ahead of male counterparts. So, it's an illogical decision by male investors to discriminate in this way.

The big takeaways for the co-authors on the issue of confidence are twofold. First, many of our female entrepreneurs overcame confidence issues by not trying to be brilliant at everything, but instead focussing on what they were really good at that delivered value for their business. They then surrounded themselves with great people who could fill their capability gaps and challenged them with pertinent questions to ensure the team stayed on track. Second, Sarah Turner's observation that women display confidence differently to men is very insightful. In our view, women shouldn't be seduced into being as masculine as the men, but should develop their own sense of self-worth and a more feminine leadership style that is true to who they are. As Tamara Gillan of Cherry London said in Chapter Eight:

> I want to embrace the bits about me that are feminine. I went to see a talk by Lynne Franks and she said: 'I like what you're wearing, it's very feminine. Do more feminine, embrace your feminine powers'. And it was one of those moments where I was like: 'Yes!'.

GREATER RETICENCE TO BE FAMOUS OR CELEBRATE SUCCESS

Many of our interviewees talked about the female tendency not to talk about or celebrate their success – in contrast to their male counterparts. They are concerned that they might not be an attractive female leader if they behave in a celebratory way and, in turn, come over to others as self-satisfied or boastful.

Tamara Gillan of Cherry London talks about the female tendency to shy away from celebrating their achievements, as it's just not feminine to brag or boast in this way. She says:

> Outside of work I don't talk about what I do. I would never say I run a company of fifty people because I'd rather die than own that success. It's something that women seem to struggle with. When you go around the room and have to say what you've done, I make myself so small as will other women. I say to my female team speak

up about yourself, be proud of what you've achieved, but that applies to me too.

I think we feel like we're boasting or bragging, which can make you seem self-satisfied. And it's more of an English thing. We've got a woman from New York who works with us who I try to emulate when introducing myself. I've done this and this and this. Women struggle with it because we don't want to say: 'Look at me, I'm great. Do you think so too?'. I always remember why Hillary Clinton was so disliked. That's probably why in my personal life I don't talk about my professional life because of fear of not being attractive as a female leader.

There has been a lot of research done on how society views female leadership differently to male leadership. For example, Caroline Criado Perez outlines in her book *Invisible Women* why Tamara is right to be concerned about how she's perceived as a female leader. She quotes an analysis of 248 performance reviews collected from a variety of U.S.-based tech companies. They found that women receive negative personality criticism that men simply don't. She says:

> Women are told to watch their tone, to step back. They are called bossy, abrasive, strident, aggressive, emotional and irrational. Out of all these words, only aggressive appeared in men's reviews at all – 'twice with an exhortation to be more of it'. More damningly, several studies of performance-related bonuses or salary increases have found that white men are rewarded at a higher rate than equally performing women and ethnic minorities, with one study of a financial corporation uncovering a 25% difference in performance-related bonuses between women and men in the same job.[5]

Victoria Mellor and Lindsay Levin go on to talk about how difficult it is for women to celebrate what they've achieved, due to being overly tough on themselves or perfectionist in nature.

As you may recall from Chapter Four, Victoria Mellor's business Melcrum went through a number of external crises that resulted in the company needing to reinvent itself multiple times, which in turn made it more successful. She recalls:

> The big external crises kept us paranoid and ensured that we never rested on our laurels. I think a lot of female entrepreneurs are very bad at self-congratulatory behaviour. They never feel really satisfied. They don't say 'I've made it' but worry about the next thing they need to do. We need to take time to recognise our success and be kinder to ourselves.

Similarly, Lindsay Levin, founder of Leaders' Quest, talks about the female tendency to push yourself harder and wanting to be perfect at everything you do. She says:

> I'm a perfectionist. Sometimes I worry about letting people down or not meeting people's expectations. I'm very motivated to do a great job. In the early days we had a slogan of 'how much is enough' which was kind of my big question and which of course is impossible to answer! That was a growing-up stage which I'm now at peace with. I've changed a lot as has everybody in our team. Today, I encourage people to focus on being their best rather than being enough.

In contrast, Melina Jacovou created a culture in her company Propel that goes out of its way to celebrate success with her team every week. She says:

> We spend a lot of time celebrating client and candidate wins. Every Friday we have a sales meeting and we ask everyone what they're proud of that week, as well as who they're proud of in the organisation and why. We celebrate a lot of stuff with loads of incentives. We make sure that people are recognised for what they do. And it's not all financial, it's also what they do to add value to our culture.

Reshma Saujani's book *Brave Not Perfect* talks about how women are brought up differently to men by being encouraged to be 'perfect rather than brave'. She exhorts women to fear less, fail more and live bolder. Reshma claims that

Girls are taught at a young age to play it safe. To strive to get all As to please our parents and teachers. To be careful not to climb too high on the jungle gym so that we don't fall and get hurt. To sit obediently, to look pretty, to be agreeable so we will be liked. Well-meaning parents and teachers guide us toward activities that we excel at so we can shine, and they steer us away from the ones we aren't naturally good at to spare our feelings and grade point averages. No one realizes how much it insulates us from taking risks and going after our dreams later in life.

She goes on to say:

Conversely, boys absorb a very different message. They are taught to explore, play rough, swing high, climb to the top of the monkey bars – and fall down trying. They are encouraged to try new things, tinker with gadgets and tools, and get right back in the game if they take a hit. From a young age, boys are groomed to be adventurous … By the time boys are teenagers asking someone on a date, or young adults negotiating their first raise, they are already well habituated to take risk after risk and are, for the most part, unfazed by failure. Unlike girls, they are rewarded with approval and praise for taking chances, even if things don't work out. In other words, boys are taught to be brave, while women are taught to be perfect. [6]

In summary, in this still male-dominated professional world, female entrepreneurs continue to have a number of barriers and challenges that they need to overcome. Most notable is the male funding bias. But alongside that is the lack of experience in pitching and selling, the less time out-of-hours available to network, the differing approach to confidence and the greater reticence to celebrate success. Much needs to be done by men and women, as well as by society as a whole, to create a level playing field for female entrepreneurs – including greater access to corporate finance training, supportive home partners who are happy to take a more equal share of the family care and female self-awareness when facing confidence issues or reticence to celebrate success.

So in this chapter we have looked at the issues that female entrepreneurs face. In the next two chapters we will turn our attention to two very important topics – how to make work work around life and how to make work work for women.

NOTES

1 'I'm a Millennial Mom and a Successful Entrepreneur. Stop Asking Me How I Manage It All' by Tori Gerbig, July 2018, www.entrepreneur.com/article/315698.

2 *The Alison Rose Review of Female Entrepreneurship*, 2019.

3 'Women Pitching the Same Exact Ideas As Men Still Get Less Funding From Venture Capitalists' by Rose Eveleth, 11 March 2014, www.smithsonianmag.com/smart-news/venture-capitalists-are-less-likely-invest-identical-companies-if-theyre-pitched-women-180950048/.

4 'Investors Don't Ask Women Founders the Same Questions as Men. Here's Why That's a Problem' by Kimberly Weisul, 8 May 2018, www.inc.com/kimberly-weisul/how-women-can-do-better-at-pitch-competitions-question-answer.html.

5 *Invisible Women* by Caroline Criado Perez (page 93).

6 *Brave Not Perfect* by Reshma Saujani, Penguin Random House LLC, page 2.

CHAPTER TEN

Making work work around life

The personal agenda

There's much in the press about how difficult it is for women to make work work around day-to-day life. Women still tend to take the lion's share of the domestic housework and be the primary carers of children and ageing parents.

A recent study conducted by University College London among 8,500 heterosexual couples living in the U.K. showed that women still shoulder the bulk of housework, even when both people work full-time. On average, full-time working women spent between ten to nineteen hours on housework weekly, whereas their partners averaged fewer than five hours per week. And fewer than seven per cent of U.K. couples share housework equally. [1]

Professor Gillian Robinson at the University of Ulster conducted a similar survey and concluded: 'It is difficult to see how women will ever have the same opportunities in the labour market if equality at home is not achieved'. [2]

Similarly, our female entrepreneurs had much to say on this subject. So, in this chapter, we look at how our female entrepreneurs make their work work around their lives, including the importance of:

1. *Really wanting it and being prepared to make sacrifices.*
2. *Having a supportive partner.*
3. *Getting the family involved and managing guilt.*
4. *Creating balance.*

REALLY WANTING IT AND BEING PREPARED TO MAKE SACRIFICES

Many of our interviewees talked about how being an entrepreneur is all-consuming. Thus, if you want to be one, you need to really want to be one and be prepared to make sacrifices.

For some, the sacrifice is less time spent with family and friends. For example, Rebekah Hall of Botanic Lab says:

> Do you want me to tell you it's going to be a bed of roses? No, it's not. At times, it's horrible, it's hard, it's difficult. Your family life suffers and your friend relationships become difficult because you can't spend as much time with them. If you have a partner they can feel neglected. There are times when it will be the pits. You can do it, but ultimately you have to decide you really want it. And I did. I don't think I really appreciated how true that statement is, but it is. Ultimately I really, really, really wanted it and I had the drive. Unless you really want it, I don't think you'll succeed, because there are times when you've got to carry on regardless.

For others such as Ellena Ophira, Vicki Willden-Lebrecht and Tash Walker, the sacrifice is more financial, particularly when starting out.

Tash Walker spoke wistfully of her first year of sacrifice starting her now successful agency, The Mix.

> The first year was rejection and the pub, The Woolpack on Bermondsey Street. There's a table in the window on the ground floor and I sat there for a good proportion of that year. I got bits and pieces of work from mates at other agencies and people making recommendations, but not enough to take a salary. I don't remember that first year being really crushing, but in retrospect I think I'd now find it really hard. At the time it was like a game. I've decided to do this thing, and so I need to work harder to make it work. In a way the stakes were low. I had no kids and no mortgage, so there was nothing to lose. So, no, it wasn't going brilliantly, but I was having fun meeting people. At the time I thought: 'Just roll with the punches and next year I'll have learnt some stuff and it will be better'.

Vicki Willden-Lebrecht now sits astride a highly successful literary agency, Bright, which operates across the world bringing artists together with publishers. But the early days were characterised by sacrifice. She told us:

> I launched the business in Frankfurt, initially staying in a youth hostel in a room with eight people. Then, in the early days when I couldn't afford an office and a flat, I valued having an office far more than a house. So I put a mattress in the office and slept on the floor. I felt quite excited at the adventure of it all. Life was fun. It was never a hardship but there was sacrifice.

She continues: 'I go to Frankfurt now and stay in smart hotels. How times have changed! I always appreciate that and never forget the journey that it took to get here'.

Ellena Ophira, founder of Weddingly, also found it financially tough when starting out, but turned the sacrifice into an advantage. She remembers:

> We soft launched the MVP in September 2017. I was getting people on-board, testing it, churning out content and seeing what people responded to. During this period, my partner and I decided to move back to my family home to minimise our outgoings. I wanted to make the best choices for the business, rather than let my own personal financial pressures impact my decision making. But this actually turned out to be a great period in the business development. I had my mother, brother and sister as amazing sounding boards – and some of the elements that we hashed out then have made Weddingly what it is today.

For Michaela Jedinak, founder of her clothing line Michaela Jedinak, the sacrifice was both financial and personal. She recalls:

> Being an entrepreneur is like training to be an Olympic champion – you're in it for the long run. You have to work hard and train hard, and you have to do different things in order to succeed. You have to find funding and support, deal with injuries and make sacrifices. You can't go to all of your friends' parties and holidays and do all

of the fun stuff. And not everyone who trains to become an Olympic champion actually becomes an Olympic champion. There's only one winner.

Nobody remembers second place. It's like training to be a champion because you need to be fully committed at any age. It's not as if your parents are saying 'You need to do that'. You have to do it of your own accord. And you can't call in sick or say 'Oh, I'm not in the mood today, I want to sleep in'. You have to get up, you need to be disciplined. But being an entrepreneur has given me a lot of satisfaction that my idea has meaning and has come to fruit. That all the efforts and sacrifices have been worthwhile. And that the way I saw the world and the business wasn't wrong. I have great satisfaction that it has paid off.

So, if you've started out and are finding the going tough, then this is something that resonates with many of our successful entrepreneurs. If you want it enough, keep going and get through this tricky phase. As Winston Churchill famously said 'If you are walking through hell, keep walking'.

HAVING A SUPPORTIVE PARTNER

Having a supportive home partner was widely cited as significantly helpful when starting out. Many of our female entrepreneurs appreciated the support of their home partner in helping to shoulder the burden and sacrifices that they needed to make during the start-up phase, as well as to share the childcare. Additionally, many valued having someone close to the business who they could share the ups and downs of building a business with, as well as to use as a sounding board when making tricky decisions and occasionally have as a shoulder to cry on.

Liann Eden, Dena McCallum and Sandra Macleod talked about the importance of having supportive partners who were prepared to put up with the inevitable sacrifices that come during the start-up phase as well as to share the childcare with.

Liann Eden and Dena McCallum, founders of Eden McCallum, commented on the huge value that their home partners bring.

> We are all in the business together. We both have very supportive partners who supported the business venture and were prepared to forego income for a while. They've always been equally supportive of the childcare. They would do the school pick-ups, sort out the nanny if they fell through and went to school plays and sports days.

They go on to comment about how their partners have good self-esteem and are very proud of their wives' achievements – qualities that they believe are essential in a supportive home partner.

Sandra Macleod of Echo Research concurs:

> It's a partnership bringing up a family. I was the one who travelled and my husband is in the property industry so he was always in the U.K. It was helpful that the two of us weren't always zipping around the world. Having that equilibrium is very important for sanity and keeping the family going.
>
> My father stayed close with all of us children and was a very wise mentor throughout. Finding similar support and encouragement in my husband and family life has been really helpful. It enables me to go headlong into things and not worry too much, because I know I've got wonderful support and love behind me. Over time, you respect where each other comes from and how you work together, and then you get to a different place. But I know it can be threatening for some men. My husband laughs because everywhere he goes he's called Michael Macleod, but it's not our married name. It doesn't bother him but I know it would bother a lot of other men. I've always said to Michael that I didn't marry him for his money or his ability to make money. I married him because I loved him and money is completely

separate. If I need money then I can go out and get it. And I think it's important to separate those two otherwise you're in a relationship for the wrong reasons.

Julia Hobsbawm and Michaela Jedinak also talked about the huge support that their home partners have given them as independent sounding boards and confidantes as their businesses have grown.

As we saw in Chapter Four, Julia Hobsbawm, founder of Editorial Intelligence, talks about the importance of having a very supportive partner. She says:

> Generally speaking, behind every high achieving person is someone propping them up. I'm very lucky that my husband has been the backstop at home and the best counsel for my business. He is one of the very small number of people that I run everything by. There is something quintessentially lonely about being an entrepreneur. In the end, the ideas come from your head and the creativity and the drive, push, and innovation is led by me too. There's absolutely no doubt that I would not have been able to build and stay in business on my own without my partner.

We also saw in Chapter Four the importance of Michaela Jedinak's partner in supporting the business. She says:

> My husband is my rock. I couldn't have done it without him. He's been an entrepreneur and so understands the emotional cycle. He gives me courage, puts things in perspective and helps me understand what I need to do. He works partly in the business and does a lot of things that I'm not good at, like marketing, strategy, finances, technology and visioning. We complement each other.

Conversely, some of our entrepreneurs suffered from having unsupportive partners. Tamara Gillan of Cherry London is one of these.

> So I've really struggled in my relationship identities outside of work with men. My husband was very threatened by my success. I met him, got engaged, married him and had a baby so quickly. And what I didn't realise was how insecure he was and how much he compared

himself to me and some of my friends who are also successful. He's a management consultant and quite strong in his field. But we didn't know each other well and we had different values. You can't be a female leader, run a company, travel around with clients and be a great mum, and not have a little bit of help – because you just can't. I'm a natural nurturer so I drove myself mad with making the home-made muesli, doing the shopping, being a wife and being a mum. But I struggled and he struggled. So actually when our relationship ended, it was a bit of a relief.

As our interviewees show, it's helpful to have a supportive partner at home. Someone who understands the pressure you're under and will encourage and help, rather than sit on the sidelines and undermine and criticise. Someone with the self-esteem to be proud of your success, even if you end up being more successful than them. We encourage single females with the entrepreneurial urge to select their future home partner wisely. As Maria Kempinska, founder of Jongleurs, advises: 'If you're going to get married, marry somebody who will support you and respect what you do.'

GETTING THE FAMILY INVOLVED AND MANAGING THE GUILT

There is much in the press about how difficult it is to be a successful businesswoman and a great mother. Women are still expected to be the primary caregiver to children and ageing parents – and so the question of how they balance both is regularly raised. Yet the same question is rarely, if ever, asked of men. As Rebekah Hall of Botanic Lab said in Chapter Nine:

Taking women seriously is a problem. I think I've done something interesting. I've built a successful business. I thought that that would be the first thing that people would ask me about. But no, they ask: 'How old are you? Are you married? Are you going to have children?'.

Those are more often the first questions that I get asked in a business and a social context. But those certainly wouldn't be the questions that would be asked of a man.

Many of our interviewees had much to say about how to balance being an entrepreneur with bringing up a family. For example, Dena McCallum and Aurée de Carbon talked about how difficult it is to juggle work and parenthood when the children are young, but how it gets easier when they are teenagers and can understand what their mothers have achieved. Dena McCallum of Eden McCallum says:

> Our teenagers are now very proud of us. Their friends think it is so cool to have mums that run successful businesses. We are always asking ourselves if we made the right choices, but our children give us permission to work. It was harder when the children were six, seven and eight, as our children constantly asked us: 'Why do you work, Mummy?', 'Why haven't you sewed me a costume for Book Day? My friends' mothers have', 'Why does the nanny always pick me up and not you? My friends' mums pick them up'. Now they say how proud they are of me and how glad they are that I work as otherwise 'Mummy's competitive edge would be focussed on us'. The moment when your child gets it is fabulous.

Similarly, Aurée De Carbon of Paris-based CARRHURE says:

> I'm not sure I would have been able to start a business when my son was younger. My son has been really supportive. He has given me permission to travel and build my business. Sometimes, when I had difficulties, he would have doubts and say: 'You won't be able to make it'. And then when the situation changed, I'd tell him: 'See, you were wrong. Remember this. Nothing is written. When you're going through a difficult journey, it's not the end of the journey, you have to fight until the end. Things can always change for the better. You just have to keep going'.

Many of our interviewees, including Di Burton, Sandra Macleod, Lara Morgan and Tamara Gillan, talked about how it's natural to feel guilty about working hard when bringing up young children. But they also talked about the importance of not beating yourself up and offered suggestions on how to manage the guilt. Di Burton, founder of Cicada Communications, confided:

> Women who work never, ever, ever get rid of their guilt. It was always hit and run, come home, and then 'Have you done your homework?', 'Have you got your gym kit?', etc. My kids would say to me: 'Forget it, don't worry, we admire you'. But I vividly remember my daughter Sarah being the only child at her primary school who had no one there on her open day. My partner was working in Preston and I was at some board meeting in Leeds. You never forget that. And yet they say they were fine. I phoned my son Rupert and he said: 'Mum, you taught me how to hustle'. And my daughter Sarah said I've taught her that she can do anything, there are no boundaries. I want to retire a little earlier, maybe next year, and spend some more time with my grand-children and put something back in that I didn't put into my kids.

Sandra Macleod of Echo Research concurs:

> You feel guilty as a mother. There's guilt when you miss major moments in their lives because you're away. But I always made sure that we had good family holidays together and that it was pure family time. I also tried to keep weekends sacrosanct by doing whatever was needed in the hours during the week. I remember my daughter being asked: 'What does your mummy do?'. And she drew a big desk and a phone and said mummy works for British Airways. I said not quite. British Airways was a client we were involved with at the time because of the Concorde disaster and the big BA strikes. So she had this strange perception of what mummy did.

Lara Morgan, founder originally of Pacific Direct and now well-being investor of Scentered, talked about the guilt she felt when her children were young and how she dealt with it. She says:

> In the last year alone at Pacific Direct, I travelled overseas for 221 nights. It wouldn't matter if I was in London or Timbuctoo, I'm just

not in my own home. That means that there were only 130 days of the year left that I could be at home, which is tough when you have very small children. I chose to sell the business when my eldest was eight years old. One of the influences was my children saying that I was never here and feeling that being too absent was the wrong thing to do.

One of the worst experiences of my life was when I went to the school playground and another mum asked me if I was picking up Kate's children. Kate's the nanny. That hurt. My children had been going to that school for the best part of five years, yet I was unrecognisable. From about the age of thirty-eight I decided that I'm not doing guilt, because I realised that feeling guilty and looking back at the past gets you nowhere.

On balance I don't have a regret about the sacrifices I made. But I did make sure that I never missed a nativity play or sports day and always made my children's birthday cakes. I might have been running round the garden at 2 a.m. trying to get the sponge to cool down because I'd just flown in from overseas, and praying I'd get four hours sleep so I could ice it in the morning. My mum had made all of my birthday cakes so that was my measure of whether I was being a half decent mum, but I was killing myself.

The other telling point was a particularly horrific week at work. I dealt with a staff member calling the police because her husband was beating her, another announcing that she was getting divorced, yet another moving house and then one of my sales people getting killed on the road in Germany. You realise that you've got nearly five hundred people around the world that depend on you for their mortgage and their living. I was flying in from all around the world arriving at Heathrow at 4.55 a.m. on a Saturday morning and driving home tired to see my kids before they went to Saturday school – and trying to fake being cheerful when actually I was pretty knackered. But the reality is I still wouldn't change any of that for what I have today.

Tamara Gillan, founder of Cherry London, talks about the importance of being kind to yourself.

> Everyone talks about the guilt, especially around children and the school gate. 'Who are you? Oh, you're the mum?'. Yep, I'm the mum! But it's important to let yourself off the hook. My son is young but he's really proud of me. I went to his nursery performance 'Cowboy Dance' last week and he was like 'That's my mum Mara Gillan'. And I'm like: 'Thank you for being so generous to me, even though I'm not here enough and you don't even seem to mind'. My advice is to have quality time with your children and lots of holidays together.

So, if you're feeling guilty about starting a business whilst trying to raise a family, then you're in good company. Many of our entrepreneurial mothers felt the same. Their advice is to not be too hard on yourself and that it will get easier as the children age into teenagers and understand the great things you've achieved. As Lindsay Levin, founder of Leaders' Quest, told us:

> Women worry, wanting to be brilliant at everything – a brilliant mother, a brilliant daughter, a brilliant daughter-in-law, a brilliant wife. I just think you have to let go. We're too hard on ourselves and we're too hard on one another. I'm astonished how my kids turned out. We've got three stunningly well-adjusted, amazing kids. I didn't do such a bad job and it took me a long time to accept that.

CREATING BALANCE

Our interviewees talked a lot about the difficulty of balancing the many issues that women face alongside building a business – including bringing up a family, staying fit and healthy and winding down for retirement. In this section we look at how they've created the balance required to be successful in each of these.

CREATING BALANCE BETWEEN WORK AND CHILDREN

First, let's look at how some of our entrepreneurs have structured their working week to balance building and running a business alongside bringing up a family.

Maria Kempinska, founder of Jongleurs, talks about the importance of building a support structure that fits you and your way of working. She says:

> Get as much help as you can in the home life. If you've got extended family get them involved, family will give you more. I didn't have that facility but I have seen it work well for other women. I don't think you have to be an amazing mother. I used to take my children to work when I needed to. But I built my working day around them, and because I worked in the evening it was a bit easier. Build your structure to fit you, not somebody else.

Liann Eden and Dena McCallum of Eden McCallum added:

> We recognise the need to respect that people have lives outside of work and the importance of leading by example day to day. We always worked our diaries so that we could go to every school play and made this obvious by saying 'It's a sports day', rather than making a false work event, so that we set the right tone for the company. Of course, it requires a huge amount of juggling, for example working in the early morning or evening. We've found that you can't set hard and fast boundaries in professional services, but being in control of how we spend our time each day has worked well.

As we saw in Chapter Eight, Gemma Greaves is a mother who has a full-time day job as Chief Executive of the Marketing Society whilst also running her own start-up Cabal. Unsurprisingly, she finds striking a balance between work and home a challenge. Gemma told us:

> The thing I find most difficult in life is time. Time is the most precious resource you have and there's not enough of it to do all the things that you want to do. There is so much going on that you've got to prioritise

the things that you really want and need to do. You have to be a little bit selfish. Life for me pivots around nursery pick-up and drop-off of Joshie, with the big things in life like global travel for the Marketing Society and my own business Cabal squeezed in-between. I sit with my husband and assistant every week and figure out when I can pick-up and drop-off. When I go to New York I ensure that I still do one pick-up and drop-off that week. It means I fly on Tuesday rather than Monday and I don't get as much time to chill out in New York. But I'm cool with that because my number one priority is my son. My advice is to take some of the stress out of being a mother and running a business by planning the week ahead with the people who are affected and making decisions together. It's about compromise and talking and accepting you can't do everything. Also, if you can combine what you love with what you do day to day, it's easier and more rewarding.

As we saw in Chapter Eight, Rebekah Hall of Botanic Lab talks about how needing to focus on children can be turned into a positive. She says:

> The entrepreneurs I know who've got children have said to me that it can be a really good thing. It's quite tough to turn off at the end of the day. And when you've got kids you have to turn off because you have to focus your attention on them. So in some ways it's quite valuable.

Many of our interviewees talked about the difficulty of juggling the growth of a new business alongside family and childcare responsibilities, particularly when children are young. Creating a schedule and support structure that worked for them was vital. One that creates the right balance of making work work around your family, as well as making your family work around work. And not being afraid to plan, prioritise and focus on what matters most. So now let's look at some of the other issues that hard-working women need to be mindful of, such as their health.

CREATING BALANCE BETWEEN WORK AND HEALTH

Some of our entrepreneurs talked about how fulfilling so many roles can take its toll on health – and thus the importance of female entrepreneurs taking time out to restore, reenergise and revitalise their minds, bodies and souls. Di Burton, Tamara Gillan and Melina Jacovou are all examples of interviewees who take looking after their health seriously.

Di Burton, founder of Cicada Communications, disclosed that:

> Every five years I had a chronic illness which is all down to work and stress. On the button I had it. The doctor would say 'Di, are you going to listen to your body. You're pushing yourself too hard'. Now I'm trying to slow down a bit. I always used to put work before me. We weren't aware of the whole health and wellbeing thing then. And I've always been a sportsman and so have been innately very fit. But, I would never take time out to do things like meditation. On reflection I would have managed my people better if I had. I was always the highly anxious, highly driven, highly shallow breath person. And people would say to me 'Di, you've been born with the hurry gene', which actually is not very attractive, is it?!

Like Di Burton, Victoria Mellor, founder of Melcrum, talks about how putting enormous pressure on herself was probably a key contributor to her getting ill. She says:

> I'm always worrying about other people and not very good at looking after myself. I put huge pressure on myself to achieve everything – like bringing up my children and running an international business. I had a cancer diagnosis during the period leading up to the sale of the business. The day after I signed the deal, I left the business with all of my belongings in a suitcase and went straight to start treatment. I'm pretty sure that this was caused by putting a lot of pressure on myself for five years. Keeping physically fit is now a really important thing for me and our culture.

Tamara Gillan, Cherry London, had some similar words of wisdom:

> My advice to new entrepreneurs is to go more steadily, don't rush everything. Take your time, manage the business. Don't do anything emotional after being affronted. Instead, write the email and don't send it. You don't succeed the more you work. The more I've taken

space and calm to go on holiday, the more I've created space to see new things. Every time I go to a speaking event, I get a piece of inspiration that takes us in a new direction.

My job is to inspire, to create vision, to take people on the journey. You need to have energy to do that. You can't just be a workhorse. You have to get sources of inspiration from listening to others. My mother said: 'If you're an entrepreneur the "to do" list will always be there. There will always be something on it. It will never go away. So, stop, get off the list for the moment and do something else'. It's so true, the list is never ending. My Dad also said: 'What you take out, you must put back in'. You have to look after your health and your energy through wellness and good food. Emotionally and physically. It's the only way I can cope with this kind of extreme pressure. I go to the gym before my son gets up and the day gets started. I also do a quick twenty-minute workout on the way home and it helps me go from my work world to having quality time with my son. It's like 'Wow, that was quite liberating'.

Melina Jacovou of Propel believes in living life to the full but staying healthy too. She says:

I love my work. To me, it's not work because I love what I do, I'm extremely passionate about it. But you've got to have energy to remain passionate. So I exercise and try to live a wholesome life. I've swum three or four times this week and I'll be spinning tonight, so I do a lot of healthy stuff. And I try and watch what I eat. But it's all about balance. I also drink and socialise a lot. I'm out three or four nights a week.

The lesson here is obvious. It's important to not be a workhorse beholden to the lengthy 'to do' list but instead to take time out to restore and reenergise yourself as well as find new avenues of inspiration. In the wise words of Tamara Gillan's dad: 'What you take out, you must put back in'.

CREATING BALANCE BETWEEN WORK AND RETIREMENT

This will be short. There's little to say about the balance between work and retirement as the 'R' word was, unsurprisingly, rarely mentioned by interviewees. Some might have been shy but none of the fifty-two interviewees were the retiring types regardless of the amount of capital made. All were passionate about their creations and even those who had sold up were on the march again. Whilst they looked back to learn and celebrate (very briefly), all were forward looking in outlook and radiant with energy. In fact, there were only three fleeting references to the 'R' word.

Jane Mosley spent a career working in the equine world. She then barely touched down in retirement before taking off again to turn her hobby of baking into a full-on vocation. Her home baking business is now on a near industrial scale for its size and has far exceeded her original hopes for success. She says:

> *Country Living* magazine is one of my luxuries. It encourages people who want to start a new business to build on their hobbies. A lot of people are farmers' wives whose families have grown up and are needing to diversify in order to keep the family farm. Or business people who have worked in London and want to move to the country. So they ask: 'Do you sew, cook, paint, or make furniture, or whatever?'. For me, it was baking cakes. I started my own business because I wanted to be able to look back with the satisfaction of establishing a reputation for great cakes. I think I've done that, cakes are a little bit of a luxury and it's great to see smiles on people's faces.

Bridget Connell spent over thirty years working for other people in corporates before starting Thinking Partnerships. She said:

> My husband stopped work six years before me. He was at home having a really nice time and I was working all the hours that god sends. So I felt I'd probably given as much as I could to working in large organisations and decided that I'd like a different quality of life. It felt time to do something different.
>
> I didn't know anything about angel investing but I accepted an invitation to go to an event. That evening, a woman stood up and told us how she got involved in angel investing. She came across a female entrepreneur who had started a personal fitness training business

and needed money to scale and grow. And so this woman invested £20,000 of her own money into this entrepreneur and used her marketing expertise as well as her capital to support her. That for me was a really simple example of what angel investing is. It was a manageable amount of money and it was in something that she could add her skills to, to help. It resonated really strongly with me as I want to support other women in growing their businesses.

Rather than leaving the corporate world to retire, Bridget started up her own business, Thinking Partnerships, offering business coaching to start-ups and senior executive coaching.

Lara Morgan (now of Scentered, but formerly of Pacific Direct) shares some experience of selling her first business, Pacific Direct. She sold it when her eldest child was eight years old, in part to spend more time with her children, but also as a pause before going on to start her next business, Scentered. She says:

> I definitely shouldn't have waited any longer to sell. I have spoilt children, but my eldest, now nineteen, knows that I'm not handing it out on a plate and so has a pub job at Christmas. My sixteen-year-old is getting to that realisation and buys vintage clothes and has her own little mini business going. My next child said to me three weeks ago: 'Mummy, what job can I get?'. And I said 'I would like you to work on the Winchester Christmas Fair stand with me on Saturday for £60'. She knows she's lucky to get the job and so works her socks off in the freezing cold. That makes her think: 'Maybe, I don't want to be serving every day on a stall' and gives her an appreciation of how hard that job is on that side of the table.
>
> I was brought up with very old-fashioned values – where 'the pennies look after themselves' and 'if at first you don't succeed try, try again'. I also don't want to hear them being negative about anybody – if you haven't got anything nice to say, then don't say it. It did me good because I don't talk about problems, I talk about opportunities. That's a great mindset and it has stood me very well. Day to day, I want the freedom to enjoy my children while they're still young. Otherwise what was the point of selling Pacific Direct.

As we can see from our interviewees, many entrepreneurs don't get round to retirement. They may change direction, turn hobbies into businesses and perhaps wind the dial down a bit. But they are essentially a restless lot, with a passion for building businesses.

So, in summary, our female entrepreneurs have found ways to make work work around life. They make time for themselves and their families. They prioritise and plan ruthlessly. They focus on what really matters. And they are kind to themselves, recognising the enormity of the roles they have to play and thus the difficulty in being excellent in all of them.

In this chapter we have looked at how to make work work around life. In Chapter Eleven we look at how to make work work for women.

NOTES

1 'Women Still Shoulder the Bulk of Household Chores', *Starts At 60*, 27 July 2019, https://startsat60.com/discover/news/women-housework-household-chores-work-employment-and-society-study-university-college-london.
2 'Working Women Still Do Housework' by Robin Yapp, *Daily Mail*, July 2019, www.dailymail.co.uk/news/article-206381/Working-women-housework.html.

CHAPTER ELEVEN

Making work work for women

The female agenda

When interviewing our entrepreneurs, the authors were struck by the number of women who had deliberately left the corporate world to do their own thing – and thus the amount of great talent the corporate world is losing. Many women talked about how business is still very male-oriented, citing the glass ceiling and lack of female role models, as well as the inflexibility of the working environment for mothers of young children. For many women it seemed too much of an uphill struggle to try to change these traditional corporations from within. Instead, they left to set up their own rules and culture.

In this chapter we will explore this issue in more depth by looking at:

1. *Why corporations are losing great talent.*
2. *The need for women to lean in <u>and</u> for corporations and governments to lean out.*
3. *The benefits to women of helping other women.*
4. *What our female entrepreneurs are doing to create a new way forward.*
5. *A win-win for all genders – the essential ingredients of a high performing work culture.*

WHY CORPORATIONS ARE LOSING GREAT TALENT

Many of our interviewees started out in the corporate world, but got to a point where they saw no future there – either because of the lack of flexibility to look after young children or because of the glass ceiling and lack of senior female role models.

Liann Eden, Dena McCallum, Tamara Gillan and Gemma Greaves all cited the lack of flexibility to look after young children as a key reason why they or their friends left the corporate world – something that still seems to be an issue for many women in business today.

Liann Eden and Dena McCallum, founders of Eden McCallum, left the corporate world when they had children as they couldn't see how to make having a full-on career and young children work. They said:

> We left corporate life due to the high level of work and commitment required to do well, not due to the glass ceiling. Weekly travelling and long hours are very difficult to do when you have young children. There are so many societal things that hinder women that don't have to be there, such as lack of childcare, meetings in the evening and travel. These barriers can be changed. But sometimes women give up too quickly. Life issues such as children, bereavement, illness and sick parents happen to men as well. But women can be more reticent than men at bringing these types of issues to the table. They should tell us 'This is what I need to make this work' rather than give up – which is something that men are more likely to do.

Gemma Greaves, founder of Cabal, has seen the same issue. She recalls:

> One of my NCT friends, a very successful woman in the city, gave up her corporate career when she went back to work after having her first baby. She had to leave soon after as she couldn't work at six o'clock in the morning until late in the evening. She needed flexibility to be at home when she needed to be and the culture wouldn't allow that. And she didn't want to be in the position where someone so talented isn't recognised because she's had a baby. She's now got her own dog-walking business. She loves dogs. The amount of women I meet who are so talented and brilliant – but who say that they're no longer working because there is no flexibility. This is a national issue of wasted talent.

To counter this, Tamara Gillan of Cherry London has deliberately created a female-friendly work culture that attracts women and she believes that corporates need to do something similar. She says:

> Women like working with women. Our culture is founded on the more feminine traits of connection, collaboration, rolling your sleeves up together. We have proactively tried to hire more men but we

struggle. I think that if you're a corporate, you have to make it more possible for women to participate in the workforce through proactive policies. So one of the things that we did is make our enhanced maternity and paternity benefits better than some of our corporate competitors.

If you make it possible for men to have more of a role in their child's life, you make it possible for women to have more equality in the workplace. Also, people need to work in the way they need to work, whether they are male or female, and so we have flexible ways of working. We try to be supportive of people who are responsible for childcare and need to go home early and do the school pick-up. We are also supportive in other ways. For example, our Managing Director of many years lived in Paris with her husband and would come to us in the middle of the week.

Tamara is giving the corporate world some much needed food for thought on how to engage the whole talent pool in employment, as well as a real-life example of how to make it work in practice. Something that corporates could and should learn from.

A second reason why many of our female interviewees left the corporate world to set up their own business was the male-dominated work culture, glass ceiling and lack of senior female role models. Tash Walker, Tamara Gillan and Bridget Connell all cited these. Tash Walker of The Mix explains:

I started my career in the early 2000s in advertising, which is quite a male-dominated industry. The lack of strong female leaders and the feeling of not being truly equal to most senior managers was a big motivation in starting my own business. If you've got that itch to be the one calling the shots and you can't see that path in front of you in male-dominated businesses, then it feels like you need to go off and do it yourself. One global agency didn't have any women on the board and there were no plans to have any women on the board, so that didn't look like a very viable option. When you're in the early stages of your career, it's really important to have senior female figures to aspire to. I couldn't see any senior female figures. There were lots of men who I had as mentors who I really valued. But there was no one that made me think: 'Yeah, that's the kind of woman I want to be when I'm a bit further down my career'.

Tamara Gillan of Cherry London agrees:

So one of the other reasons I started my agency was the very visible glass ceiling in Orange where I was working. If you looked around our big open plan floor in marketing, 70% of the team were women – yet the leadership were men. Which is ironic because I think as a female leader, you have so many more tools in your toolkit. I thought there must be an easier way to do this, by creating and playing to my own rules, rather than trying to break through that corporate environment.

A female friend of mine went to one of the big four where they had a working mothers 'Come Back To Work' programme. She managed to get onto the programme out of something like five thousand applicants. But after three months she resigned as she kept having 7 p.m. meetings and conference calls. On the one hand, they were saying we're going to help women with children come back to work. But in reality the culture made it untenable for them to actually come back to work. I look at women who have stayed and are saying that they've got to play by those rules – and I think that the price is too high.

Bridget Connell's story is even more alarming. Before setting up Thinking Partnerships she worked at DHL. She says:

I worked there for ten years and I left because I couldn't get any more senior. It was a very male environment, with networking done in Europe and Africa when we were travelling together. People built their network and allies and strong collaborative working relationships with senior people whilst drinking ten pints of beer in casinos and gentlemen's clubs. When I got to a certain level I thought: 'I'm never going to get anywhere in this organisation'. If there were more senior women there, I could have probably gone further.

The lack of senior female leaders is very real. Men do indeed still run the world. As Sheryl Sandberg quotes in her book *Lean In*, of the 195 independent countries in the world only seventeen are led by women. Women hold just 22% of parliament seats globally, with 23.5% of U.K. seats held by women. The percentage of women in leadership roles in the corporate world is even lower. A meagre 5% of the S&P 500 CEOs are women. In the U.S., women hold only 25% of senior executive positions and 19% of board seats. In the U.K.'s FTSE 100, these figures are 21% and 23.5% respectively, so fairly similar. In 2015, only five female CEOs sat in the FTSE 100 companies and nine in the FTSE 250. Additionally, after years of protests and battles, women's pay is still significantly lower than men's. In 1970, American women were paid 59% of what a man was paid. By 2010, that had gone up to 77% – still well below the pay levels of their male counterparts. In Europe and the U.K. women earn 84% and 82% of their male counterparts. A woeful situation.[1]

A study conducted in 2015 by researchers at Columbia Business School and the University of Maryland's Business School among 1,500 of America's biggest companies also showed how women are still disadvantaged when trying to achieve senior-level positions. The study discovered that when a woman had been appointed as CEO, other women were more likely to be promoted to senior positions. But when a company was headed by a man, it was much harder for more than one woman to make it into senior management. In fact, the probability of a second woman becoming a senior manager fell by 51% when the CEO was male.[2]

Unless big corporations address the male cultural bias that makes it difficult for women to see themselves as having a place at the top table or enjoy a full-on career whilst having children, they will continue to lose out on half of the country's top talent – females. One can only ask why big corporations aren't waking up to this harsh reality more quickly and doing more to address this.

THE NEED FOR WOMEN TO LEAN IN AND FOR CORPORATIONS AND GOVERNMENTS TO LEAN OUT

In 2015, Sheryl Sandberg wrote the provocative book *Lean In*, which was countered by the equally provocative book *Lean Out* by Dawn Foster. These two books raised the heated debate of whether women should be working harder to fit into the male-dominated corporate world (by 'leaning in'), or whether the corporate world should be doing more to accommodate women (by 'leaning out'). We asked our interviewees to comment on this – with many believing that a mixture of the two is needed to address this issue.

Martha Lane Fox is one of them. She says:

> I think we need to both lean in and lean out. I think Sheryl got a bad rap. I think she was trying to say that just because you're in a room full of men it doesn't mean your voice isn't valid and you shouldn't use it. For me, that's a helpful and important message. But the other message is valid as well. It needs to be a two-way process – you have to be listened to by men. Women can't solve these challenges by themselves and men also can't solve them by themselves. To me, it's about fundamental equality and both sides leaning in to each other a bit more.

Martha continues with the need for corporations to do more to lean out and make the workplace more attractive to females. She says:

> Companies are having a lot more conversations and action in groups about representing women more and better. But that doesn't mean that it's being followed through with real action, legislation and tangible differences to people's lives. That's the bit that I think we need to focus on now. I really hope that women are encouraged to be more entrepreneurial and are given the chance to develop different skills – and that real progress keeps being made. I hope we sort the gender pay gap and improve childcare. That doesn't mean enabling women to

do the childcare, it means men and women sharing childcare. Unless we think dramatically, a lot of these things won't shift.

She also talks about the importance of men as well as women stepping up, right from the moment that children start education.

You can't just rely on women to make the changes, it's got to come from men as well. There are a lot of male teachers and heads of schools. And there are a lot of men working in the department of education, including education ministers. So, the change needs to come from men as well as women. It would be impossible to argue that the education system was geared equally to encourage women. I think it's patchy. I'm sure some schools do a great job but some less so. You just have to look at the numbers to know that it's not geared towards encouraging entrepreneurship, particularly digital entrepreneurship. There's a huge amount that needs to happen to make people more resilient. But it's not just down to the education system. It's also the responsibility of parents, the wider community and employers. It's the responsibility of anyone employing, funding or helping women succeed in the workplace.

Rebekah Hall of Botanic Lab agrees with Martha, both on the need for women to lean in and for corporations to lean out. She says:

By nature I'm more of a 'lean in-er'. This probably comes from being in a male-dominated industry that doesn't have many women in it, with women needing to scrap to get to where they've got to. If you'd asked me that question when I was in the midst of that career, I would say: 'Lean in and get on with it. It's not that bad. I do it. Why shouldn't everyone else?'. But when I look back now, with the benefit of experience and fresh eyes, I can see that there are a lot of things that actually weren't right about that experience. So my mindset around it has changed. I'm not on the ultra-politically correct end of the spectrum. I think some of the rhetoric around what's going on now is not good for the equality cause. Sometimes women, like men, just aren't good enough and I think defaulting to 'I haven't been promoted because I'm a woman' is a dangerous territory to step into. You've got to take responsibility for yourself and your actions and career. However there are industries like the one I work in where there are blatant problems for women who want to get to the top. There are barriers in the way that aren't always obvious that women need help with.

Similarly, Victoria Mellor, who financed and sold her company Melcrum, saw a lot of discrimination when seeking funding. She says:

> There's an opportunity to change the investment world. It's the classic old boys' network that doesn't encourage women to get involved. The same is true when it comes to non-executive opportunities. Since selling my business, I've received a number of invitations to join all male boards because they want a 'token woman', which is fairly insulting. I want to be involved because I'm valued for my experience rather than my gender.

If society wants to leverage the huge female talent pool, it needs to lean out by challenging its traditional male-oriented ways of working and creating a more equal working environment fit for the 21st century. It needs to make work for young mothers a tenable choice and the ability to rise to the top a credible and aspirational option for females. That said, women also need to help drive the change by leaning in and working hard – and taking responsibility for their careers, decisions and actions.

THE BENEFITS TO WOMEN OF HELPING OTHER WOMEN

In a male-oriented world, you'd think that successful women who have fought their way up would want to help other women get up the ladder too. But our interviewees suggested that this isn't always the case. Some of our female entrepreneurs talked about how the people who had encouraged them most in their careers were men. And, in some cases, it even seemed as if some successful women have gone out of their way not to help other women succeed too.

Rebekah Hall of Botanic Lab was one of these. She explains:

> In my experience, the most encouraging people in my career have
> been male. I've always found the least encouraging to be women.
> I was at a dinner recently with forty very impressive women. One of
> the consistent themes was that women are often our worst enemies.
> This sort of women say: 'I have to do it, so you've got to do it' and
> are a bit protective of what they've achieved. Now I may not have
> come across the right women but, conversely, I've had some great
> men in my career. Two of them are investors in my business who've
> been hugely supportive and have really put their hand out and pulled
> me up.

Tamara Gillan of Cherry London has also seen women shying away from
helping other women. She explains:

> I've worked with women who aren't pro-women and almost don't
> want to be seen to help other women because they don't want to come
> over as nepotistic. But more often I am inspired by the generosity of
> other successful women. The WealthiHer Network which I founded is
> populated by incredible female changemakers determined to help and
> support other women. I have a huge network of very trusted female
> connections – both clients and partners we work with – and I reg-
> ularly see them and know about their lives. They are deep personal
> connections that I respect greatly. I honour them, protect them, pro-
> mote them and advise them if things are not going well for them. But
> I would never work with my personal friends and would never ask
> my friends to involve me in their business. Whereas men, it's almost
> like the opposite. They say: 'We know each other, so let's do business
> together'.

Sherry Roberts, founder of The Longest Stay, is even more pessimistic.
Her view is that:

> Women will never be treated equally to men. Women are amaz-
> ing. They make amazing businesses, amazing mothers, amazing

loads of things. They need to recognise this and help themselves and each other more. Women should invest in and mentor other female businesses. But instead they often get jealous and so don't want to help.

She adds:

When I meet other female entrepreneurs, I try to invest in them, introduce them to others in my network and buy one of their products. For women it's not fair, it's harder. Helping each other is the only way we can make it a little bit better and create change. It doesn't need to be perfect, we just need to improve. And we have to do this for the next generation.

Some of our entrepreneurs are describing the 'Queen Bee' syndrome, which was first defined by psychologists at the University of Michigan in 1973. There has been a lot of research done into this syndrome, where behaviour ranges from women disparaging typical female traits, emphasising their own masculine traits, seeing claims of gender discrimination as baseless and being unsupportive of initiatives designed to address gender inequality. Professor Dame Sally Davies, the U.K.'s first female Chief Medical Officer, used the term in 2014 when describing her own experiences in the health sector. 'I saw it particularly in medicine – queen bees preening and enjoying being the only woman.' Margaret Thatcher, the U.K.'s first female prime minister, has also been described as a queen bee for not promoting or furthering the careers of women in her cabinet.[3]

Marianne Cooper in her 2016 article in *The Atlantic* says that 'Queen Bee' behaviours emerge when there is gender bias and a lack of gender solidarity. Or, put another way, when women who don't see their womanhood as a central aspect of their identity experience gender discrimination. They think their gender should be irrelevant at work but, when discriminated against, realise that others see them first and foremost as women. Because of negative stereotypes about women, for example being less competent than men, they get concerned that their career path may be stunted. So they distance themselves from other women. For example, by describing themselves in more typically masculine terms and denigrating other women, such as: 'I'm not like other women, I've always prioritised my career'. It's not that women are inherently catty. Instead, 'Queen Bee' behaviours emerge in male-dominated environments where women are devalued. Other marginalised groups respond similarly when they are discriminated against. For example, gay men try to distance themselves from being seen as effeminate by emphasising hyper-masculine traits. While social distancing can enable an individual from a disadvantaged group to advance, it does a disservice to the group as a whole because it can legitimise inequalities.[4]

Many of our female entrepreneurs commented on being encouraged in their careers by successful men rather than successful women. And, in some cases, successful women not helping other women to succeed. The 'Queen Bee' syndrome may have worked for female individuals in the past but, sadly, has also helped to perpetuate gender inequality. On reflection, if we want to make the corporate environment more gender equal, it seems important for successful women to support other women, as well as help create a more gender-neutral working environment and culture that the whole workforce will want to be part of. Madeleine Albright's famous quote seems to sum it up well: 'There is a special place in hell for women who don't help each other!'.[5]

WHAT OUR FEMALE ENTREPRENEURS ARE DOING TO CREATE A NEW WAY FORWARD

Interestingly, many of our female entrepreneurs talked about how they were deliberately creating more female-friendly working environments – to both create a culture that they want to work in and to tap into the huge female talent pool that is often disenfranchised by the corporate world. Perhaps our female entrepreneurs have more permission and capability to create this culture due to the lack of ingrained gender bias in their companies that so many corporates still suffer from.

For example, Rebekah Hall of Botanic Lab has created a female-oriented company, but has done so unconsciously. She says:

> We have a very female organisation, but that wasn't on purpose. Hiring people who want to work flexibly actually works quite well for me because I don't have to pay a full-time salary. So we don't have that many men in the organisation. But one thing I'm conscious of is, at the advisory and shareholder levels, I have no women. We're just coming to the end of this investment round and I've left a space on the advisory board because there has to be a woman on it. If you look at angel investors then, broadly speaking, you've got a few successful female entrepreneurs but the majority tend to be guys advising people like me. And so the chain continues. I've got a board that's entirely made up of men, so I'm now part of the problem. So I have one advisory board space left for a woman and I've got a few women in mind.

Lindsay Levin, founder of Leaders' Quest, has also built a female-friendly culture. She explains:

> We're strongly female, not deliberately, but we have a lot of really talented women. We had a lot of people on maternity leave last year which we just had to cope with, but now there are a number of people back on a four-day week. We're hard-working because of the nature of our work, but we've also put in place things that accommodate family which has been an intuitive thing for us to do. I think that one of the attractions of Leaders' Quest for women is the type of work we do. It's all about being human in the broadest sense and, of course, everybody is interested in that. A lot of women are very motivated by doing something purposeful and I think that helps to make us attractive to them.

As we saw in Chapter Eight, Tash Walker of The Mix has gone one stage further. She says:

> About nine months ago, we decided to go to a four-day week. Our people are the most important thing to us. So getting a life balance for our employees, including me, is another way to show how we are disrupting ourselves and the market – and demonstrates how we are staying true to our business purpose which is being interested in human behaviour. We're quite female-dominated at the moment, with two females at the top, five guys and ten other females. It's not intentional. In a way I'd want more balance. But regardless of who we employ, our values are clear in the sense that we're people-orientated. So going to a four-day week was imperative. We wanted our people to get some balance in their lives. To enjoy life and be happy, and to turn up and give us their all. I really believe in that. Additionally, bringing women into the business is important to me. I speak most months at an event about flexible working and equality in the workplace – and the need to develop more empathy both as business owners and marketers. We can all be more empathetic in the way that we treat the people around us.

Liann Eden and Dena McCallum, of Eden McCallum fame, are also proud to be driving equality in the consulting world. They told us that:

> Eden McCallum's consultancy business is helping to make male and female salaries more equal. Our consultant survey shows that, in their previous job before Eden McCallum, women's salaries were about 30% lower than men's, even after accounting for all other differences. Amongst our consultants there is only a 3% difference in day rates. Additionally, if a person (male or female) is good then we want to make this work. We recognise how valuable they are. People have different things that matter to them in life – and we need to stop judging people, as all are legitimate choices. People need to ask for what they want and be clear about what will and won't work for them. As long as they deliver for our clients, they can do what they like in-between.

Bridget Connell of Thinking Partnerships concludes with some very sage advice for both new and successful female entrepreneurs. She says:

> There aren't that many female entrepreneurs out there. So there's masses of benefit in supporting each other and sharing contacts and lessons learned. Also, the more senior you get, the less women there are around you and so it can be very lonely. You need allies, people you can identify with and who will support each other. So it's important for women to be there for each other.

We end this section with a *Forbes* article written by Caroline Castrillon, published 10 March 2019: 'Why Women Need To Network Differently Than Men To Get Ahead'. In it, she argues that women benefit from having a strong female support group and so should nurture building one. She quotes Rachel Thomas, President of LeanIn.org, as saying: 'I think men are socialised from the get-go to understand that mixing business and friendship is what you do to get ahead. We, as women, aren't as comfortable doing that'.

She goes on to say that when men network they form alliances. Their networks tend to be larger and broader, which increases the probability that they will be introduced to someone who can help them with their career. And men generally network with a clear short-term goal in mind and are more comfortable asking for what they want. Conversely, women are more focussed on building long-term personal connections or friendships. They often make contacts through people they know and tend to form smaller, deeper networks based on trust. They generally hesitate to ask for what they want when networking. Instead, they ask what they can do for the other person first.

Additionally, many women don't want to attend events after work because they want to be at home with their families. A study conducted by the Kellogg School of Management showed that women who try to network like men actually do the worst, as they don't have a tight-knit female group who will provide job opportunities and support. In contrast, 77% of the highest-achieving women in the study had strong ties with an inner circle of two to three other women. Similarly, women who form a strong inner circle with other women who can share career advice are nearly three times more likely to get a better job than women who don't have that support system. So for women to advance professionally it's important that they build a strong, tight female support group with whom they can mutually benefit.[6]

Female entrepreneurs are recognising the need to build a more female-friendly culture and flexible working environment, and are achieving a competitive advantage by doing so. This gives them access to a highly talented workforce who feel disenfranchised by the corporate world, yet are keen to work.

Corporations and the public sector should look at and emulate some of the initiatives that female entrepreneurs are taking to build a more female-friendly culture rather than making minimal politically correct nods to women at work. This will enable them to attract talented people who will enjoy a more female-friendly collaborative culture – as well as mothers of young children who need a more flexible working environment.

By doing this, corporations can help the U.K. leverage a huge asset and talent pool that is being neglected today, as well as attract top talent that finds it difficult to work in the more traditional and inflexible male working environment. If our female entrepreneurs can make these changes and make them pay for everyone, then why can't big business implement them too?

A WIN–WIN FOR ALL GENDERS – THE ESSENTIAL INGREDIENTS OF A HIGH-PERFORMING WORK CULTURE

This chapter looks at the world largely and intentionally through a female lens. But the broader aim is to make the work environment attractive to all genders. In this final section, we summarise the essential ingredients of a harmonious and high-performing work culture to help leaders and managers maximise the benefits for all. These essential ingredients divide into those that are tangible and those that are intangible. Let's start with the tangibles.

TANGIBLES

Mutual trust

As outlined at the beginning of this chapter, many female entrepreneurs start out in the corporate world as employees in what is essentially a male domain. This contributes to some leaving the corporate world to start their own company where they can shape the working culture.

To counter this, both the employer and employee need to take responsibility for creating a great working environment. The employer needs to create a more flexible and collaborative working environment that works for all genders. The employee needs to respect the trust that has been given to them in a less 'rules-based' environment. To retain the benefits of a lighter touch regime, it is beholden on them to collectively self-police.

Some may write this off as going soft on performance at work. But we should remind ourselves of the research referenced earlier in this work that suggests that female-led start-ups that create more flexible working environments often enjoy better business performance.

Flexible hours and presence

Flexible hours were cited by our interviewees as a key characteristic of the high-performing work culture. The 'nine to six' working day spent at company locations is just not tenable for those, male or female, who have other responsibilities – many of which have absolutely non-negotiable schedules such as the school run, helping with homework, providing meals for ageing parents and more.

In male-dominated workplaces it's assumed that care will be provided by people's partners, male or female, but traditionally female. The entrepreneurs who left corporate life because of this presumption have created more flexible working environments. This has been made possible by technology and will increasingly be the norm in the future. To manage this, more time needs to be spent in 'air traffic control' mode, to ensure that the work is covered and that everyone knows who's where and who's doing what. That requires good communication and mutual trust between owners and employees. John Smythe notes that, with his company's (SmytheDorwardLambert) workforce of 130 people split between Boston and London, trust was self-policed by everyone rather than being top down. It's not a 'dosser's charter' and, if trusted, people will rise to it – though from time to time a 'mickey taker' will have to be heaved overboard.

Anti-social fixtures in the early mornings, evenings and weekends

Also widely reported by our interviewees was the expected need to work anti-social hours that is so prevalent in many male environments. As we saw earlier in the chapter, a friend of one of our interviewees who was employed by one of the big four accountants applied for family-friendly employment status. But there were still phone calls and meetings in the early mornings and evenings so she resigned very soon after taking up the post.

Much of the talk about flexibility appears to be worthless rhetoric. We seem to be still in the 'band-aid phase' of revolutionising working cultures to meet the needs of all genders. In reality, it's probably less about banning work in anti-social hours and more about good 'air traffic' organisational skills, with great care taken to listen to and resolve resourcing black spots. That said, no one should work weekends except in exceptional circumstances or unless they choose to for convenience. This is especially true of vacuous team-building activities in some 'gilded cage resort' miles from home. If it can't be done during the working week, don't do it, it can't be that crucial.

Taking holiday is not optional

Owners and partners should ensure that colleagues take all of their leave. They should be careful not to allow a culture of presenteeism to become the norm by being a great role model themselves. They should take their holidays and not stay late into the evenings. A rested colleague will make a better, more even-tempered team member.

Equitable pay and benefits

Perhaps the greatest gender imbalance still lies in pay and benefits, in spite of it being illegal to pay people differently based on their gender. The business model needs to work if there is equality. If it only works if half the employees are paid less, then the business model is likely to be unsustainable as word spreads. Unequal pay is paying for something else – such as subsidised rates for clients or additional profits for investors and owners. It's within shouting distance of modern-day slave labour. Enough. Entrepreneurs should be saying 'If my idea depends on inequality, which is essentially deception, then it can't fly for long'.

INTANGIBLES

Intangible ingredients are just as crucial and in their absence may be more significant than the tangible ingredients. They include the following.

Setting the right tone

Values are experienced through day-to-day attitudes, language, tone of voice and patterns of behaviour. To set the right tone, entrepreneurs should think through which values they want their company to have and embed them day to day by leading by example. It can also be helpful to outline the values and behaviours they don't want to see as well as those they do. Entrepreneurs shouldn't merge these qualities into the corporate wallpaper that is 'corporate values'. Corporate values are for bigger companies who want to hold onto what originally made them successful – helping a maturing organisation to stay in touch with its five-year-old self. Rather than write corporate values down in stone, smaller companies should 'walk the talk' in practice.

Additionally, it's important for entrepreneurs to ensure that these values are being actioned. One of the best ways to do this is to carry a notebook and jot down oft-repeated language, the tone it is delivered in and patterns of repeated behaviour, rather as a tourist might when making sense of a new experience. If everyone does it for a day or so and then compares notes, a common picture will emerge and any necessary course correction can be identified and taken.

Collegiality, collaboration and courtesy

Words like collegiality, collaboration and courtesy abound in our interviews. Many of our interviewees wanted to create a culture where collegial, courteous and collaborative interactions are the day-to-day norm. These types of behaviours and attitudes need to start at the top and then filter down through the organisation – much as primitive tribes passed down beliefs, mores, manners and identity in song and dance. They should be made visible in day-to-day processes and interactions and bad behaviour pointed out and corrected to ensure it doesn't become the norm.

Creating 'our community'

It's important to create a sense of family and community. To achieve this, entrepreneurs should embed occasions and rituals that create a unique company experience. These could be Friday afternoon drinks on the terrace, end-of-project celebration dinners, internal best client awards, a team trip on Eurostar to Disneyland Paris or insightful external speakers over breakfast, to name a few. Over time, the events that people look forward to most should be retained and the 'if we have to' events dropped, with leaders changing the tune when ennui sets in.

We end Chapter Eleven with a plea to all companies, especially large corporates kidding themselves with skin-deep gender-friendly policies, to stop losing top talent by making their working environment attractive for all genders and, in turn, creating a higher performing working culture.

In our final chapter the two co-authors conclude the book with reflections on the learnings and insights that most resonated with them.

NOTES

1 *Lean In* by Sheryl Sandberg, Penguin Random House LLC, 2015 (page 6).

2 BBC article, 'Queen Bees: Do Women Hinder the Progress of Other Women', Reality Check Team, 4 January 2018, www.bbc.co.uk/news/uk-41165076.

3 BBC article, 'Queen Bees: Do women Hinder the Progress of Other Women', Reality Check Team, 4 January 2018, www.bbc.co.uk/news/uk-41165076; 'Why Women (Sometimes) Don't Help Each Other', Marianne Cooper, *The Atlantic*, 23 June 2016, www.theatlantic.com/business/archive/2016/06/queen-bee/488144/.

4 'Why Women (Sometimes) Don't Help Each Other', Marianne Cooper, *The Atlantic*, 23 June 2016, www.theatlantic.com/business/archive/2016/06/queen-bee/488144/.

5 'Why Women (Sometimes) Don't Help Each Other', Marianne Cooper, *The Atlantic*, 23 June 2016, www.theatlantic.com/business/archive/2016/06/queen-bee/488144.

6 www.forbes.com/sites/carolinecastrillon/2019/03/10/why-women-need-to-network-differently-than-men-to-get-ahead/#6a6bb792b0a1.

CHAPTER TWELVE
'Yes, she can'

Authors' reflections

We've written this book to encourage every woman who has dreamt of being an entrepreneur but hasn't yet taken the leap to take the first steps towards realising their dreams – as well as every woman who has not yet thought about running their own business to consider it. In the words of Ruth Davidson: 'Yes, she can'.[1]

Additionally, we want to encourage the Government and the corporate world, particularly investors, to recognise and embrace the huge value that female entrepreneurs bring to our society and economy.

Previous chapters largely feature the opinions of our fifty-two interviewees. In Chapter Twelve the authors leave you with their analysis and reflections on the fifty-two interviews, as well as an entrepreneurs' 'readiness checklist' to help budding entrepreneurs take the first steps as well as to scale up to the next stage. Carpe diem.

Let's start with some wisdom and insights to inspire budding entrepreneurs who are keen to start their own business but who have not yet taken the leap.

- ***You can start your business at any age***. *Being an entrepreneur is not just the preserve of thrusting youth with a gilded technology breakthrough. In our interviews we met entrepreneurs who started their businesses before the age of ten and into their sixties – some with the aim of being a sole trader and others making it into big business. The younger ones felt that they had less to lose and more time to make and learn from their mistakes. The older ones used their previous life experiences to help them hone their business idea and build their confidence. No one is too young or old to take the leap.*
- ***You can start your business at any lifestage***. *For some, the appetite to be an entrepreneur emerges early on in life when a childhood passion or hobby becomes a business. For others, it comes after working in the corporate world for some years, driven by a desire to create a more balanced and enjoyable life, such as combining a career with a family or working in a more collaborative, female-friendly workplace. For some, it's born out of necessity such as needing to make money or rebuild a life after facing difficulties. And for others it originates later in life when*

turning a hobby, passion or product or service that solves their own life issues into a business. If you're not an entrepreneur today, the passion and drive to be one may well come in the future.

- **Not knowing your proposition isn't a hindrance to success.** *The main predictor of entrepreneurial success is the desire to be an entrepreneur, even if you don't know your proposition. Some budding entrepreneurs honed their skills within another company before breaking off to do something similar for themselves. Others looked back over their life's journey to find an idea that they were passionate about and could turn into a commercial entity. Others didn't have a clear business idea and so looked externally for one, for example by disrupting a traditional market or researching overseas markets for new ideas or surrounding themselves with interesting people who inspired them.*

- **Validate whether the world needs your idea.** *When deciding whether to launch an idea, many cited the litmus test of 'Would you buy or subscribe to this product or service if it was offered to you by someone else? Or would someone you know buy or subscribe to it?'. If not, then perhaps think again.*

- **Balance the 'perfection versus getting on with it' dilemma.** *Many of our entrepreneurs faced the dilemma between getting their idea up and running and hopefully making money versus perfecting their product or service before launch. Most advised to launch as quickly as possible but to recognise that constant improvements would most probably be needed and thus the importance of seeking feedback early on.*

- **Enjoy the journey.** *Not all business launches succeed in the way that founders might have initially hoped. In fact, some reports suggest that just 7% of start-ups result in a sale. Consequently, our entrepreneurs advise people to start a business in something that they're passionate about so that they can 'enjoy the journey'. In their view: 'If you're doing it solely for money, then it's probably not going to work'.*

Once you've discovered and honed your winning idea, you need to set your business up for success. Below are some nuggets of advice on what to think through at this stage.

- **To partner or not to partner.** *When deciding whether to start a business with partners or to go it alone, we advise people to know their control needs. Some of our interviewees wanted partners as they needed a broad set of skills at the top or wanted to share the risk and responsibility of the new venture. Others wanted almost absolute control and opted for employees rather than fellow partners who would want to influence the direction. It's far better to 'know yourself' upfront and make decisions with this self-knowledge, rather than face high colleague turnover. If you are having trouble figuring out your control needs then ask family, past business associates, friends or even a counsellor.*

- **Surround yourself with the right people.** *When building the right day-to-day team, people can be tempted to recruit in their own likeness. Conversely, we encourage people to 'know yourself' – both your strengths that you can play to and your weaknesses or gaps that others need to fill. Incorporate your strengths into your day-to-day entrepreneurial role and recruit people around you who can fill your gaps. Assessment tools like Myers Briggs, Hogan, Gallup StrengthsFinder, 16 Personality Factor, the Obsessive Compulsive Inventory (OCI), SHL's OPQ and many more may help you avoid recruiting in your own likeness.*

- **Seek investment or self-fund.** *When it comes to outside investment, our female entrepreneurs encourage people to self-fund if they can so that they reap all of the benefits of their hard work. But if they need outside money, they advise bringing in 'smart money' from people with relevant experience and contacts. They should select their investors wisely, bringing in people who have a shared vision and values and who will be supportive every step of the way. And they should always retain a majority share. Ask close contacts and female angel investors for recommendations.*

- **To plan or not to plan.** *Start-ups that need the investment of other people's money need a plan showing how the money will be used and when a return might be expected – with progress reviewed at regular intervals. In contrast, 'resource-lean' start-ups often survive at the beginning by putting one foot in front of the other without much of a plan. The choice of whether to plan or not seems to primarily mirror personality. Some like to plan, to squeeze as much into their day as* *possible or to give them the confidence to take the next leap. And others believe that 'planning' should paint a future business direction that doesn't over-influence daily decision-making. There seems to be no right way, just the one that best suits your preferred working style.*

- **The power of behaving courteously**. *Being courteous and kind was widely seen as essential to good business. Our entrepreneurs advise others to treat everyone in the same manner that they would want to be treated themselves – and to support others at every stage. In their view: 'If you invest in that support, the rewards are incredible'.*

There comes a time where the start-up phase is over and you need to decide if you have the desire and capabilities to scale up. We have these words of advice.

- ***Adapt your leadership style as the company grows***. *To successfully scale up, entrepreneurs need to transcend from being the main driver of the business and often, in turn, the main bottleneck. Instead they need to put in place the team and structure needed to scale up, as well as to keep the team motivated and aligned around a clear vision, strategy, goals and plan. As Victoria Mellor wisely said: 'Get out of the way of your business and let your management team take up the reins'.*
- ***Adapt the team structure to enable the business to scale***. *As the business grows, your team structure may need to change. For example, you and your partner may have increasingly different visions and need to go your different ways. Or you may need to build a strong management team around you to set up the processes and structure needed to scale up. Or you may need to let someone who doesn't fit, go. It can be easy to hang on to people for too long because you're dealing with people's livelihoods, which is emotional. Instead, don't be afraid to make difficult people decisions quickly, professionally and as kindly as you can. If it's not working, then it's unlikely to improve.*
- ***Lift yourself off the shop floor to look forward to the future***. *If you have identified a great commercial opportunity, it is imperative to keep refreshing your business idea once launched to keep it ahead of the competition. To achieve this, entrepreneurs need to strike the right balance between being 'hands on' on the shop floor and 'rising above the dance floor of the daily*

grind to think in the present and to the future'. Our interviewees talked of 'inking in time away from the office', where they can step back to see the bigger picture and be inspired. They go to external conferences or on long walks, have regular blue-sky offsites facilitated by someone outside of the business so that all of the top team can participate, look at what the brands they admire are doing and how to emulate them within their business and mystery shop competitors. These can all help to spark new ideas on where to take the business going forward.

- **Know your destination**. *Some of our entrepreneurs planned their desired destination from the outset. Deciding whether to sell or float their business helped them to frame some of the operational decisions they made along the way. For co-author John Smythe, a sale was always the target for the change management consultancy he co-founded with Colette Dorward and Jerome Reback. Consequently, key decisions like new hires, office locations, target clients, whether to create an advisory board and more were considered with a sale in mind. Our advice is to think through what your destination might be and, if you plan to sell, then scale the company with this in mind.*

We had a number of reflections about how to stay sane along the journey. These include:

- **Separate yourself from the business**. *While some fully identified with their businesses, others separated themselves and their identities from their enterprise in order to make better commercial decisions. They deliberately walked away and left business at the door each day to focus on other things and live a more balanced, well-rounded life. Again, this is a personal choice – there's no right way, just your way. Our advice is to make a conscious rather than an accidental choice.*
- **The value of a supportive partner**. *A constant theme in our interviews was the value of a supportive home partner. They can act as a foil, critic and cheerleader, challenging you to think differently and nudging you to make things happen. They can also help to shoulder the responsibilities of family care. Both Warren Buffett and Sheryl Sandberg agree that the most important career choice you'll ever make is whether you will have*

a life partner and, if so, who that person is. We encourage single female entrepreneurs to choose wisely. [2]

- **The value of a supportive network**. *Some people don't have a home partner or one that plays a supportive role. And so many of our entrepreneurs talked about the importance of having a supportive network of people who believe in you. People who you can bounce things off or who will pick you up and encourage you when you need support. They can be family. Parents are a great source of candour – they know you better than most and will say the unsayable – as are wider family like siblings. They can also be friends, teammates or even pets. Co-author John had dogs that took him for a walk after a busy day for a reflective drink in a local pub.*

- **Handling guilt over children**. *Women tend to be the primary carer of children, making all kinds of sacrifices to look after both their family and business. Our pages are littered with examples of women managing this divide with grace, humility, hidden energy reserves and the ability to deflect exhaustion. Many experienced guilt at being absent from their young children. Our advice is to not be too hard on yourself and that it will get easier as the children age into teenagers and understand the great things you've achieved. Also remember that you are not alone – there are lots of people in the same boat. And there are sites out there like Elizabeth Cowper's WOMO and Justine Roberts' Mumsnet that can give you much needed advice and support.*

- **Keeping the plates spinning**. *Whether true or false, it has long been said that women are experts at juggling multiple roles. That hypothesis tested positive in our fifty-two interviews – with many of our female entrepreneurs running a start-up, raising a family and, in some cases, managing pro bono work or day jobs as well. Their secret is to create a schedule and support structure that works for them and to not be afraid to plan, prioritise and ruthlessly focus on what matters most. Ours is qualitative validation that women can successfully keep many plates spinning at a sobering rate – although we are reasonably sure that many men will also resonate with these traits.*

- **Be proud of what you've achieved**. *Some of our interviewees expressed discomfort at being labelled 'an entrepreneur'. And most were reticent to* *talk about their success. We concluded from our conversations that this is perhaps due to modesty, a sense that 'anyone could do what I've done', as quite a few inferred. Our culture disincentivises women from expressing confidence and pride in themselves. Reshma Saujani's book Brave Not Perfect talks about how women, unlike men, are brought up to be 'perfect rather than brave'. She exhorts women to fear less, fail more and live bolder. This is slowly changing and we encourage female entrepreneurs to be a part of that change by being proud of taking the entrepreneurial leap and celebrating their achievements to date.*

Many of our entrepreneurs talked about the challenges they faced when building a business. Many have overcome significant issues to get to where they have got to. We name a few of those challenges here:

- ***Overcoming a lack of confidence***. *Some of our entrepreneurs disclosed suffering from a lack of confidence or even the imposter syndrome when they started out. Female entrepreneurs, whilst catching up fast, are still a minority in the business world, which is still mostly shaped and financed by men. There are far fewer female role models and support networks for female entrepreneurs. And women are largely doing business with men. Our advice is to not expect to be good at everything. Instead step back, focus on what really matters for the business, play to your strengths and surround yourself with people who can cover your weaknesses. You don't need to be an expert in areas where you are weak. Instead, you need to ask your team pertinent questions to ensure that they stay on track.*
- ***Overcoming fear of failure***. *Similarly, some of our entrepreneurs suffered from a fear of failure. Those who had overcome it talked about failure as an essential part of the journey and an inevitable driver of their growth curve. It isn't necessarily bad or something to be scared of. Moreover, it is something to embrace and learn from, recognising that it will most probably lead to the next growth spurt. They advised others to identify and accept the worst thing that could happen and, when failing, to not be overly hard on themselves, but, instead, to pick themselves up, learn from their mistakes and not repeat them a second time. As Sherry Roberts*

said: 'I don't really know what failure is. I look at it as experience, deepening your soul, making you smarter and wiser'.

- **Losing your way by emulating the bling of big business**. *Every start-up that wants to be the next big thing must put in place the minimum necessary systems and processes to grow, rather than continue to 'make it up as they go along'. However, the danger expressed by some was moving away from the entrepreneurial mentality that had served them well in the early days. Instead they had been seduced into adopting more expensive, big business practices that used up cash fast and resulted in them becoming unprofitable. As you scale, it's important to stay true to who you are and what you know by maintaining your vision as well as remaining lean, flexible and cost-efficient. Beware of anything that is style over substance, such as corner offices, big marketing budgets and unproductive perks. Avoid anything that makes it difficult to stay agile and flexible, such as long leases and overly large workforces. Instead, invest in the things that will make a difference to the day-to-day client and employee experience such as technology, people and culture. Rewarding people for going the extra mile with a cocktail at the end of the week is worth its weight in gold. As Melina Jacovou wisely said: 'Never believe your own hype'.*

- **When the going gets tough, the tough get going**. *Many of our successful entrepreneurs talked about how, at times, building a business is tough, challenging and all-consuming. They advise that if you want it enough, then be prepared to make sacrifices. For some, this is less time spent with family and friends. For others, the sacrifice is financial. Our interviewees agree that these sacrifices are worth it. They have much more control over their lives, as well as the satisfaction of growing their own business and seeing their idea come to fruition. They also advise to keep going through any tricky phase. As Winston Churchill famously said: 'If you are walking through hell, keep walking'.*

We continue with some reflections that society should be mindful of.

- **A policy opportunity for U.K. government**. *When it comes to female-led start-ups, the U.K. continues to lag behind the U.S., Canada, Australia and some European countries. There is an extraordinary* *opportunity for the largely male-dominated political parties to make the U.K. a leading global power in helping female entrepreneurs to succeed. We exhort our leaders to not put off until tomorrow something great that they can do today.*

- **The scandalous lack of funding for female start-ups**. *The comparative numbers between male- and female-led start-ups are stark. Ninety-one per cent of venture capital money continues to fund businesses founded solely by men, with only 1% of venture capital money invested in businesses founded solely by women. The reason is that most investors are men. Research shows that male investors treat female entrepreneurs more sceptically when pitching and prefer to invest in more male-oriented business ideas that resonate with them. Being a woman pitching for money in those arenas takes courage and patience. Many successful and more female-oriented ideas are being left to fall by the wayside. Wake up boys! Research suggests that female start-ups are more profitable than their male-led counterparts, so it's time to invest in them.*

- **Supporting the changing nature of the U.K. workforce**. *A huge theme in our interviews was the use of part- or full-time associates to minimise the risk and overhead of employing people. Businesses like Mélanie Chevalier's Creative Culture can muster a global army in moments using technology and a mutually agreeable arrangement that rewards both parties. Governments should seize the opportunity to mobilise the associate workforce and encourage enterprises to enter into productive partnerships with them – through tax breaks, education, recognition, social awards and the like. Long live the associate!*

- **Corporates are missing out on a large talent pool**. *Many of our female interviewees began their working lives as employees in corporates but left due to the male-dominated work culture. On the one hand, the glass ceiling and lack of senior female role models. On the other, the inflexible working arrangements when needing to care for family. The corporate working environment continues to be male-dominated. It asks people to work early in the morning or late into the evening, or five days a week, or even at the weekend. And senior female role models continue to be few and far between. Unless the corporate world addresses the male cultural bias that* *makes it difficult for women to see themselves as having a place at the top table, or enables women to enjoy a full-on career whilst having children, they will continue to lose out on one of the country's largest talent pools.*

- **Taking women in business seriously**. *Women are still not taken as seriously as men in business. Our interviewees are regularly asked about their age, marital status and family, and how they manage to juggle both children and career, over and above their entrepreneurial venture and business success. Yet the same questions are rarely if ever asked of men. As Tori Gerbig, a millennial mum and a successful entrepreneur, says:*

  'How different would this conversation be if we stopped quietly judging our ambitious young women and successful female business leaders, but instead started asking them what they love about work? What gets you excited about work each day? Which of your professional accomplishments most shifted the trajectory of your career? Why do you do what you do? Perhaps before we can reach the point where we embrace our ambitious working mothers, we need to better understand their points of view.' [3]

- **Men need to help women**. *There's much in the press about how women still tend to take on the lion's share of the domestic housework. A recent study showed that, on average, full-time working women spend between ten to nineteen hours on housework weekly, whereas their partners average fewer than five hours per week. And fewer than seven per cent of U.K. couples share housework equally. As Professor Gillian Robinson who conducted a similar survey says: 'It is difficult to see how women will ever have the same opportunities in the labour market if equality at home is not achieved'. We implore men to step up and shoulder more of the household chores and for society to make gender equality at home the only acceptable norm.* [4]

- **Women need to help other women**. *Many of our female entrepreneurs talked about successful men encouraging them in their careers rather than successful women. And, in some cases, successful women not helping other women to succeed. 'Queen Bee' women think that their gender should be irrelevant at work but, when discriminated against, realise that* *others see them first and foremost as women. They get concerned that as women their career path may be stunted, so they distance themselves from other women, for example, by saying: 'I'm not like other women, I've always prioritised my career'. If we want to make the corporate environment more gender equal, it's important that successful women support other women. As Madeleine Albright said: 'There is a special place in hell for women who don't help each other!'.*

- **Women need to help themselves, leaning in AND leaning out.** *The dilemma between 'leaning in as women to emulate men' or 'leaning out and being true to the female gender' is often presented as a binary choice. However, many interviewees believe that both need to happen, at least until the playing field is levelled. If society wants to leverage the huge female talent pool, it needs to 'lean out' by challenging the traditional male-oriented ways of working. Corporations need to make work for all women, including young mothers, a tenable choice, as well as make the ability to rise to the top a credible and aspirational option. That said, women also need to help drive the change by 'leaning in' – driving their own success by taking responsibility for their careers, decisions and actions.*

WE END WITH OUR ENTREPRENEURS' READINESS CHECKLIST

If you're interested in becoming an entrepreneur, or are already on the journey, then we suggest you review our entrepreneurs' readiness checklist. If you are thinking about becoming an entrepreneur then we suggest you ask yourself:

- Are you by nature an entrepreneur, intrapreneur, freelancer or intern?
- Do you really want to be an entrepreneur? Are you willing to ride through the inevitable tough times and the sacrifices?
- Do you have a winning idea or know someone who has that you can team up with?

- Is your winning idea something that you're passionate about?
- Have you validated your idea with your target market?
- Is the idea a first footer or an improvement on existing ideas? Can you legally protect it and, if so, have you protected it? If not, you must.
- Have you got your nearest and dearest on board?
- Are you ready to take the entrepreneurial leap and launch your idea? If not, what's holding you back and how can you resolve this?

If you are setting up your business:

- Do you need a partner(s)? If so, will your control needs enable or disable them?
- Do you need a day-to-day team? If so, what are your strengths that you can play to? And what are your weaknesses that others can help with?
- Do you need other people's money? If so, can you find 'smart money'? Do your potential investors have a shared vision and values for your business?
- Do you have a plan that you can work to? If so, will it persuade potential partners and investors to come on board?

If you are scaling up your business:

- Have you adapted your leadership style to lead the scale up?
- Have you adapted the team structure to enable the business to scale?
- Do you have an inspiring business vision?
- Are you staying ahead of your competitors?
- Are you remaining lean, flexible and cost-efficient, rather than being seduced into behaving like a corporate?
- Do you know your desired destination? If so, are you scaling up the business with this in mind?

If you are running your business day to day:

- Can you separate yourself from the business to make the right commercial decisions?
- Do you have a supportive home partner? If so, are they supporting you in the ways you need?

- Do you have a supportive network? If so, are they supporting you in the ways you need?
- Are you experiencing guilt at being absent from your children? If so, are you being too hard on yourself?
- Are you keeping all of the plates spinning? If not, are you focussing on what really matters most?
- Are you proud of what you've achieved? If so, are you celebrating those achievements?

We also ask society and Government to:

- Build the U.K. into a leading global power in helping entrepreneurs, including female entrepreneurs, to get going and succeed.
- Encourage funding of female start-ups.
- Spearhead the rise of part- and full-time working associates.
- Encourage corporates to make workplaces female-friendly by getting rid of glass ceilings and promoting more flexible working arrangements.
- Embrace our ambitious working mothers by allowing them to celebrate their success and encouraging more gender equality in the home.
- Encourage successful women to inspire and support other women.
- 'Lean out' by challenging the traditional male-oriented ways of working.

'Yes, she can'. We finish on the commonly expressed view that being a woman entrepreneur is not the preserve of Wonder Woman. It's for **every woman** who wants to make it happen. We encourage anyone who wants to make the entrepreneurial leap, and wants it enough, to do it, just as our female entrepreneurs did. They have succeeded, so why shouldn't you? It matters not whether you want to build an empire spanning the globe or simply turn your hobby into a money-making venture from your spare room. What matters is reflecting on your insight, experiences, strengths and circumstances and turning them into a viable proposition. You don't have to leap over the edge and give up the day job at the beginning. You can sacrifice downtime to work on it until you have enough momentum to make the risk bearable. The only regret you may have is having left it so long. Just do it. **Yes, she will.**

Thank you for 'coming into the club with us'. It has been a pleasure and a privilege to write this book – and a final thank you to our fifty-two interviewees.

Good luck and enjoy the journey!

NOTES

1 *Yes, She Can* by Ruth Davidson, published in 2018 by Hodder & Stoughton.

2 'Warren Buffet and Sheryl Sandberg Agree on the Most Important Decision You Will Ever Make' by Kathleen Elkins, 7 February 2017, CNBC News, www.cnbc.com/2017/02/07/warren-buffett-and-sheryl-sandberg-agree-on-most-important-decision.html.

3 'I'm a Millennial Mom and a Successful Entrepreneur. Stop Asking Me How I Manage It All' by Tori Gerbig, Entrepreneur.com, 5 July 2018, www.entrepreneur.com/article/315698.

4 'Women Still Shoulder the Bulk of Household Chores', *Starts At 60*, 27 July 2019, https://startsat60.com/discover/news/women-housework-household-chores-work-employment-and-society-study-university-college-london; 'Working Women Still Do Housework' by Robin Yapp, *Daily Mail*, July 2019 www.dailymail.co.uk/news/article-206381/Working-women-housework.html.

Interviewee biographies

SARAH ALI CHOUDHURY – EASY CURRY

Sarah is a multi-award-winning Indian food expert and columnist whose recipes and articles have featured in print and online publications locally, nationally and internationally, including *Forbes*, the *Sun*, the *Telegraph*, *iNews*, the *Guardian* and various other publications. Her work has been highlighted by *Forbes* who recognise her as 'The Curry Queen' and as a leader for Asian women in catering.

Sarah is also an inspirational and motivational public speaker and is listed in the F: Entrepreneur #ialso100 List for being in the top 100 female entrepreneurs in the U.K.

Company overview. Through Easy Curry, Sarah takes great delight in teaching people simple meals and recipes from all over India via cookery classes and demonstrations, YouTube videos and recipe columns. Sarah loves to dispel the myth that all curries need numerous complex spices – and loves to tackle the intimidation that can so easily lead people to pick a jar of curry sauce off a shelf rather than cook from scratch.

KATE ANDREWS – LOCO2

Kate is an advocate for low-carbon travel. She has circumnavigated the world without planes, taking a cargo ship across the Atlantic, with 6,000 tonnes of fruit and forty Russian sailors, and a yacht across the Pacific. She's travelled by tuk-tuk in Thailand, by yak across the Gobi Desert and by train everywhere from Singapore to London. Having travelled around the world without flying, Kate returned to London to establish Loco2, an online booking service for train travel in the U.K. and Europe.

Company overview. Loco2 was launched in 2012 by a team of committed train travellers, led by brother and sister Jamie and Kate Andrews. It sells tickets, without booking fees, through its website and smartphone apps. Loco2 – which is shorthand for 'Low CO_2' – set out to simplify the online rail booking process, helping travellers to ditch the plane for a lower-carbon journey by train. In 2017, Loco2 was acquired by Voyages-sncf.com, a subsidiary of SNCF, and is now part of the wider Oui-SNCF group.

ALEX BEER – FEED THE SOUL VEGAN CAFÉ

Alex grew up in Dorchester, she has two older sisters and a younger brother and she found out at five that she was deaf. In her teenage years she developed anxiety which led to an eating disorder. As a vegetarian she enjoyed making food and did a two-year cooking apprenticeship. She suffered from stomach problems and so went to a nutritionist who advised her to try a vegan diet. The effect on her health was immediate and she took to it straight away.

Company overview. Nestled in the beautiful Cerne Valley, Feed the Soul is a speciality vegan café and shop that serves beautiful, fresh, vibrant food. All the food in the café and shop is organic, gluten free and home-made. The raw vegan meals are made from seasonal organic produce. The Feed The Soul holistic shop sells organic seasonal produce and local lifestyle products.

DI BURTON – CICADA COMMUNICATIONS LIMITED

Di is originally from South Africa, with a background in film and TV production. In the early 1990s Di studied for a PGCE and attended Harvard Business School. Di has spent the past thirty years working in public relations and communication. She operates at board level across government, private and voluntary sectors. Her experience includes transforming organisations through cultural change and working with leaders on communication techniques. She is a Fellow of the CIPR and of the CIPD. In April 2015 she sold Cicada and launched Di Burton Limited.

Company overview. Di started Cicada thirty years ago and grew it into a full-service communications agency operating regionally, nationally and internationally. The company managed all aspects of communications for companies, whether in the service, manufacturing, public or not-for-profit sectors. Di's team took over the business which continues to operate from its Harrogate base.

Di Burton Limited launched in 2015 and Di operates within a network of trusted advisors and partners, bringing in expertise when needed. Her clients now include Phillips 66, The European Union Agency for Cyber Security and the Association of Commonwealth Universities.

AURÉE DE CARBON – CARRHURE

A urée is fluent in both French and English. She began her career as a sales manager for a number of French media companies and then moved to the banking sector working as a private advisor. She holds an undergraduate degree in Arts and Communication from Université Paris Nanterre. She is certified in DISC Model and is also a professional coach and NLP technician.

Company overview. CARRHURE was established in March 2012. With consulting recruitment as its core business, CARRHURE helps companies to hire the best of the best. It specialises in identifying, gauging and attracting leaders in the non-profit and non-government organisation (NGO) sectors. It aims to help organisations create concrete, productive and long-lasting bonds with their workforce.

HELEN CATON – THE FORTON GROUP

H elen is a qualified leadership and team coach working hands-on with international organisations. Her clients include the U.N., the U.K. National Health Service (NHS), BT and Network Rail. She is a published author and has a Master's Level degree and a Diploma in Marketing. She is currently co-writing a book on transformational leadership.

Company overview. Founded in 1992, the Forton Group operates around the world, specialising in leadership development through consulting, research, coaching and training. Doubly accredited by the International Coach Federation (ICF) and the Chartered Management Institute (CMI), it works with partners who deliver their programmes and with qualified associates located around the world, all committed to professional excellence in leadership.

MÉLANIE CHEVALIER – CREATIVE CULTURE

Mélanie has over fifteen years of industry experience in cross-cultural communications. She has lived around the world, including in countries such as Taiwan, Brazil, Cameroon, France, Spain and the U.K. She truly understands the importance of culture and local norms in global campaigns.

Company overview. Creative Culture is a cross-cultural consultancy that specialises in international marketing. It makes a client's global vision a reality in local markets by providing local market intelligence, cross-cultural audits and adaptation from global into local content including transcreation. Its main objective is to help brands and agencies to get their cross-market messages right. Cultures, languages and strategies are the three pillars of the business.

BRIDGET CONNELL – THINKING PARTNERSHIPS

Bridget is an experienced and qualified business coach with over twenty-five years of commercial experience in senior executive roles. She is a board adviser, mentor and angel investor concentrating on technology-based start-ups.

Company overview. Thinking Partnerships is a specialist coaching consultancy. Clients include ambitious start-ups looking to raise external investment and senior executives responsible for leading change in global organisations.

ELIZABETH COWPER – WOMO NETWORK

Elizabeth is a mother of three children (two daughters and a son). She has worked for over twenty years in HR, including roles at Network Rail, Fenn Wright Manson, Planet Organic, LVMH and Harvey Nichols. She is currently Vice President of HR Europe and Global Wellness Lead for a multi-brand fashion house in the U.S. Additionally, she is CEO of her online support business for other working mothers, WoMo. She was inspired to create this after having children of her own and returning to a full-time career in HR, where she saw the process of maternity leave and time away from the office managed both brilliantly and poorly.

Company overview. WoMo is an affectionate term for the modern Working Mother. The WoMo Network is transforming the working world for the working mother. It guides a woman through the journey of being pregnant, going on maternity leave and returning to work. It's a vehicle that keeps the woman in touch and connected to her employer. As we go to print, Elizabeth is in the latter stages of launching a SaaS platform to support WoMos through this life-changing transition. It will advise individuals on how to better manage the process themselves, as well as companies and HR leaders on how to help the woman through the process in a really positive way that benefits the company and the employee.

The WoMo Network is on a mission to support, empower and inspire more mothers to become WoMos, helping them to pursue their career and balance this with being an awesome mum.

HELEN DUNNE – HARDY MEDIA

An economics graduate, Helen began a career in financial journalism in 1988. She has worked for *International Financing Review*, the *Daily Telegraph* and the *Mail on Sunday*, while contributing to other publications. Helen went freelance in 2005 and joined *CorpComms Magazine* as a contributor shortly after its launch. She led a management buy-out in 2008. Issue 30 was the first published under her ownership.

Helen has written three novels, published by Orion, including *Trixie Trader* which was based on a popular weekly column in the *Telegraph*.

Company overview. Launched in 2005 as a bi-monthly publication by Cross Border Group, *CorpComms Magazine* was the subject of a management buyout by Helen, its long-standing freelance editor, in July 2008. The magazine is now published by her business Hardy Media.

CorpComms Magazine is the only monthly magazine targeted at the in-house communicator. Written in a lively and engaging manner, the 48-page publication offers advice and informative articles on a range of topical subjects, such as corporate reputation, sustainability, social media and the evolving role of the in-house corporate communicator.

LIANN EDEN – EDEN MCCALLUM

Liann was raised in upstate New York but most of her career has been in Europe. Before founding Eden McCallum in 2000 with Dena McCallum, she was a consultant in McKinsey's London office, worked for Unilever in European brand management and was in business-to-business marketing for OSRAM, the Siemens lighting business, based in Munich. Liann holds an MBA from INSEAD and BA from Smith College.

Company overview. Eden McCallum is redefining management consulting. From their offices in London, Amsterdam and Zurich they support clients to resolve their most pressing issues of strategy, operations and organisation. Working with a group of independent consultants of the highest calibre, they have pioneered an approach that delivers tangible impact, client ownership and great value.

VERITY DREW FIRTH – LIMES HOUSE FILMS

V erity is a young actress and filmmaker with a wide range of professional credits to her name. Verity was born in London and showed an interest and aptitude for performing arts at an early age. Her father Andrew Firth is a portrait and reportage photographer, her uncle Richard MacPhail (of Genesis fame) is a musician and business owner and her aunt Maggie Cole is the renowned classical harpsichord pianist. She was signed by an agent who saw her at drama and singing classes when she was six.

As well as working across pantomime, musical theatre, dance and modelling, Verity's acting experience, interest in film and talent for photography led her to also start making movies at the age of eleven.

She is an animal lover who is adored by her two pet Tonkinese cats and she enjoys walking the two family dogs when she can. At the time of publication Verity had recently turned thirteen.

Company overview. Verity's stage credits include the powerful adaptation of *1984* (Robert Icke, Duncan MacMillan), appearing as The Child, and the opera *Madam Butterfly* appearing to great acclaim as Sorrow (Directed by Paul Higgins). TV, radio and film roles include Greg Davies's *Man Down* as Dan's niece Lucy (Channel 4 TV), the BBC's *The Cazalet Chronicles* in the role of Juliet (Radio 4 adaptation), the short film *Lacrimosa* (Steven Bakewell) and the music video *Rhythm Inside* for Loic Nottet as the Rebel Child (Belgium Eurovision).

Verity recently made her first solo film, which she wrote, cast, directed, produced, filmed and edited, and is now working on her next ones. Verity has gained experience working with film production companies as well as with The London Film School and she participated in RADA's film development workshops.

TAMARA GILLAN – CHERRY LONDON

Tamara is the Founder of The WealthiHer Network and CEO of Cherry London, after heading up e-marketing at Orange and setting up an integrated agency. Today Cherry London is one of Europe's fastest-growing marketing agencies specialising in brand partnerships.

Company overview. Cherry London is a brand relationship building company. It was founded in 2009, creating a strategy for VISA to unite the world-leading brands sponsoring the London 2012 Olympics. Working globally, Cherry London builds meaningful relationships through the power of partnership and collaboration to create value. Cherry London uses data and insight, supercharges loyalty and creates profitability results through strategic partnership marketing, customer loyalty and engagement programmes and brand creation.

GEMMA GREAVES – CABAL

Throughout her career, Gemma has believed in and championed three things close to her heart: being brave, the power of connections and the belief that together we can make a difference. Gemma is the Chief Executive of the Marketing Society and, over the past decade, has spearheaded the Society's international expansion, transforming it into the leading global community for marketing leaders.

An entrepreneur at heart, Gemma also founded Cabal in 2013, a private members club for extraordinary people. She is currently developing two other side projects – Nurture and Seers – both rooted in her belief that meaningful connections lead to better business. In 2016 Gemma became the first female president of the Solus Club in its ninety-year history. She is also a regular speaker at events, on podcasts and a writer of industry articles. Gemma lives in Twickenham with her husband Andy and Joshie, their son.

Company overview. Gemma founded Cabal in 2013 – a handpicked private members club of extraordinary people. Today it has grown into a tight-knit community boasting a membership of creative leaders, innovators, authors and storytellers to name a few. At the core of Cabal is the belief that if you bring good people together, good stuff happens – with the aim of creating unforgettable experiences, meaningful connections and strong relationships that together inspire change.

KATE GRUSSING – SAPPHIRE PARTNERS

Kate is a former consultancy and banking executive whose career and functional expertise is in strategy, corporate governance, corporate finance, talent management, financial services, professional services and diversity and inclusion. She is a regular commentator on diversity, women's careers and advancement in executive and non-executive roles. Kate has an MBA with honours from the Tuck School at Dartmouth, a BA with honours from Wellesley College and has studied at the London School of Economics. She is a trustee of the New London Institute of Imagination and an active member of the British Association of Women Entrepreneurs. Kate is a Companion of the Chartered Institute of Management. She has also been on the advisory board of Rare Recruitment, supporting black and ethnic minority students, for over a decade.

Company overview. Sapphire Partners are passionate believers in diversity and have a unique expertise in providing creative and balanced shortlists. Working closely with their clients and candidates they promote and bring diverse professional talent to deliver business excellence. In their searches they place exceptional professionals who can meet the demands of world-class organisations. They have a global reach, consistently delivering inclusive and innovative results.

REBEKAH HALL – BOTANIC LAB

Rebekah is in her late thirties, single and lives in London. She grew up near Glastonbury and practised traditional ashtanga yoga with her mother. She started her career in corporate finance, buying and selling businesses, but always wanted to work for herself. At the age of thirty she was bored, unhappy and wanted a change. So she set about founding a functional drinks business, Botanic Lab, through her contacts in and knowledge of the wellness industry.

Company overview. Botanic Lab is an award-winning innovative drinks brand disrupting the U.K. market with its 'drinks that do something'. Creating premium functional drinks with a focus on botanical ingredients and unique flavour profiles, Botanic Lab has built a reputation as a pioneer whilst making next-generation products available to an ever-increasing U.K. audience. It has championed the use of plant-based ingredients that have a functional benefit to the body. Renowned for its cold-pressed Performance Juices, non-dairy Grown Up Milkshakes and first-to-market adaptogenic Hotshots, Botanic Lab launched the U.K.'s first Cannabidiol (CBD) soft drink, Dutch Courage, in 2018.

MURSAL HEDAYAT – CHATTERBOX

Mursal was three years old when she, her older sister and her mother had to flee war-torn Afghanistan. Her mother, a civil engineer, hoped to continue her work when they arrived in the U.K. Her mother's perseverance was the inspiration behind Chatterbox, an online education company that matches employees in need of language training with refugees able to teach them.

Company overview. Chatterbox launched in August 2016 and is a multi-award-winning language learning service employing refugees to teach their native languages. It delivers language lessons online both to individuals and enterprises. While the clients learn, the refugee tutors earn a living and improve their employability.

EMMA HILL – REDEFINE HAIR SALON

Emma has over twenty-five years of experience in the hairdressing industry. Emma started her journey at the age of fourteen. During her career Emma has managed several salons and for ten years she enjoyed a very successful business partnership in an award-winning salon. Emma has a degree in teaching and uses her six years of lecturing experience to continue training within the salon and provide for the future of the profession she is so passionate about.

Company overview. Redefine is a hairdressing salon based in Poundbury that provides the ultimate in cutting, colouring and all hairdressing services. Redefine welcomes clients of all ages, meeting the demands of men and women in today's ever-changing industry. With decades of experience, their qualified hairdressers are the perfect choice when redefining your style.

JULIA HOBSBAWM – EDITORIAL INTELLIGENCE

A mother, wife and step-mum, Julia Hobsbawm OBE is a British writer and speaker on Social Health, simplicity in a complex world and the role of the human in a machine-led workplace. She is the author of the acclaimed book *Fully Connected: Social Health in an Age of Overload* (Bloomsbury paperback, 2018), which was shortlisted for several major awards. She is Honorary Visiting Professor in Workplace Social Health at Cass Business School, editor-at-large for Arianna Huffington's global wellbeing portal Thrive and a columnist for *Strategy + Business Magazine*. An entrepreneur who founded the knowledge networking company Editorial Intelligence in 2005, she was awarded an OBE in the Queen's Birthday Honours list in 2015. In addition to her books, articles and speeches, Julia is a broadcaster. She has written and presented two series for BBC Radio 4 and regularly appears on television and radio networks and podcasts. Her new book *The Simplicity Principle* is published in 2020.

Company overview. Editorial Intelligence runs a network and provides network and media-based services for businesses and individuals ranging from salons to podcasts and a social mobility social enterprise called the Social Capital Network.

CAROLYN HOPKINS – THE TRUCKLE TRUCK

Carolyn runs The Truckle Truck, a 'cheese shop on wheels'. Having learned the trade working for and alongside renowned cheese judge Charlie Turnbull for many years, Carolyn started The Truckle Truck in 2018. Since hitting the road in the converted Citroen HY van that is The Truckle Truck, she's discovered the joys and advantages of being a peripatetic trader, as well as the pitfalls of operating in a fifty-year-old vehicle. Carolyn is already a judge for The Great Taste Awards and is looking forward to joining the esteemed judges at this year's World Cheese Awards for the first time.

Company overview. The Truckle Truck is a 'cheese shop on wheels'. Operating from a lovingly restored 1969 Citroen HY van, the business curates the best cheeses and accompaniments to go with them. Only the best, most extraordinary cheeses make it into The Truckle Truck's bijoux counter, with many of them coming from the business's home region in the West Country.

ROWENA IRONSIDE – WOMEN ON BOARDS

Rowena spent twenty-five years as an executive in the ICT sector, starting out writing software in Australia, building an IT services business in London and running international services businesses in the software and hosting industries. Rowena has been a non-executive member of boards in the private, public and not-for-profit sectors since 2006. She has been Chair of Women on Boards in the U.K. since its launch in 2012 and currently sits on the boards of the Digital Catapult and the Cabinet Office Elections and Registrations Division.

Company overview. Women on Boards UK (WOB) exists to help women make the right connections and career choices to take on a board role as a non-executive director, trustee or governor, or to get to the top within their own company. WOB also works with individuals within companies who are trying to navigate a successful path to directorship. It runs in-house career and leadership workshops for organisations as diverse as PwC, Linklaters, Scottish Water and Carillion plc.

MELINA JACOVOU – PROPEL LONDON

Melina has twenty-five years of experience in London's digital high growth tech sector and is one of the most recognisable figures in the industry. She has invested in and advised many high growth tech companies and mentored founders in the digital ecosystem. She takes a real interest in female founders and is often seen speaking on behalf of women in business and digital business leaders at a wide range of industry events. She also runs regular events that challenge current debate around future technology, gender pay gaps, diversity, the effects of the gig economy, the importance of company culture and values among other issues. In recent years Melina was named in the Hospital Club's 'Top

100 Influential People in Digital' and won the inaugural MARA Award for 'Best Human Resources Boss'.

Company overview. As a pioneer of talent for the digital economy, Melina founded Propel in 2001. The agency is now one of the U.K.'s largest independent digital talent businesses. It has helped hundreds of businesses to grow through the acquisition of skilled digital professionals. In 2012, Propel was named 'Best Large Agency' at the MARAs and continues to grow and develop high growth tech companies in the U.K. and internationally.

MICHAELA JEDINAK – MICHAELA JEDINAK

Michaela is a fashion entrepreneur and dress designer of her own label, Michaela Jedinak. Her mission is to empower women to feel and look confident so they can focus on what matters in their day. Michaela has a Law degree and unique range of experiences from the fashion, media and design industries in London, New York, Milan and Prague. Prior to moving to London, she was Managing Director of *Cosmopolitan* in Prague where she deepened her passion for colour and style. Michaela is a dog owner, great animal lover and supporter of animal causes including the preservation of our remaining wildlife and the elimination of poaching, killing and cruelty to animals for fashion.

Company overview. In 2005 Michaela founded one of the leading colour and style consultancies, Joy of Colour. In 2009 she launched Joy of Clothes to share her personal styling experience with a wider audience. In 2013 she launched her first dress collection, Michaela Jedinak. Her dresses are worn by international leading businesswomen around the world, including European royalty, aristocrats, politicians and TV personalities.

ALICE JOHNSEN – ALICE JOHNSEN LIFE COACHING

Alice lives near Sherborne in Dorset and is married with three children. She has worked for the Foreign & Commonwealth Office, the Countryside Alliance and has served with the Territorial Army. She also ran her own catering business, a national political campaign on rural issues, various fundraising campaigns and farmed her own beef and sheep. She recently worked with the charity Key 4 Life in the south west, supporting their emotional resilience work with young offenders as they left prison. Between 2015 and 2019, she was a Foundation Governor for Thornford Church of England Primary School. She has Grade A Foundation and Higher Diplomas in Life Coaching and a Grade A Foundation Diploma in Stress Management. She is accredited to The International College of Holistic Medicine and is an Associate Member of the School of Natural Health Science.

Company overview. At Alice Johnsen Life Coaching, Alice coaches clients on a one-on-one basis or in groups throughout London and the south west. She covers a wide range of life issues including:

- Preparation for and support during divorce.
- Support in running your own business.
- Menopause.
- Communication.
- Confidence.
- Maintaining a healthy work–life balance.
- Stress management for adults and children.

MARIA KEMPINSKA – JONGLEURS COMEDY CLUB

Doctor Maria Kempinska MBE is an award-winning businesswoman, a mother of two and works tirelessly around the U.K. for various charities. In 2004 Maria was awarded her MA in Psychotherapy and

Healing, having been inspired by her reading of the works of Carl Jung. With this qualification Maria is able to practice psychotherapy. She then gained a PhD in Psychoanalysis at Essex University and is now a practising counsellor, couples' therapist and mediator. Maria has a passion for music of all genres. She is a music producer and owner of the Dingwalls brand.

Company overview. Maria established and opened the first Jongleurs club in 1983, in Battersea, London. Using her bicycle and £300 as collateral to fund the project, she set out to form a chain of fun venues from a humble ballroom in Battersea which had lost its sparkle. By 2000, there were eight Jongleurs venues and she sold the rights to use the Jongleurs name in pubs to Regent Inns. By 2009, there were sixteen Jongleurs venues and the company that owned the club use of the brand went into liquidation. The rights to the brand reverted to Maria and the Jongleurs business was rebuilt again. Maria left the company in 2013 and, two years later, the Jongleurs business went into administration.

RENOU KIEFER – REWRITE THE NARRATIVE

Renou is a communications consultant, lecturer and writer living in Guildford. Her interests include entrepreneurship – particularly entrepreneurship as a vehicle for social justice – writing, causes, psychology and running.

Company overview. Rewrite the Narrative is a brand-led strategic communications consultancy with a social purpose. Its aim is to bring about positive change at three levels: individual, organisational and societal. Rewrite the Narrative believes that the stories that we write for ourselves have power – they can build or break us. It then harnesses the power of storytelling to develop brand-led communication strategies that empower individuals and organisations to engage with, challenge and rewrite these narratives in order to bring about change. Clients include an Infantry Unit of the British Army, start-ups and senior executives embarking on major career pivots. At least 10% of the Rewrite the Narrative's income forms the 'Tree of Life Fund' which invests in ventures undertaken by entrepreneurs who are also single parents.

MARTHA LANE FOX – DOT EVERYONE

Born in London in the early 1970s, Martha is the daughter of academic and gardening writer Robin Lane Fox, the scion of an English landed gentry family seated at Bramham Park. She was educated at Oxford High School and at Westminster School. She read ancient and modern history at Magdalen College, Oxford, and graduated with a BA degree, advancing MA.

Lane Fox co-founded lastminute.com during the dotcom boom of the early 2000s and has subsequently served on public service digital projects. She sits on the boards of Twitter, Donmar Warehouse and Chanel and is also a trustee of The Queen's Commonwealth Trust. She previously served on the board of Channel 4. She entered the House of Lords as a crossbencher in 2013, becoming its youngest female member, and was appointed Chancellor of the Open University in 2014. She serves as convenor of More United, a cross-party political movement.

Company overview. Martha is founder and executive chair of Doteveryone.org.uk, an independent think tank and charity championing responsible technology for a fairer future. The charity explores how technology is changing society, creates products and prototypes that show what responsible technology looks like and catalyses communities to create change.

ETTY LANIADO – CHEF LANIADO

Etty was born to a family of food lovers. Her father was the head of a large department, managing forty employees. She started cooking at a very young age and never stopped enjoying it, developing her own touch in the kitchen. She holds a Chef Diploma from The Chef

Academy of London. She then trained at Gauthier Restaurant in London, Hibiscus Restaurant in London (Two Michelin Star) and at Il Bottaccio Montignoso in Tuscany, Italy.

Company overview. Chef Laniado cooks in a variety of styles but always, being partly of Italian heritage, with a hint of Mediterranean and Middle Eastern flavours. Her ethos is using first-class and fresh ingredients to prepare all meals. Whether simple or complex she provides superb dishes, all meticulously prepared and tailored to specific requirements, providing customers and guests with a memorable gastronomic experience.

MELANIE LAWSON – BARE BIOLOGY

Melanie is founder and CEO of Bare Biology, as well as a mother of three children. Prior to setting up Bare Biology, she worked in advertising with big brands such as Sainsbury's and Coca Cola. Melanie's own experience of anxiety and postnatal depression was the inspiration behind her business.

Company overview. Founded in 2013, Bare Biology is a small independent U.K. company specialising in marine-based supplements. It's known for its leading premium Omega 3 range and marine collagen. All of its products are independently tested and certified for strength, purity and freshness. At the time of publication, stockists include Liberty, Whole Foods, Harrods Pharmacy, Victoria Health and Planet Organic.

PHOEBE LEBRECHT – GLASS DIGITAL MEDIA

Phoebe is a social media marketer working with early stage start-ups and fast-paced tech companies. She is motivated by creating engaging content that cuts through the noise and drives results. Phoebe is now working in-house at GoCardless. Phoebe is also a keen triathlete who has combined sport and her experience into a passion project. Working with a small group of fellow entrepreneurs, she has grown Got To Tri Triathlon Training camps into a viable product.

Company overview. Glass Digital Media is a social media agency focussed on helping companies build their brand awareness, develop a social strategy and create human conversations that engage audiences and amplify content. Got To Tri is now in its fourth year of business, offering Triathlon Training camps to clubs, universities and individuals.

VICKI WILLDEN-LEBRECHT – BRIGHT AGENCY

Vicki has run her own business since the age of seven, when she sold bracelets made of shells from a stall in the garden. After stints pitching T-shirts to classmates and hawking frozen food out of the back of a van during university holidays, she set up the Bright Agency, specialising in children's books, in 2003. She funded the business in part by selling her car and last year was shortlisted for literary agent of the year at the British Book Industry Awards.

Company overview. With experience as a graphic designer and a love of stories told through images, Vicki set up the Bright Group in 2003. Since then, the agency has gone on to represent some of the best-known talents in children's publishing and has expanded into full rights management including film, TV and licensing deals. The agency prides itself on being more than just an ordinary literary agency and, instead, being a 'bespoke career management service' which operates globally. After all, the creation of the product is just the beginning of the story.

SOPHIE LE RAY – NASEBA

Sophie was born in France. She started out in PR and now has over twenty years of experience in producing and organising business platforms, specialising in B2B conference production. She has a Master's degree in Ancient History. She is co-author of *Game Changers: How Women in the Arab World are Changing the Rules and Shaping the Future*, which looks at the transformative power of female inclusion in the Arab workforce.

Company overview. Naseba offers business facilitation services in growth markets. It supports clients in a range of sectors including fintech, cybersecurity, real estate and hospitality. It helps clients to raise capital, close sales, enter new markets, secure partners and educate workforces. It has offices in the Middle East, India, Pakistan, China, the U.S. and Europe. Naseba is also a proud supporter and signatory of the UN Global Compact and the Women Empowerment Principles.

LINDSAY LEVIN – LEADERS' QUEST

Lindsay lives in New York with her husband David and three sons. She has written a book *Invisible Giants: Changing the World One Step at a Time*, published in 2013. Lindsay was CEO of the Whites Group in the 1990s and sold the business to create a host of entrepreneurial companies. She founded Leaders' Quest as her 'last start-up' in 2001.

Company overview. As Founder and CEO of Leaders' Quest, Lindsay works with corporate CEOs and their leadership teams on the role and purpose of business, company values and culture change. As a co-founder of the Future Stewards partnership, she also supports leaders who are working on complex systemic problems in order to build a regenerative future.

DENA MCCALLUM – EDEN MCCALLUM

Dena grew up in Toronto and joined McKinsey there following her MBA. She transferred to Frankfurt, then London, where she served clients in retail and financial services and co-led McKinsey's global CRM practice. Dena joined Condé Nast International as Director of Strategy and Planning. She and Liann Eden founded Eden McCallum in 2000. She holds an MBA from INSEAD, an MPA from the Woodrow Wilson School at Princeton and a BA from the University of Toronto.

Company overview. Eden McCallum is redefining management consulting. From their offices in London, Amsterdam and Zurich they support clients to resolve their most pressing issues of strategy, operations and organisation. Working with a group of independent consultants of the highest calibre, they have pioneered an approach that delivers tangible impact, client ownership and great value.

SANDRA MACLEOD – ECHO RESEARCH

Sandra is an Expert Witness in Reputation and cited as 'among the 100 most influential people in PR'. She is also Group CEO of Echo Research, which provides brand and reputation research for clients globally, and Director of Reputation Dividend, which values reputation for listed companies. After an early career at PA Management Consultants, Sandra set up the first international media analysis franchise in 1989 before launching Echo Research. Sandra is also Ambassador to the International Integrated Reporting Council <IR>, a Companion of the Chartered Institute of Management, member of the McKinsey Women as Leaders' Forum and Visiting Professor on Reputation at NYU. She is founder of the International Association of Measurement & Evaluation Companies (amec) and has been a Trustee and Board Member of the Arthur W Page Society, the Institute of Public Relations, the International Business Leaders Forum (IBLF) and the University of Oxford's Public Affairs Advisory Group. Sandra is also a recipient of the 2018 Page Distinguished Service Award.

Company overview. Echo Research offers customised research specialising in the evaluation and measurement of corporate reputation, branding and communications for leading clients globally. Initially trading as CARMA International in 1989, the group changed its name to Echo Research in 1999 when it extended its media analytics with market research capabilities. With offices in the U.K., France, Singapore and the U.S.A., it was acquired by Ebiquity PLC in 2011 and integrated into the Market Intelligence division. In 2018, Echo Research was bought back by its original founder, Sandra Macleod.

MAYA MAGAL – MAYA MAGAL JEWELLERY

Maya is the Founder and Creative Director of her eponymous jewellery brand, Maya Magal. Maya comes from a long line of creatives and apprenticed for the legendary jeweller Tony Thomson while she studied for her Textiles BA at Chelsea College of Art. But it was the time she spent as Head Designer at Miquella jewellery that gave Maya the confidence to set up her own brand in 2013, all from a humble Hatton Garden studio. The Maya Magal business was born and she hasn't looked back.

Company overview. Maya Magal crafts modern jewellery by hand. Whether a birthstone charm or a mixed-metal ring, all their pieces are designed by the founder, Maya, and then handmade in small batches by skilled artisans. Maya spent years learning her craft in Hatton Garden, before opening up a workshop and creative studio where her contemporary designs come to life. Today in their three shops across London they invite customers to experiment and play with their designs. In their view, rings are made for stacking, necklaces for layering and silver and gold for mixing.

VICTORIA MELLOR – MELCRUM PUBLISHING

Victoria has been an entrepreneur for over two decades. After reading Economics at Exeter University she started her career as a business schoolteacher in Spain. She founded Melcrum in 1996 from her kitchen table and grew it as CEO and Chairman into a $10m business which she sold in 2015. She then went on to start other business ventures, including her latest one, Kademy. She is married to her long-term business partner Robin and is an accomplished long-distance open water swimmer.

Company overview. Victoria co-founded Melcrum in 1996, providing thought leadership research and services to the top internal communication leaders and organisations around the globe. She led Melcrum from a humble kitchen table start-up and grew it into a $10m industry leader, prior to its sale to CEB (now Gartner) in 2015. Her latest business, Kademy, is a learning and development platform for corporate communication teams.

LARA MORGAN – PACIFIC DIRECT; SCENTERED

Lara founded her first business, Pacific Direct, in 1991 at the age of twenty-three. Having arrived in the U.K. from Hong Kong with little or no hotel experience, Lara quickly grew Pacific Direct into a global company and sold it seventeen years later for £20 million. Lara now invests in British brands including Dryrobe, Gate8, KitBrix and Yogi Bare. Her passion for fragrance and functionality in natural aromatherapy products also led her to develop, design and produce Scentered, a mood therapy brand that breathes renewed positivity into busy lives. Lara is a proud mother of three teenage girls and a committed volunteer and philanthropist.

Company overview. Pacific Direct Ltd is a specialist global supplier of luxury high-end brands for five-star hotels. The company offers fragrances, toiletries and grooming products, and concierge accessories and services, and has operations in the Czech Republic, the United Arab Emirates, Germany, Hong Kong, Singapore, the United Kingdom and the United States.

JANE MOSLEY – GRANNY OLIVE'S KITCHEN

With a childhood in farming, horses and countryside, Jane owes her love of cooking, particularly baking, to her grandmother, the original Granny Olive, and her mother, who both taught and encouraged her from an early age. On leaving school, Jane trained as a secretary, which led to her first job at the Porlock Vale Riding School on Exmoor. Alongside her office work, she was given the opportunity to further her equestrian career and qualify as a British Horse Society Instructor. Following a number of 'all equally wonderful jobs' in the horse industry, Jane moved to the New Forest to work at The Fortune Centre of Riding Therapy, a registered charity which provides Equine Facilitated Education and
Therapy for a wide age range of people with additional needs. After thirty happy years there, she retired and set up Granny Olive's Kitchen. Jane and her husband Richard have two grown-up children and are enjoying being grandparents.

Company overview. Granny Olive's Kitchen is a small business based in Alderholt, Hampshire. Jane produces home-baked cakes, cookies, savoury and sweet pastries and desserts using as many locally sourced ingredients as possible and often old family recipes. Her gluten-free products are very popular. Granny Olive's Kitchen can provide personalised catering packages for teas, picnics and special occasions. Jane regularly sells her produce at local markets and supplies local businesses.

FIONNUALA O'CONOR – OPDEM

Fionnuala has founded three successful start-ups and has over twenty years of experience as an innovator and advisor on people and technology. She is CEO of AI start-up OpDem, as well as being available for consulting projects and speaking engagements. Her key areas of expertise include human and technology co-working, behavioural change via technology and emotional intelligence, people strategy, assessment and optimisation in complex and disruptive political and technological contexts.

Company overview. OpDem optimises technology for the benefit of humanity. In June 2019 it launched Project Kindi, an independent research project into the non-technical success factors for great data science and AI. The company gathers robust, detailed, evidence-based data on what works best and what can be done better across different sectors and specialisms. They share the resulting data and insights with the data science and AI communities, as well as offer development and implementation support to data scientists, advanced technologists and those who work with them.

ELLENA OPHIRA – WEDDINGLY

The CEO and Founder of Weddingly, Ellena is an ambitious entrepreneur who started her first successful business in her early twenties. Ellena has worked with leading brands and SMEs alike, with over ten years of experience in marketing and strategy. She now brings her knowledge and passion to niche markets. As pioneers in WedTech, Ellena and her female-led team are on a mission to bring innovative technology to the dated wedding industry. She is a proud international speaker and a dedicated advocate for entrepreneurship in women and women in tech.

Company overview. Wedding planning just got smarter. Weddingly is an intuitive platform that uses the latest technology to offer a personalised planning experience. Matching couples to their perfect vendors, Weddingly celebrates the individual and their own unique choices. Weddingly provides a streamlined and unique experience for the couple, the bridal party and the guests, helping them find what they need when they need it.

CLAIRE RANDALL – CLAIRE RANDALL CONSULTING

Claire Randall Consulting was founded in 1996 by Claire Randall, previously a broadcast producer at Saatchi & Saatchi, London. In 1996, she formed the company to manage all TV production for a large global advertiser across all categories of their business on an exclusive basis. Claire is a well-known figure in the industry, consulting and advising for industry bodies such as ISBA (Incorporated Society of British Advertisers), the IPA (Institute of Practitioners in Advertising) and the ANA (Association of National Advertisers).

Company overview. Claire Randall Consulting's original remit was to manage all TV productions across Europe on an exclusive basis for a leading food and beverage company. It has grown steadily since then and has a large team in London and on-the-ground resources in Los Angeles, Boston, Miami, New York, Strasbourg, Dubai, Moscow and Singapore. In 2001 it extended beyond TV production into all media, recruiting experienced digital and print specialists to bolster its TV offering. In 2003 it became non-exclusive and opened its doors to all creative brands across the world to become one of the leading creative production consultancies in the industry. It now offers comprehensive consultancy in TV, video, print, animation, digital content, digital builds, retail and experiential production, as well as other production management specialist services.

SHERRY ROBERTS – THE LONGEST STAY

American by birth but European in spirit, Sherry's career began at the age of fifteen at Blue Cross Blue Shield where she worked every day after school. Her ambitions continued throughout university where she turned her dorm room into a travel agency. She started her first corporate job at AT&T in San Francisco at the age of twenty-two. She then moved to Germany and extended her corporate career with Mannesmann Arcor, Bertelsmann Media

Group and Symbian for a total of fifteen years while completing her EMBA at J.L. Kellogg-WHU. Having spent many years in Italy working with design manufacturers and attending École hôtelière de Lausanne, Sherry identified the need for consumers to buy what they see in hotels and home decoration magazines and created the company The Longest Stay.

Company overview. The Longest Stay is creating the world's first shoppable hotels. It furnishes luxury hotels and then enables customers to buy what they see in the rooms through an easy-to-use, editorial-driven website. The Longest Stay has launched phase one of the business selling designer furniture on its website and is now launching the concept in hotels in Europe and in the U.K.

NAOMI SAUTTER – NAOMI SAUTTER WEDDINGS & EVENTS

Naomi has a First Class Honours degree in Business Management from the University of Winchester and a Diploma in Wedding Planning from the Blackford Centre for Professional Wedding Planners.

Company overview. Naomi Sautter Weddings & Events provides first class planning, design, coordination and management for weddings and events in Hampshire and the surrounding counties. The company prides itself on creating beautiful and unique celebrations that are unforgettable. Its professional team alleviates the stress of planning, working alongside its clients to create an exclusive wedding or event that is glamorous, elegant and planned to perfection.

HILARY SCARLETT – SCARLETT & GREY

Hilary is a consultant, author and speaker, and Director of Scarlett & Grey. Her work has spanned Europe, the U.S. and Asia and concentrates on the development of people-focussed change management programmes and leadership development. Hilary regularly works with leadership teams in the private and public sectors to help them build resilience and high performance through better understanding of the brain. Hilary holds an MA from Cambridge University, has a post-graduate Certificate in the Psychology of Organisation Development and Change and is an accredited executive coach with the Institute of Leadership and Management. Her book *Neuroscience for Organizational Change: An Evidence-Based, Practical Guide to Managing Change* has been widely praised; a second edition was published in 2019.

Company overview. Scarlett & Grey's work enables employees to perform at their best. They build understanding about what helps people to focus and thrive at work. In particular, they believe that if people have some understanding of their brains, they can work with that knowledge and have more good days at work. Scarlett & Grey work with scientists to bring neuroscience out of the lab and into the workplace – making it relevant and practical. They designed and led the Neuroscience of Leadership Masterclass for Senior Civil Servants in the U.K. – one of Civil Service Learning's most highly recommended products. They have conducted research into the impact of leaders learning about applied neuroscience. Participating organisations included Lloyds Banking Group, Orbit Housing Group, Department for Business, Innovation and Skills and BAE Systems.

GABRIELLA SUGG – THE ELLA-PHANT KITCHEN

Gabriella has been an aspiring chef since a very young age. She went to Ashburton Cookery School at the age of eighteen where she gained a Certificate in Culinary Arts. Shortly after Cookery School, Gabriella got a job as Head Chef at a new local restaurant, learning an array of new skills that she then used to set up her own business, The Ella-Phant Kitchen.

Company overview. The Ella-Phant Kitchen launched in March 2019. It offers boutique catering for a wide range of events as well as supplying cakes to cafés. The business is based in Yeovil and mainly operates around Somerset and Dorset.

SIAN SUTHERLAND – MAMA MIO

Sian started in advertising back in the heady 1980s. She created her first business when twenty-six – a Michelin star restaurant in Soho, London, where she met her husband, Christian. She then moved back to her marketing roots, setting up brand creation agency Miller Sutherland with Kathy Miller, who remained Sian's business partner for twenty-four years. Sian got involved in film production along the way and eventually, out of a totally selfish need, Sian and three business partners created their first skincare range, Mama Mio, in 2005. They successfully sold the business to The Hut Group and exited in 2016. Sian is now co-founder of A Plastic Planet, using her entrepreneurial and marketing experience for a very different goal – to ignite and inspire the world to turn off the plastic tap.

Company overview. Established in 2005, Mama Mio began as one of the very first brands dedicated entirely to pregnancy skincare. Their founders, four mamas themselves, struggled to find high quality efficient skincare during their pregnancies. It all began with the iconic Tummy Rub, which quickly became a globally renowned cult-pregnancy range. Loved by countless mamas to be all around the world, their award-winning stretch mark prevention oil and butter became a pregnancy saviour.

SARAH TURNER – ANGEL ACADEME

Sarah is a technologist, entrepreneur and angel investor. She's spent most of her career working in digital technology in the U.K., U.S. and Asia as an advisor and connector for start-ups, scale-ups and corporates. In 2014 she co-founded the award-winning angel network, Angel Academe. Sarah is also a Non-Executive Director and Chair of the Investment Committee of the Low Carbon Innovation Fund and is on the board of the U.K. Business Angels Association.

Company overview. Angel Academe is a fast-growing and award-winning angel investor network and the largest mainly female angel network in the U.K. The network invests in women-founded and co-founded technology businesses with high growth potential. It also introduces more women to angel investing through education, mentoring and collaboration with experienced investors. Many of the Angel Academe investors are entrepreneurs and others are senior professionals with portfolio careers or on career breaks.

TASH WALKER – THE MIX

Tash's early career was in branding and packaging agencies, with invaluable experiences of working on big brands – a diet of Hovis and Bacardi with playtime on the 2012 Olympics. She was a planner in packaging brand agency BrandMe and in client services at both FutureBrand and jkr, cutting her teeth in the world of supermarkets. Throughout this time her curious and uncompromising nature resulted in frustration at the bland world of research and insight. A chance meeting with a researcher offered some hope that 'research' could indeed not just be useful but also inspiring. She realised that her love of brands was misdirected and that her driving passion was in understanding why normal people do what they do, and so she started The Mix. Tash is now a regular speaker at events such as Food Matters Live, Marketing Week Live and Ad:Tech. Tash also founded thequiff.org, dedicated to supporting women in leadership roles.

Company overview. Founded by Tash Walker in 2012, The Mix is an immersive research agency. It figures out the difference between what consumers say and what they really do and then helps clients work out solutions that offer consumers a different choice. The agency creates innovative ways to get great insight from consumers, using a variety of technology and immersive experiences, and then brings this together with great planning and strategy.

SUSIE WATSON – SUSIE WATSON DESIGNS

Susie founded Susie Watson Designs in the belief that using beautiful handmade things everyday can be a source of great pleasure. An obsessive love of colour and fascination with form and balance play a huge part in what she does. Her influences come from both the palette of the English countryside and her travels, resulting in unique, interesting designs that always have an English feel. It was art in the everyday that inspired her first pottery collection – a beautiful mug can bring people as much pleasure, if not more, than a piece of art on the wall. It was many years of doing up houses and working as an architectural designer that sparked her passion for interiors.

Company overview. Susie Watson's designs are contemporary yet timeless, ensuring they will bring joy for many years to come. Everything has been meticulously designed by Susie and her team. Finding the right factories to bring their designs to life was far from easy, resulting in long periods working in India and Sri Lanka. It has proved worthwhile as they now work with some wonderfully skilled artisans using traditional techniques. Susie firmly believes that a truly sustainable business must work for everyone involved. So the family-run business is built on creating kind understanding relationships among both staff and suppliers. Their teams in the U.K. and India are part of a close working family with strong professional and personal ties inside and outside of work.

SARAH WOOD – UNRULY

Sarah is the co-founder of Unruly, the global video advertising marketplace acquired by News Corp in 2015. She currently sits on the boards of Tech Nation and City Ventures and is an ambassador for The Prince's Trust Women Supporting Women Programme. Sarah has been named Veuve Clicquot Businesswoman of the Year, City AM Entrepreneur of the Year and has been awarded an OBE for services to technology and innovation. Having co-founded City Unrulyversity, a free pop-up university in London with a mission to inspire the next generation of Tech City entrepreneurs, Sarah was awarded an honorary doctorate from City University, London. She is also the author of best-selling career handbook *Stepping Up: How to Accelerate Your Leadership Potential*, which calls for more diverse and empathetic business leaders.

Company overview. Unruly was founded in 2006 and specialises in distributing, publishing and tracking video advertising across multiple channels as well as targeting consumers. It has racked up two trillion views to date, working with brands like Dove, Adidas, Evian and Renault – 95% of the world's top 100 brands. It has 300 employees in twenty locations worldwide. Unruly was responsible for helping the Evian Roller Babies campaign and Dove's Real Beauty Sketches go viral, which are in the *Guinness Book of World Records* for the most viewed ads in 2010 and 2013 respectively.

STEPHANIE WRAY – CRESSWELL ASSOCIATES; RSK BIOCENSUS

Stephanie studied Zoology at Reading University and then did a PhD in Ecology at Bristol. After a couple of short post-doc contracts (including a year studying bats in the tropical rainforest) she took a temporary role in a consultancy. She worked as an environmental consultant in the U.K. construction industry for about twenty-five years, having built a successful ecology consultancy, Cresswell Associates, with her husband Warren. She is an ecologist, EIA practitioner and sustainability consultant and has worked on several hundred development projects in the transport, energy, property and water sectors.

Company overview. RSK Biocensus was started in 2002. It provides expert ecologists to the U.K. construction and development industry, helping its clients manage ecological risks and maximise opportunities. Its projects range from individual developments to major national infrastructure projects, with the company providing anything from a single expert witness to a 100-person strong field survey team. Its national network of ecologists enables it to provide local expertise where needed. The company was acquired by the RSK Group, an international environmental services company, in 2019.

INDEX

Page numbers in *italics* indicate interviewee biographies and company overviews.

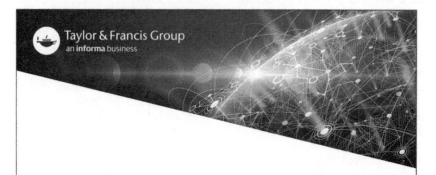